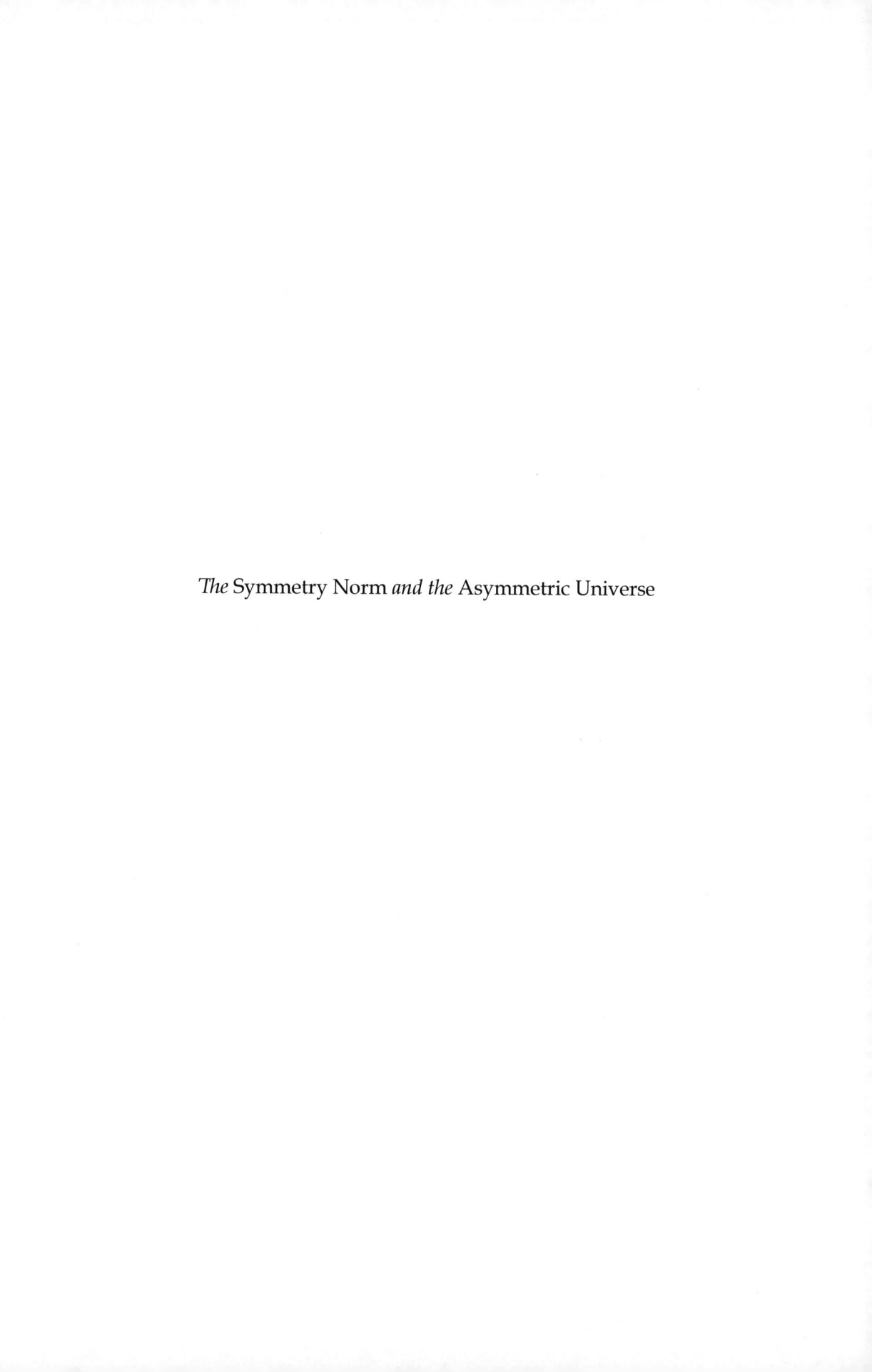

The Symmetry Norm *and the* Asymmetric Universe

THE CATHEDRAL OF NOTRE DAME, ST. LO, NORMANDY The early-medieval façade of the cathedral was almost completely destroyed during World War II. This 19th. century stereoscopic photograph by S. Thompson shows that the structure was asymmetric in virtually every detail. The flanking doors and windows do not mirror each other; and the towers, with their spires, have different dimensions and designs. Even the main portal into the cathedral is off-center.

The
SYMMETRY NORM
and the
ASYMMETRIC
UNIVERSE

Michael Selzer

"The universe is asymmetric and I am persuaded that life, as it is known to us, is a direct result of the asymmetry of the universe or of its indirect consequences." - *Louis Pasteur*

"There is no center about which everything turns in the universe." – *Leon Lederman*

KeepAhead Books
Colorado Springs, 2015

This book is dedicated
with abiding affection and gratitude
to the memory of
Lilly and Morris Fleming

The quotations on the titlepage are from
Comptes Rendue de l'Académie des Sciences (June 1, 1874) and Lederman 2008, p.65

First Edition

© Michael Selzer 2015. All Rights Reserved

CONTENTS

Foreword: The Symmetry Norm	1
Note 1: Asymmetry and Symmetry	4
Note 2: The Asymmetric Universe	10
Note 3: Symmetry in the Classical World	42
Appendix: Is the Parthenon Symmetric?	64
Note 4: The Question of Medieval Symmetry	98
Note 5: The Asymmetry of Primitive Art	128
Note 6: The History of the Concept of Symmetry	160
Appendix: Alberti's *Collocatio*	192
Note 7: The Natural Garden in England	212
Note 8: Wittkower and the Façade of Santa Maria Novella	236
Works Cited or Consulted	255

0.1 BASILICA OF ST. MARK, VENICE (north entrance). This magnificent portal exemplifies "the dense, unpredictable" asymmetry characteristic of the medieval (in this case, Byzantine) aesthetic – and of Nature herself. The rectangular grid has been superimposed on the photograph, and the dark vertical line identifies the central axis as defined by the peaks of the innermost arches.

FOREWORD: THE SYMMETRY NORM

The idea of shapes whose left and right halves mirror each other across a vertical axis – the idea of symmetry, as we now usually call it - originated in Italy at the beginning of the Renaissance. Almost immediately, it was put to use as the foundation of a bold new norm that aimed at recasting the ways in which we perceive the world and shape our habitats. I call this the symmetry norm.

Its proponents took as their starting point the premise that no shape can be beautiful unless it is symmetric. This was a radical departure from the aesthetic of the Middle Ages, that had evoked the dense, unpredictable and asymmetric forms of Nature (*fig.* 0.1).

The advent of the symmetry norm testifies to the appetite for change that marked the first century of the Renaissance. But as the very term "Renaissance", or *re*birth, implies, that appetite was not an unbounded one. It was constrained, rather, by an innate conservatism that made it more likely for a new idea to be embraced if it was presented, not at all as an innovation, but as a recently-recovered fragment of the heritage of ancient Greece and Rome that was now being acknowledged as the standard of everything fit and proper.

The advocates of the new symmetry norm understood this perfectly well. They seldom argued their case on the merits (and invariably did a poor job when they tried to do so). Instead, they claimed that the concept of symmetry had been discovered in ancient Greece, and that the Greeks, as well as the Romans after them, always saw to it that their buildings, works of art and decorated artifacts were symmetric.

This patina of Classical antiquity – for all that it was completely spurious - may well have sufficed on its own to secure the new doctrine's adoption. The advocates of the symmetry norm went on however to embellish it with an even bolder set of claims. The Greeks, they declared, had discovered that everything Nature makes is symmetrically shaped; and because Nature's creations are the templates of

Beauty, the Greeks understood that nothing made by human hands can be beautiful unless it, too, is symmetrically shaped.

The ingenious triangulation of history ("the Greeks"), of science ("Nature"), and of philosophy ("Beauty") proved to be a winning formula, and within less than a century the symmetry norm had become deeply entrenched throughout western Europe. Indeed, it literally changed the face of Europe, for its enthusiasts not only insisted that henceforth all new buildings must be symmetric, but also that the asymmetric facades of important medieval churches and other public buildings be demolished and replaced with symmetric facades. The free-flowing and visually-complex textures of the medieval *hortus conclusus*, too, were replaced by the stiff, symmetric and instantly-comprehended forms of the Renaissance garden.

Since that time the authority and scope of the symmetry norm have continued to be enlarged. It became and remains a byword among Classical archeologists that Greek temples are symmetric; among physicists that crystals, and most prominently, snowflakes, are symmetric; among anthropologists, that the art of primitive peoples everywhere and at all times is symmetric; among psychologists, that humans prefer symmetric shapes to asymmetric ones. These axioms, along with others that we examine here, are all incorrect. So of course is the foundational axiom of the symmetry norm that only symmetric shapes can be beautiful.

The effect of the symmetric norm therefore was not only to change the appearance of Europe but to enervate significant aspects of Western cultural and intellectual life. The Notes in this book aim at tracing the origin, survival and consequences of these fallacies.

Humbly rather than boastfully, I would point out to the reader that this book covers a great deal of new ground. To the best of my knowledge the fact (as I conceive it to be) that the concept of symmetry was first formulated at the dawn of the Italian Renaissance – and therefore that it was unknown in the Classical era, in the Middle Ages and in primitive cultures worldwide – has not been acknowledged previously, except in a brief and tantalizingly unelaborated aside by James Fergusson more than 150 years ago.[1] Exploring this new ground

---

[1] Fergusson 1849, p.399. See also p.161, *below*.

has taken me far beyond my competence into realms of science, anthropology, and art and architectural history. This book, therefore, is not an authoritative study of the symmetry norm. It is merely a first step; and I will be more than repaid for my effort in writing it if, in future, someone else extends our understanding of the subject beyond the limits I have reached here.

ACKNOWLEDGEMENTS

In my research for this book I have enjoyed the valuable assistance of librarians at the Alumni Library of Simon's Rock College, the Clark Art Institute Library, the Architecture and Environmental Design Library of Arizona State University, the Special Collections Library of the University of Arizona, the Tutt Library of Colorado College, the Archivio dell'Opera di Santa Maria del Fiore and the Biblioteca Nazionale Centrale di Firenze.

Michael Selzer
Colorado Springs
April, 2015

ASYMMETRY

Columbus, Indiana: First Christian Church
(Eliel Saarinen, architect)

AND

SYMMETRY

Columbus, Indiana: North Christian Church
(Eero Saarinen, architect)

Note One

Symmetry, in the words of the noted mathematician Hermann Weyl (himself author of an influential study of the subject), is an "absolutely precise" concept.[1] By that token, of course, asymmetry too is an absolutely precise concept. The terms moreover are not only unambiguous but mutually exclusive, which is to say that symmetry and asymmetry are opposites and not points on a continuum like "hot" and "cold", for example, are. Thus, if a shape is not symmetric it must be asymmetric, and if it is not asymmetric it must be symmetric: there is no such thing as a shape that partakes of both qualities.[2] Nor is there a shape that is neither the one nor the other. Careless usage sometimes obscures the distinction between the two with terms such as "almost symmetric" or "broken symmetry", and so on. These refer to shapes that are asymmetric and should be called that. It is curious that we never encounter their opposites, which would be terms like "almost asymmetric" or "broken asymmetry". This, I suspect, reflects the presumption that symmetry is the norm and asymmetry is not – see my discussion of this point on pages 7-8 and 190-192, *below*.

That said however it is also the case that asymmetry (and sometimes symmetry, too) can be more apparent in some designs than it is in others. Indeed, on occasion it can only be detected by careful scrutiny. But no matter how discrete the asymmetry is, it must always be recognized as such and not be thought of as a weakened or defective form of symmetry.[3] Many shapes have a pronounced *bilateral* quality but unless

---

[1] Weyl, 1952, p.4. The insistence that symmetry requires the two halves of a form to mirror each other precisely goes back to the earliest days of the concept, when Alberti (1966, IX.7; see also the appendix, "Alberti's *Collocatio*", to Note Six) insisted that the right must always accord with the left (*dextra sinistris convenirent*) even in the most minute details (*in minutissimis*).

[2] I use "symmetric" and "asymmetric" throughout this book. Their longer forms add sound but not meaning to the words, and therefore should not be encouraged. See the entry "-ic(al)" in Fowler's *Dictionary of Modern English Usage*.

[3] The fact that some asymmetries are not recognized consciously need not mean that they do not register themselves on the unconscious mind. White for example (1967,

the two halves are mirror images of each other these shapes must not be considered symmetric. The two sides of our bodies, for example, resemble but are not mirror images of each other. Our bodies accordingly are not symmetric, let alone *almost* symmetric. They are, rather, what for want of a better term I call bilaterally asymmetric.

There is nevertheless a legitimate question about the degree of precision one must use in deciding whether a shape is symmetric or asymmetric. Clearly, in all but the very rarest instances it would be fatuous to demand for this purpose that the reflection of the two sides be identical down to a sub-atomic level. Yet sometimes extremely fine measurements, whose precision far surpasses the capabilities of the naked eye, may reveal unsuspected symmetries. Such is the case, or so it has been claimed, with certain portions of the Parthenon, whose symmetry is reported to be accurate to the astonishing degree of 1:10,000 or even more.[4] Precision of this order can only be detected using modern optical or, better yet, electronic instruments. The fact that it is not apparent to the naked eye does not mean that we should ignore it or assume that it was created unwittingly, for except in the rarest instances symmetric forms are only created intentionally.

The example of the Parthenon shows that the determination of whether something is symmetric cannot always be treated in absolute terms. For example, the - alleged - exceptionally precise symmetry of parts of the Parthenon requires that we designate other parts of this structure that fall short of this standard as asymmetric. Yet on another building the latter may well appear precise enough to be considered symmetric. The important criterion that symmetry is an "absolutely precise" concept is therefore *not* an entirely absolute one; and the context in which something was made must not be ignored. But the example of the

---

p.158) plausibly suggests that people whose attention is held by the appearance of the façade of Santa Maria Novella in Florence are unwittingly responding to its "hidden asymmetry, a half-felt difference on the fringes of consciousness". The same point is made more generally by Ruskin, who noted (*Stones of Venice*, 2.5.12) that the eye "is continually influenced by what it cannot detect". But whether such "discrete" asymmetries were created intentionally is another question. Goodyear claims that the asymmetry and other "refinements" of Greek temples were not intended to be noticed consciously; and in this he appears to echo Ruskin's claim in *The Lamp of Life* that builders sometimes created a "pretended symmetry" to conceal asymmetric arrangements. One must doubt, however, whether it is possible to know the undeclared intentions of craftsman who lived centuries or even millennia, and who moreover almost certainly were unfamiliar with the concept of symmetry.

[4] The reliability of these measurements still awaits confirmation. The matter is discussed in some detail in the appendix to Note Three.

Parthenon is highly unusual, and similar instances will not be encountered very often. For the rest, we can safely take as our standard for deciding whether something is symmetric or asymmetric the one that guides careful observers when they look at a shape with the naked eye, or when they examine a photograph with the help of a divider or ruler or, far better yet, any of the elementary graphic software programs that are now easily obtained. I have used one of these programs to analyze the head of Leonardo da Vinci's "Vitruvian Man" drawing (*fig.* 0.1; illustrations are to be found at the end of each Note) and in this simple way have been able to demonstrate conclusively that it is asymmetric.

That such observations should be made meticulously deserves to be emphasized, for in the modern world there is an undoubted cultural bias in favor of assuming that most forms – especially ones regarded as attractive or important - *are* symmetric.

One instance of this bias can be found in the decision taken in the 1970's by the University of Florence's Department of Architecture to survey only the left side of the façade of the church of Santa Maria Novella (*fig.* 8.1) on the grounds that "the façade's perfect symmetry" - *la perfetta simmetria della stessa facciata* – made it unnecessary to measure the other half, too.[5] As it happens this great and mysterious façade is markedly asymmetric. Some of its asymmetries can be seen with the naked eye, while others can be found through rudimentary analyses of photographs.[6] But of course none are likely to be discovered by an observer who is convinced *a priori* that they are not there! We will see numerous other instances of this bias at work throughout this book.

There is a further point – not directly about the concepts themselves so much as about the terms used for them – that deserves to be considered. The word "asymmetry" means literally that which is "without symmetry". It carries with it the implication, not only that asymmetry lacks that which symmetry possesses, but also that symmetry is somehow the appropriate standard for shapes, while asymmetry is a falling off from that standard.

But is that really so? Of the two churches illustrated at the beginning of this Note, which is the defective one? Is it the church by Saarinen *père* because it is so markedly and pervasively *without* symmetry? Or is it the church by Saarinen *fils* because it is so markedly and pervasively without *asymmetry*? Which more draws in the eye – and perhaps the

---

[5] Bardeschi 1970, text vol. p.23.

[6] See Note Eight, especially fn.37

soul? Which proves more elusive the longer one's gaze moves over it, and which reveals all that it has at the very first glance? Which suggests more the mystery of spiritual reality – and which, little more than an upturned martini glass?

Or consider the face of Leonardo's so-called "Vitruvian Man". The symmetric images that consist of the mirrored left and right halves of the original are flat and little more than caricatures; we would not be surprised to find them on the pages of a comic book. But when the two halves are combined asymmetrically in a single portrait, the guileless passivity of the one half and the intimidating hostility of the other interact to suggest the inner complexities and conflicts of an authentic human being.

The superiority of these asymmetric forms would not be surprising, I suspect, if our perceptions were not so strongly determined by the notion that asymmetry is inherently defective. How unfortunate it is that we do not have a word-pair that indicates that (what we now call) asymmetry possesses what symmetry in today's parlance lacks: terminology that implies that symmetry is best understood as a defective form of asymmetry!

The issues raised by the normative juxtaposition of asymmetry and symmetry are therefore not merely etymologic or stylistic. The symmetry norm distorts every aspect of reality that it addresses. The universe is far more complex, elusive, problematic, intriguing, challenging *and true* than this norm will allow: and so, it diminishes us. For although the endeavor to see things as they really are is one that can never be completely successful, undertaking it is both an intellectual and a moral obligation. The alternative is to distort reality by forcing it into the predictable grids of symmetry, thereby evading our duty to experience both our limitations and our potentials. Every symmetric design we see is an indictment of its creator, who has preferred the trite to the arduous, and has succumbed to the false doctrine that symmetry is the universe's norm.

The left side doubled

1.1 The asymmetric face of Leonardo's "Vitruvian Man"

The original face

The right side doubled

THE ASYMMETRIC UNIVERSE

2.1 Arizona Landscape

Note Two

> *"These urbashus borders, altogether too 'ap'azard... Sloppy. That's Nature."* [1]

It has been a commonplace since the middle of the 15th century that the shapes made by Nature are symmetric. Leon Battista Alberti, the Renaissance polymath, was among the first to voice this opinion. "It is of the essence of Nature (*tam ex natura est*)", he declared in *De re aedificatoria*, his treatise on architecture, "that things on the right should correspond in every respect to those on the left (*ut dextra sinistris omni parilitate correspondeant*)".[2] Alberti also claimed that it was "from the lap of Nature (*ex naturae gremio*)" that the ancient Greeks deduced the fundamental principle that in works of art and architecture "the right must accord with the left (*dextra sinistris convenirent*) even in the most minute details (*in minutissimis*)".[3]

With certain exceptions this view of the shapes Nature creates has been upheld ever since Alberti's time, and it remains current today, even among scientists. The physicist Leon Lederman, for example, a Nobel laureate, writes of "the graceful symmetry" that characterizes Nature's forms. Symmetry, he says, affirms the perfect order and harmony which underlies everything in the universe.[4] For his part, Alexander Voloshinov, also a physicist, declares that "symmetry is the universal principle of Nature, the principle permeating the whole universe and revealing its unified picture from atomic nuclei and molecules to the solar system and the metagalaxy".[5] Such views are not considered controversial among scientists today. Indeed, I am unaware of any who repudiate them. It should be noted that the claim is not usually that Nature's forms are symmetric only in some hypothesized ideal state –

---

[1] Ngaio Marsh, *A Man Lay Dead* (1934; Kindle ed. at 2402).

[2] Alberti 1966, IX,7.

[3] *ibid.*, VI, 3. See Gadol (1969, p.111*ff.*) who, in common with other Alberti scholars, failed to recognize that Alberti's belief that Nature's forms are symmetric was a basic element of his concept of *collocatio*.

[4] Lederman 2008, p.13. See also fn.75, *below*.

[5] Voloshinov 1996. Even perceptual psychologists share this opinion – *vide* McBeath 1997: "Symmetry is a pervasive structural characteristic of 3-D objects in the [natural] world."

that they are "theoretically" rather than actually symmetric. The claim, rather, is that Nature's forms *as we see them* are symmetric.[6]

Yet in truth Nature disdains symmetry. Draw an imaginary line, if you doubt that, between the right and left halves of any of her artifacts – down the middle of a cloud, perhaps, or the canopy of stars in the night sky; of a mountain, or a tree growing on its slopes; of a meandering river, the fish swimming in it, or the boulders resting on its bed; of a snowflake or the cells of a honeycomb; of your own face and body: indeed, down the middle of anything animal or vegetable or mineral that has not been tampered with by the likes of topiarists or "cosmetic" surgeons - and you will always discover that the features of one of those halves do not mirror those on the other (*figs*.2.1 – 2.5).

And this hold true regardless of the size of the objects we look at, for Nature's asymmetry is just as apparent in molecules of a few Ångstroms seen through an electron microscope (*fig.* 2.4) as it is in the Eagle nebula's colossal "Pillars of Creation" (*fig.* 2.5).[7] Nature's penchant for asymmetry, indeed, may well be as old as the universe – as old as Nature – itself. That, at least, is what seems to be implied by the asymmetrically-shaped and distributed clusters of radiation left over from the Big Bang which have been mapped by the COBE, WMAP and Planck spacecraft (*fig.* 2.3). Prudence, to be sure, requires us to recognize that somewhere in the far reaches of our universe (or perhaps in the parallel universes posited by some cosmologists) there could be regions in which natural forms are always symmetric rather than asymmetric: even worlds where – who knows? – symmetrically-shaped people speak to each other in palindromes. But in the universe as we have been able to see it so far we have encountered nothing, anywhere or on any scale, that challenges the notion that Nature's forms are bilaterally asymmetric in appearance.

This point, one suspects, would have seemed self-evident to archbishop Olaus Magnus of Uppsala (1490-1557). Olaus is the first person we know of who wrote about the appearance of snowflakes. What struck him in particular about them was the great variety of their

---

[6] Inherent in the concept of symmetry is the concept of simplicity, for a form whose left half contains identical information to that in the right is bound to be more simple than it would be if one of the halves contained different information. We take up the implications of this in Note Six, but it should be pointed out now that in the Italian Renaissance the claim that Nature's forms are symmetric was conjoined to the idea that they are simple, too. Palladio, for example, who was a vigorous proponent of symmetric design, wrote of "the simplicity of the things created by Nature" – *quellu semplicita che nella cose da lei [i.e la Natura] create*.

[7] Scientists using NASA's RHESSI spacecraft have recently established that the sun is not a perfect sphere: see nasa.gov/topics/solarsystem/features/oblate_sun.html

shapes. During a single day or night, he reported, one might see "fifteen to twenty distinct patterns, or sometimes more".[8] His illustration of them (*fig. 2.6*) shows 23 different forms. One looks like an arrowhead; others resemble a bell, a human hand, a crescent moon, a six-pointed star. All are asymmetric

For Olaus the varied shapes of snowflakes was, as he put it, "more a matter for amazement than for inquiry". Not so, half a century later, for the great mathematician and astronomer, Johannes Kepler (1571-1630). Crossing a bridge in Prague one winter's night, Kepler looked at the snow that was settling on his coat and asked himself why snowflakes always fall (*"perpetuo cadant"*) as equilateral - regular - hexagons.[9] We may suppose that this did not at first seem like a particularly difficult question to him. Kepler, after all, had recently revolutionized astronomy by codifying the laws of planetary motion. In comparison to this awesome achievement the challenge of accounting for the shape of snowflakes may well have appeared trivial. Kepler discussed his findings in a book entitled *De nive sexangula* ("the hexagonal snowflake") that was published in 1611 in Frankfurt-am-Main, two years after his work on the laws of planetary motion. The book is a very short one, of about 8,000 words. Somewhat fatefully for the history of science he began it by examining another natural form that he believed also has a regular hexagonal structure.

"*Quo ordine structi sint apum alveoli*" he asked: what principles guide bees as they build their honeycombs? Kepler claimed that he first approached this question empirically with a simple look – "*ex intuitu simplici*" – at a honeycomb, but it would seem that in fact his starting point were some ideas developed by Pappus, a fourth-century mathematician in Alexandria. Pappus knew that, of the shapes that can be packed together without leaving any empty space between them, it is the hexagon that has the most angles and therefore the largest storage capacity: and so he marveled at the "geometrical foresight" that led bees to make their cells regular hexagons. Centuries later the bee in *The Arabian Nights* would echo Pappus' assessment by boasting that Euclid himself might have learned a thing or two about geometry from the bees.

There are two layers of cells in the honeycomb, with each layer facing in the opposite direction. The outward-looking faces are open so that a bee may enter and leave, while the part of the cell that is within the honeycomb is closed. Kepler focused his investigation on the point where the closed end of each cell (he called it the *carina* or "keel") meets those abutting it; and he asked himself what kind of a shape these ends

---

[8] Magnus 1996, Bk.1, cap.22.

[9] Kepler 2010.

must be if they met (as he thought was the case) without any empty space between them. He determined that the shape that bees form in their honeycomb – *"haec inquam est quam effingunt in suis alvearibus"* – is that of an incomplete rhombic dodecahedron.[10] He added that this design is based on material necessity – *"rationes materialem"* – not only because (as Pappas had already noted) the hexagon is the most capacious of the space-filling solids but also because its many obtuse angles best protect the delicate bodies of baby bees. The lattice of shared walls moreover, each reinforcing the others, imparts greater strength to the entire comb than any other form could.[11]

It is unclear how, really, Kepler's inquiry into the shape of bees' cells contributed to his understanding of the shape of snowflakes, but it did take on a life of its own. In 1712, a century after he published his book, Kepler's hypothesis about the *carina* received (or seemed to receive) empirical validation in a paper on the structure of the honeycomb that a certain Giacomo Maraldi delivered to the Académie des Sciences in Paris. In his paper, Maraldi declared that he had measured – *not calculated*! – the angles of the rhombs at the base of bee cells and found that they were 70° 32′, and 109° 28′, respectively.[12] These are the angles of the rhombic dodecahedron, and as such they confirmed the accuracy of Kepler's mathematical calculations.

Some years later a young Swiss mathematician called Samuel Koenig was asked by the great René Antoine Ferchault de Réaumur, who was interested in the economy and efficiency of the honeycomb's design, to calculate what configuration of a hexagonal cell, terminated by three similar and equal rhombs, requires the least amount of material for its construction. Koenig's calculations produced a result which differed from the angles that Maraldi claimed to have measured by a mere 2′ – that is, one-thirtieth of a degree. Koenig's comment on this finding was that the bees had long ago solved a problem which had been beyond the capacity of human beings before Newton and Leibnitz.[13] Upon learning of Koenig's calculations Fontenelle, the Academy's Sécretaire Perpétuel, declared that the bees, lacking intelligence as they undoubtedly did, could only have achieved this optimal result

---

[10] Kepler 2010, p. 45.

[11] *ibid*, pp. 62-3. These explanations, Kepler added, are "sufficient, and thus I do not feel the need at this point to philosophize about the perfection, beauty or nobility of the rhombic figure, or to busy myself so that the essence of the little soul within the bee may be elucidated by contemplation of the shape it produced. If the shape in question were of no discernible utility, we might have to proceed in this manner".

[12] Thompson 2005, p.110.

[13] *idem*.

through divine guidance. Later, it was determined that the tiny discrepancy between Maraldi's observations and Koenig's calculations was caused by an error in the logarithmic tables that Koenig had used.[14] It was then said that the bees had been right all along and the mathematician wrong![15]

Maraldi's measurements, now vindicated mathematically down to the last second of a minute, would remain unchallenged for over a century. When Lord Brougham (d.1868) – a former Lord Chancellor of England and author of *Observations, Demonstrations and Experiments upon the Structure of the Cells of Bees* – heard someone say that mathematical calculations and empirical observations "nearly agree" about the shape of the cell, he responded with some *hauteur*: "The 'nearly' is quite incorrect. There is an absolute and perfect agreement between theory and observation".[16] Among those who also accepted Maraldi's claims were the great French naturalist Buffon (d.1788) and, a century after him, Charles Darwin (d.1882) himself. Darwin spoke for many when he referred to "the extreme perfection of the cells of the hive-bee", which he also declared is "absolutely perfect in economizing labor and wax"; and he made the pronouncement that natural selection "could not lead … beyond this stage of perfection in architecture".[17]

But Maraldi's claims, despite their acceptance in scientific circles, are manifestly implausible. As Thompson has pointed out:

> The fact is that, were the angles and facets of the honeycomb as sharp and smooth, and as constant and

---

[14] *ibid*, p.112.

[15] A modern echo of these claims is to be found in the report on recent research findings by Klarreich (2000): "The full honeycomb consists of two layers of these cells, stacked together so that the caps of one layer fit into the gaps of the other, like a jigsaw puzzle. For many years it was believed that this was the best two-layer arrangement, but in 1964 the Hungarian mathematician L. Fejes Tóth showed that a hexagonal cell capped off by part of a truncated octahedron would produce a tiny saving. Tóth pointed out, however, that the bees could have excellent reasons for choosing a slightly less efficient structure. Because the honeycomb walls have a definite thickness, it is not clear that Tóth's structure would indeed be an improvement. In that respect, the honeycomb is more like a wet foam than a dry foam. Recently, Weaire and Phelan undertook to construct two-layer foams with equal-sized bubbles, and they found that the dry foams did take on Tóth's pattern. But when they gradually added liquid, they wrote, something 'quite dramatic' happened: The structure suddenly switched over to the bees' configuration. It seems, then, that the bees got it right after all." It should be pointed out that these are mathematical or laboratory findings, not real-world ones, and they do not obviate the need *to look* at actual honeycombs!

[16] Henry Brougham, *Natural Theology* 1856, p.350, as quoted in Wyman 1866, pp. 4-5.

[17] Thompson 2005, p.114.

uniform, as those of a quartz-crystal, it would still be a delicate matter to measure the angles within a minute or two of arc, and a technique unknown in Maraldi's time would be required to do it. The minute-hand of a clock (if it moves continuously) moves through one degree of arc in ten seconds of time, and through an angle of two minutes in one-third of a second; - and this last is the angle which Maraldi is supposed to have measured![18]

The established view that bees' cells were constructed in such a way as to optimize their capacity and use of materials - and that they were therefore also regular in shape, and completely filled the spaces between themselves and the cells bordering them – was thus based on claims that *could not* have been valid. Yet it was not until 1866 that the implausibility of this view was empirically demonstrated. In that year Jeffries Wyman, a professor of anatomy at Harvard, published his findings about the extensive series of measurements that he had made of bee cells.[19]

Wyman reported that he had failed to discover even one cell whose six sides were all the same length and that, on the contrary, in any given cell the sides varied in length by between 10% and 100%. Their interior angles, moreover, far from being the 60 degrees of a regular hexagon, were in fact "nowhere sharply defined" (*fig* 2.7). Wyman added that the shapes of the rhombic faces – Kepler's "keel" – were also markedly irregular and variable; and indeed that some cells had four and not three rhombs. Wyman summarized his findings with fine understatement. "The cell of the bee", he declared, "has not the strict conformity to geometrical accuracy so often claimed for it". And that, indeed, is what anyone who looks with reasonable care at the cells of a honeycomb must also conclude (*fig.* 2.8)

Wyman sent a copy of his study to Darwin, and the two men corresponded with each other about it. We should be clear that Wyman's findings conclusively refute all the claims that had been made about the shape of the bee's cell from at least the time of Pappus. They are also supported by common sense and by the kind of simple observation of honeycombs that anyone can make.

Wyman must therefore have expected – as indeed we might have expected – that in the next edition of *The Origin of Species* Darwin would replace his earlier description of the bee's cell with remarks that reflected Wyman's findings. But that is not what Darwin did. Instead,

---

[18] *ibid*, p.112.

[19] Wyman 1866.

he retained his entire original text, with its admiration of the "perfection" of the honeycomb's design, and to it merely added a single sentence:

> I hear from Prof. Wyman, who has made numerous careful measurements, that the accuracy of the workmanship of the bee has been greatly exaggerated; so much so, that whatever the typical form of the cell may be, it is rarely, if ever realised.[20]

In this one sentence Darwin tacitly acknowledged that Wyman had refuted everything that he, Darwin, had previously written on the subject. Yet Darwin deleted nothing from his earlier discussion. His analysis and Wyman's refutation of it appear in subsequent editions of *The Origin of Species* as a single, ostensibly consistent, narrative in which Darwin continued to refer to the "extreme perfection" of the bees' cells, and their "absolute perfection" in economizing materials.

Despite Wyman's findings, the view of the bee cell's structure that originated with Kepler and was seemingly validated by Maraldi's observations has not only outlived Darwin but remains the standard account today. D'Arcy Thompson, whose *On Growth and Form* was described by Stephen Jay Gould as "the greatest work of prose in twentieth-century science", is a particularly striking case in point. Thompson himself sums up the evidence against the standard view by noting that although "all the geometrical reasoning in the case postulates cell-walls of uniform tenuity and edges which are mathematically straight", in reality "the [cell's] base is always thicker than the side-walls; its solid angles are by no means sharp but [are] filled with curving surfaces of wax ... the Maraldi angle is seldom or never attained".[21] But then, as if he had not just made these remarks, Thomson went on to refer to "the beautiful regularity of the bee's architecture", to the "regularly hexagonal" sides of their cells, and to their "all but constant" angles. He ended his discussion by quoting at length and with approval Buffon's rhapsodic description of the bee's cell as *"toute geometrique et toute reguliere"*![22]

The second edition of D'Arcy Thompson's work appeared in 1942. Ten years later Hermann Weyl published his influential *Symme-*

---

[20] Darwin 1998, p.342. The alert reader will have noted that Wyman had stated flatly that the bee's cell does not conform to geometrical accuracy. Darwin's "rarely, if ever" is therefore misleading in its implication that *some* cells may perhaps be geometrically accurate.

[21] p.114. Actually, there is no reliable evidence of the Maraldi angle *ever* being found in a honeycomb.

[22] i.e., "altogether geometric and regular". Buffon, *Histoire naturelle*, 1753 vol.4, p.99, as cited by D'Arcy Thompson, *ibid.* p.118-9.

try. Weyl's lengthy discussion of the bee cell in this book is little more than a detailed (though unacknowledged) précis of Thompson's own discussion. Indeed, Weyl adopted Thompson's ambivalence about the subject by declaring that bees' cells are "not as regular" as had been assumed and then nevertheless admiring the "geometrical talents" that had constructed them.[23]

More recent writers, throwing even this much caution to the winds, have reverted to what we might call the pre-Wyman position. Thus Frisch marveled at the "astounding precision" of the bee's cell, adding that "human craftsmen could not do work of this nature without the use of carpenter's squares and sliding gauges."[24] "The combs are natural engineering marvels", a paper of the authoritative Darwin Project declares, "using the least possible amount of wax to provide the greatest amount of storage space with the greatest possible structural stability."[25] And in a book published in 2008 by Marcus du Sautoy, a distinguished Oxford mathematician, we find the statement that "symmetry is nature's way of being efficient and economical. For the bee, the lattice of hexagons allows the colony to pack the most honey into the greatest space without wasting too much wax on building its walls."[26]

But back now to that fateful winter's night in Prague, and Kepler's observation that the snowflakes falling on his coat were "all" in the shape of a regular hexagon (*"omnes sexanguli"*). Even at first glance this statement seems implausible.[27] Street lighting in Prague at the beginning of the seventeenth century was quite rudimentary, and it seems unlikely that there would have been enough light on that stormy evening for Kepler to see precisely what the shapes of the snowflakes that were falling all around him really were.[28] Nevertheless, as far as Kepler

---

[23] Weyl, 1952, pp.90-92. In the preface Weyl refers to Thomson's *On Growth and Form* with the remark, merely, that in it "symmetry is but a side issue".

[24] Frisch (1975), quoted Bergman and Ishay 2007. Frisch even specified standard measurements for the honeycomb: "The thickness of the cell walls is 0.073 mm with a tolerance of no more than 0.002 mm." Bergman and Ishay refer to "the very precise hexagonal lateral symmetry" of hornets' cells, a claim the authors attempt to bolster with a photograph that – as one might expect – shows them instead to be asymmetric.

[25] darwinproject.ac.uk/the-evolution-of-honey-comb downloaded March 12, 2009.

[26] Sautoy 2008, p.13.

[27] One might say that it should perhaps be taken with a pinch of another crystal, that of sodium chloride.

[28] The only street lighting in Prague at this time took the form of coal or wood flames in iron baskets affixed to the walls of houses on street corners. See praha.eu/jnp/en/extra/light_in_streets/history.html accessed Feb.7, 2011.

was concerned those snowflakes were indeed regular hexagons. Exclaiming *mehercule!* – "by Hercules" – he began to ponder the reason for that. "Why", he asked himself, "do snowflakes always come down (*"perpetuo cadant"*) as hexagons?" He assumed that there must be a specific cause for their six-sidedness, for if their shape were merely a matter of chance, "why would they always fall with six corners, and not just as well with five, or with seven?" The answer, he felt, must lie in the "formative force" which "built its nest in the center" of the snowflake and from there distributed itself equally (*"equaliter"*) in all directions.

Within days however Kepler began to discover snowflakes that were not hexagonal at all but had "varying numbers of radii which spread in every direction"; what is more, these snowflakes were irregularly shaped. Kepler described them as lumpy and roundish, and thought that they were quite without beauty. He had believed that the hexagonal snowflakes which he noticed initially were produced by the "supreme reason" which had existed "from the very beginning in the plan of the Creator". This suggested to him that the unattractive ones he now observed must have been "abandoned by the Master Builder". Further observations led Kepler to conclude that the hexagonal snowflakes that had originally caught his attention were clearly the "rarer" of the two kinds (*"duorum generum"*). More startlingly, he then decided that they were in fact not really six-sided at all but had "a seventh little radius bent down, like a kind of root, on which they settled as they fell, and on which they were propped up for a little while".

One might have supposed that Kepler, upon discovering that most snowflakes are not regular hexagons and that even the seemingly hexagonal ones are not, in fact, hexagonal at all, would have recognized that the question he asked himself that wintry night in Prague was based on a false premise and therefore could not be answered. But Kepler never did reach this conclusion. He neither abandoned his original question – why do snowflakes always fall as regular hexagons? – nor modified it to fit the fact, ascertained by himself, that they are *not* hexagons. Instead, much to our bafflement, he stuck with his original delusory question to the very end, and concluded his essay with the bizarre comment, "I have not resolved this matter. Much remains to be said on the subject before we know its cause".

It goes without saying that Kepler's refusal to acknowledge the implications of facts that he himself had obtained is inconsistent with the norms of scientific inquiry.[29] Yet, as we shall see, research into

---

[29] Comp. the helpful insight of Hauser (1965, p.47) that Kepler, as well as Copernicus, "cannot be regarded as typical representatives of the new, unbiased scientific spirit that based itself purely on observation. In the development of their ideas and the description of their systems they allow themselves to be guided by all sorts of

snowflakes has always been marred by a willingness – one might almost call it a compulsion - to ignore, and even to bend, the evidence in order to support the *a priori* belief that snowflakes are shaped as regular hexagons.

Thus Descartes, in his Sixth Discourse on Meteorology, marveled at the snowflakes he observed in Amsterdam on the night of February 5, 1634.[30] They were, he persuaded himself, "perfectly-cut in hexagons, with their sides so straight and their six angles so equal, that it would be impossible for human beings to make anything so precise". Like Kepler, he failed to explain how he was able to determine their shape, particularly at night, with such precision.[31] Descartes had never heard anyone speak of such accurately-shaped snowflakes before ("*je n'avois jamais ouï parler*"), which suggests that he had not read Kepler's work; and he wondered "what could have formed and proportioned those six teeth with such precision around each grain?" The next day however he noticed that the snowflakes which were falling were not as regularly formed ("*pas si régulièrement formées*") as those of the previous night, though apparently all of them, too, were hexagonal. Descartes' investigations did not lead to any conclusion, but he never altered his conviction that *some* flakes, at least, are "perfectly-cut" hexagons. He did not come up with a theory of how either the regularly, or the irregularly, shaped flakes are formed.

Three decades after Descartes, Thomas Hooke was also at first impressed by the regular hexagonal form of snowflakes, which he reported in his *Micrographia* were "all of equal length, shape and make, from the center, being each of them inclined ... by an angle of sixty degrees".[32] The branches of each flake, he added, "were for the most part in one flake exactly of the same make ... so that whatever Figure one of the branches were, the other five were sure to be of the same, very exactly " However, when Hooke looked at them under his microscope he found that they were not after all "so curious and exactly figur'd as one would have imagin'd"; and the more he magnified their images, he reported, "the more irregularities appear'd in them". In his view, however, these irregularities were caused by "the thawing and breaking of

---

mystical, metaphysical and aesthetic fancies; all sorts of fascinating geometrical and ornamental patterns hover alluringly before their mind's eye ... and they create the impression that their great discoveries were due to chance and sudden inspiration."

[30] Descartes 1824, v.5, pp.226-239.

[31] According to *moonpage.com* the moon over Amsterdam that night was about 86% full, but it was snowing and the cloud cover would presumably have screened out some or perhaps much of the moonlight.

[32] Hooke 1665, observation 14.

the flake" during its descent, and so were to be construed as accidents and "not at all" as "the defect ... of Nature". Hooke suggested ("I am very apt to think") that if it were possible to view snowflakes through a microscope when they are first formed in the clouds, and thus "before their Figures are vitiated by external accidents", they would be seen to exhibit "an abundance of ... neatness" (i.e., to be regular hexagons) no matter how greatly their images were magnified. However, he offered no evidence to support this idea.

Hooke's findings were echoed a few years later by Nehemiah Grew, the plant physiologist. "Many parts of snow are a regular feature", he declared in a paper to the Royal Society in London, and he suggested that those with irregular shapes are probably broken fragments.[33] The arctic explorer and scientist William Scoresby also confronted, in a fashion, the fact that not all snowflakes have regular shapes. His *Account of the Arctic Regions* (1820) contains a lengthy analysis, illustrated with engravings, of snowflakes which he had observed over the course of several voyages. These snowflakes, he declared, included "almost every shape of which the generating angles of 60 degrees and 120 degrees are susceptible"[34]. A pious man who would later be ordained in the Church of England, Scoresby ascribed the beauty and variety of these snowflakes to "the will and pleasure of the First Great Cause whose works, even the most minute and evanescent, and in regions the most remote from human observation, are altogether admirable".[35] In another passage, aspiring perhaps to a somewhat more scientific tone, he remarked of the "perfect geometrical figures" of snowflakes that "... the constant regard to equality in the form and size of the six radii of the stellates; the geometrical accuracy of the different parts of the hexagons; the beauty and precision of the internal lines of the compound figures, with the proper arrangement of any attendant ramifications, and the general completion of the regular figure, compose one of the most interesting features of the Science of Crystallography."[36]

Elsewhere in his discussion, however, Scoresby acknowledged

---

[33] Grew 1673.

[34] Martin 1988, P. 40, writes that Scoresby "meticulously measured and drew the symmetry of hundreds of individual snowflakes ...Scoresby's drawings are the first accurate visual descriptions". Martin does not identify the reasons for her confidence in the accuracy of Scoresby's drawings or question whether snowflakes are ever symmetric. It should be pointed out, too, that Scoresby himself did not use the term "symmetry".

[35] Scoresby, I: 426-7. Kepler, it will be recalled, had attributed the shape of regularly-shaped snowflakes to "the plan of the Creator".

[36] *ibid*, pp. 431-2.

that "flakes of snow of the most regular and beautiful forms" only fell when the weather was exceptionally cold.[37] Indeed, even under those conditions it was not *all* but only "the greatest proportion" which were – not certainly, but - "*probably* perfect geometrical figures".[38] At other times, when the temperature was within a degree or two of the freezing point, the snow which fell typically consisted of "large irregular flakes such as are common in Britain". The fraught question of why it was that "the will and pleasure of the First Great Cause" had not shaped these flakes, too, was not one which Scoresby discussed with his readers. At about the same time as Scoresby a Japanese scholar by the name of Sekka Zusetsu published his own drawings of snowflakes, and it is notable that while the two men would surely have differed about the identity of the First Great Cause, the snowflakes which Zusetsu drew are as impeccably symmetric as those drawn by Scoresby.

A few comments are in order at this point regarding the notion that snowflakes are symmetric, specifically, rather than regularly hexagonal. The Japanese physicist Ukichiro Nakaya, who is recognized as the founder of the modern scientific study of snowflakes, criticized Olaus Magnus, the sixteenth-century archbishop of Uppsala whom we met on an earlier page, because he did "not indicate that snow crystals have hexagonal symmetry".[39] In view of the fact that there are no symmetric snowflakes, or at least none that have ever been recorded, it is perhaps Nakaya rather than Olaus who is deserving of censure. We should note, though, that even if Olaus *had* believed that snowflakes have the shape of regular hexagons it is doubtful that he would have seen them as symmetric. The concept of symmetry after all had been formulated for the first time (see Note Six) a mere century before Olaus wrote his work, and in Olaus' day was used largely by architects and others interested in aesthetics. Indeed, it is noteworthy that not just Kepler, but his intellectual descendants up to the beginning of the nineteenth century, did not describe the regular hexagonal configuration (as they thought of it) of snowflakes and bees' cells as symmetric. To be sure, the perfectly regular hexagons which both Kepler and Descartes imagined they had seen *are* indeed symmetric shapes, but what interested each man was the problem of accounting specifically for the hexagonal shape of snowflakes, and for the regularity of the hexagon: they were not interested in its symmetry and we have no reason to believe

---

[37] Note Scoresby's equation of "regular" and "beautiful".

[38] *ibid*, pp. 425, 431. My italics.

[39] Nakaya 1954, p.1.

that they were even aware of it.⁴⁰ Hooke and Scoresby too referred to the regular hexagonal shape of snowflakes without describing them as symmetric.

It is only quite recently that snowflakes have come to be described, specifically, as symmetric, rather than with terms like "perfect geometrical figures", "regular hexagons" and so on that had been used earlier. The symmetry of at least *some* snowflakes was first alleged, in 1800, by the French crystallographer Haüy, who wrote that snowflakes quite often (*"assez souvent"*, i.e., not always) have *"un charactière particulier de symétrie"*. It took English scientists three-quarters of a century to follow this lead. T. H. Huxley, was evidently the first to do so, referring to Scoresby's illustrations of snowflakes as being "always true to hexagonal symmetry".⁴¹ The first description of snowflakes as symmetric in the German language was, curiously enough, by the architectural theorist Gottfried Semper (1803-1879), who used the snowflake's alleged symmetric shape to justify his call for symmetry in the design of buildings.⁴²

There are those who, retroactively as it were, attribute the perception of snowflakes as symmetric to people in past ages. The British mathematician Ian Stewart, for example, does so with his assertion that "the sixfold symmetry of snowflakes has been remarked on for thousands of years".⁴³ Stewart provides no evidence for this statement, and

---

⁴⁰ The failure to perceive the symmetry of a symmetric form does not occur only among students of snowflakes. In Note Three I point to the likelihood that although the ancient Greeks knew of forms that we regard as symmetric they did not recognize them as such. Plato's solids, notably, are symmetric, but neither he nor Euclid, in his mathematical elucidation of them, ever referred to them as such. This distinction should not be minimized, for all that its implications are elusive. Not all symmetric forms are regular polygons, and the distinction between a form whose two halves mirror each other and ones whose angles are identical seems to be a quite fundamental one.

⁴¹ Huxley 1888, pp. 60-62.

⁴² Semper, *Der Stil...* 2ⁿᵈ ed., 1861-3, as quoted Rykwert 1972, p.31. I have not seen a copy of Semper's work.

⁴³ Stewart 1995, p.3. Other untenable claims by Stewart are that the branches of a snowflake are "all identical" though its symmetry is only "almost perfect" (p.9, a neologism - see Note 1 - which means that they are in fact *asymmetric*); "the human form has approximate bilateral symmetry" (p.32; the same neologism); "butterflies are bilaterally symmetric, each wing bearing a mirror image of the pattern on the other" (p.32; "orchids are a glorious, exuberant example of flowers that nearly all have striking bilateral symmetry" (p.49); and "an asymmetric snowflake would be little more than an irregular speck of ice" (p.190). Stewart documented his claim that "bilateral symmetry has been around for a long time" by reference to the Ediacaran worm Spriggina which lived some 560 to 580 million years ago" (p.32); however, a fossil of this worm - see ts4.mm.bing.net/th?id=HN.608007618 236319991&pid=15.1&H=133&W=160 - shows that it was asymmetric. Stewart ac-

in view of the fact that the concept of symmetry can be traced no further back than to the middle of the fifteenth century we may safely regard it as incorrect.[44] The same can also be said of Stewart's claim that Kepler "came up with a pretty good explanation of the snowflake's sixfold symmetry", for Kepler did not use the word "symmetry" in his essay on the snowflake and, as we have already noted, he frankly acknowledged that he had not, in fact, come up with *any* – let alone "a pretty good" - explanation of the shapes of snowflakes. Nor is Stewart alone in making such remarks. The distinguished physicist Mario Livio claimed that Kepler had wanted "to explain the symmetry of snowflakes", while the equally distinguished physicist Ken Libbrecht claimed that both Kepler and Descartes had hoped to understand "the precise sixfold symmetry" of snowflakes. Libbrecht documented this claim, with regard to Descartes, by quoting from a mistranslation which has the Frenchman wondering "what could have formed and made so exactly *symmetrical* these six teeth" – symmetrical in this sense being a word which Descartes did not use.[45]

The description of snowflakes as symmetric was popularized in the German language by the novelist Thomas Mann, who wrote in *The Magic Mountain*, first published in 1924, of the "absolutely symmetrical, icily regular" form of "all" snowflakes. Stranded on the mountain in a storm, Mann's hero Hans Castorp found that the flakes were "too regular, as substance adapted to life never was to this degree – the living principle shuddered at this perfect precision, found it deathly, the very marrow of death". And Mann added: "Hans Castorp felt he understood now the reason why the builders of antiquity purposely and secretly introduced minute variations from absolute symmetry in their columnar structures".[46] Mann's recognition of the contradiction between symmetry and "the living principle" is profound; we will return to it on a later page.

We may note parenthetically that Mann's musings are quoted by Hermann Weyl in his book *Symmetry*. Snowflakes, Weyl declared

---

knowledges (p.56), but without accounting for it, that the human brain is shaped asymmetrically.

[44] See Note Six, "The History of the Concept of Symmetry".

[45] Frank (1974), whose translation was the one Libbrecht used, claimed that he had translated Descartes' French "rather literally". In fact, he thrice erroneously rendered Descartes' *compassé* ("measured", or "well-shaped") as "symmetric".

[46] There is little if any evidence that Classical buildings were symmetric (see Note Three), but the popular belief, here echoed by Mann, in the deliberate breaking of the symmetry of ancient buildings is implausible. Symmetry is a concept that was unknown to the makers of ancient as well as primitive artifacts (see also Notes Four and Five *passim*).

there, "provide the best known specimens of hexagonal symmetry" in nature. However, the twelve photographs (one of them is reproduced as *fig*.2.9) with which he purported to illustrate this claim all show snowflakes which, it is easy to see, are unambiguously asymmetric![47]

It was not until the 1930's that it became conventional for scientists to describe snowflakes as symmetric.[48] Nothing did more to entrench this misconception than the publication in 1936 of *Snow Crystals natural and artificial* by Ukichiro Nakaya, whom we met him earlier in this Note criticizing Olaus Magnus for having failed to recognize that "snow crystals have hexagonal symmetry".[49] The importance Nakaya attached to the notion that snowflakes are symmetric is evident from the very first page of his book, where he claimed (inaccurately, as the reader of these pages will now know!) that "the extraordinary symmetric nature of the six branches of a snow crystal ... has long been an object of wonder and mystery". This, and his statement that "snow crystals have hexagonal symmetry" can only be understood as applying to *all* snowflakes. It is curious, therefore, that Nakaya presented a number of photographs that he said showed snowflakes "having bilateral symmetry" or "showing a perfect symmetry of design"[50]. One might suppose these descriptions to be superfluous, for if all snowflakes "have hexagonal symmetry" why would it be necessary to single out the symmetry of some for special mention? By implication, at least, Nakaya's opening remarks raised the question of how many snowflakes "have hexagonal symmetry". Are all symmetric? Or only some? Or – perhaps – *none*?

Nakaya's attempts to deal with this problem were hesitant and ambivalent, and bring to mind Kepler's reluctance to acknowledge that his own data contradicted his *a priori* belief that snowflakes are regular hexagons. Thus, after referring to snowflakes "having bilateral symmetry", Nakaya commented that "it is surprising that crystals of such a unique form were observed again and again", a remark that implies that symmetric snowflakes are distinctive.[51] In another passage he acknowledged that asymmetric snowflakes "are not less often observed" than symmetric ones. Then, seemingly under the momentum of this disclosure, he went on to declare rather strangely that, "considering the frequency of [their] occurrence, these asymmetrical crystals may be

---

[47] Weyl 1955, pp.63; 64-5 and fig.38.

[48] Seligman 1980, p.36.

[49] Nakaya's achievement in creating the world's first artificial snowflakes is commemorated by a granite marker in the shape of a perfectly hexagonal snowflake on the campus of Hokkaido University – see illustration in Hargittai, 1986, p.78.

[50] Nakaya 1954, crystals # 512-515 and pp. 407-8; p.103, # 208.

[51] *ibid*, p.41.

more common than the symmetrical ones". Next, and as if retreating from this acknowledgment, he added: "Of course, the question is a matter of degree ... the criterion of regular crystals and asymmetrical ones is rather arbitrary". Questionable in itself, this is not a point he had thought to make earlier when he declared that snowflakes are symmetric. Nakaya's two-step continued with the even bolder – but still insufficient! – acknowledgement that "a perfectly symmetrical crystal is rarely observed."[52] At no point did he provide evidence that "a perfectly symmetrical" snowflake has *ever* been observed.

To the very end Nakaya remained uncertain about the conclusion to which his data pointed. His findings, he declared in his summary of them, "lead us to the conclusion that snow crystals do not always show complete hexagonal symmetry". In the very next sentence however he modified this with the statement that, "as a matter of fact, *most* [my emphasis] of the natural snowflakes of the hexagonal plane type do not exhibit ... complete hexagonal symmetry", adding that they "deviate more or less" from symmetry.[53]

This statement implies a need to reconsider what the norm for snowflakes really is, but Nakaya chose instead to declare that snowflakes (by which he presumably meant *all* snowflakes) "have a tendency to grow" symmetrically.[54] But he offered no theoretical or empirical explanation for this claim, which I think is inconsistent not only with the empirical data but with some of his own observations; it also of course begs the question of how far this "tendency" determines their ultimate shape.

All in all, then, and by his own reckoning, Nakaya failed to justify his enthusiastic reference at the outset of his book to "the extraordinary symmetric nature of the six branches of a snow crystal". Did he ever think, one wonders, that he perhaps owed old Olaus an apology?!

Later works by popular and scientific writers also express a thoroughly ambiguous attitude to the question of how snowflakes are shaped. Edward LaChapelle, for example, in his *Field Guide to Snow Crystals*, declared rather strangely that "most snowflakes are ... often asymmetric".[55] In somewhat the same vein the organic chemists István and Magdolna Hargittai refer to "the magnificent hexagonal symmetry" of snowflakes, but then retreat to the statement that the symmetry of snowflakes is "practically perfect" – a construct that careful readers will take to mean that snowflakes are asymmetric.[56] Corydon Bell ac-

---

[52] *ibid*, p.38; and comp. p.19.

[53] *ibid*, p.106; comp. p.37.

[54] *ibid*, p.37.

[55] LaChapelle 1960, p.10.

[56] Hargittai 1994, p.128.

knowledged that asymmetric snowflakes "probably fall in greater number and more frequently than other types of snow" but then added that "By most standards they cannot be called beautiful. They give the appearance of having been born in troublesome times or on the wrong side of the storm". [57] The physical chemist Joe Rosen, who has written extensively on symmetry, somewhat more circumspectly declared that "snowflakes *generally* [my emphasis] possess a single axis of sixfold ... symmetry", and cited in support of this claim some photographs which according to Nakaya were doctored (and which moreover do *not* show symmetric forms!) as well as a statement by - Kepler himself.[58] Other scientists however affirm the snowflake's symmetry unhesitatingly. Burke, in his study of the history of crystallography, flatly declared that "the snowflake exhibits hexagonal symmetry".[59] The physicist Leon Lederman, a Nobel laureate, wrote of the "graceful symmetry" of Nature's creations, among them the snowflake.[60] Weyl, for his part, declared he was inclined to think with Plato that "the ... mathematical laws governing nature are the origins of symmetry in nature", one of the best known expressions of which he claimed is the hexagonal symmetry of the snowflake.[61]

The most prolific scientific writer on snowflakes today is Kenneth G. Libbrecht who, although chairman of the physics department at Caltech, has written mainly popular works on the subject. Even in his scientific publications however Libbrecht continues the long tradition of ambiguity regarding the snowflake's shape. "Most snow crystals", he wrote in *Reports on Progress in Physics*, are "usually [!] without the high degree of symmetry present in well-formed specimens". The simple meaning of this statement is of course that snowflakes are "usually" asymmetric. Further on in the same paper however Libbrecht reversed course with the statement that a "combination of complexity and symmetry" is in fact to be "seen in many specimens" – a claim that he illustrated with a photograph showing a snowflake that he claimed pos-

---

[57] Bell 1967, p.207.

[58] Rosen 1975, pp.86-88.

[59] Burke 1966, p.35.

[60] Lederman 2008, p.13. "Graceful symmetry", according to Lederman, is also characteristic of a flower's petals, a radiating seashell, and "a noble tree's branches and the veins of its leaves"; he also refers to "the ideal symmetrical disks of the Moon and Sun". Of course, none of these are symmetric.

[61] Weyl 1955, pp.7-8. Weyl offered nothing to support his implication here that Plato recognized, let alone explained, "symmetry in Nature". On Plato's evident ignorance of the concept of symmetry see pp. 43-44, *below*.

sessed "especially precise sixfold symmetry". It is readily apparent however that the photograph shows an *asymmetric* snowflake (*fig.* 2.10).

Libbrecht's descriptions of the growth of snowflakes extend this confusion. "The six arms of an individual crystal travel together" as they fall from the clouds, he writes, and "grow in synchrony, simply because they each experience the same growth history."[62] We need not tarry here on the point that synchrony has nothing to do with the matter – things can grow at the same time, after all, without growing in the same way – but instead will note Libbrecht's acknowledgment further on in the discussion that, except when conditions are "ideal" the six arms merely develop merely "*roughly* [my emphasis] the same pattern". In other words, they are asymmetric. Libbrecht did not describe the "ideal" conditions which allegedly produce symmetric snowflakes or vouchsafe his readers so much as a hint as to the frequency with which these conditions occur or indeed his evidence for suggesting that they *ever* occur. "Symmetry is inherent in snow crystals", he declared at another point, though again without identifying either the meaning of this statement or his evidence for making it. Reversing himself again, he acknowledged that the symmetry of snowflakes is "fragile and *never perfect* [my emphasis]", and that their forms are merely versions of "imperfect ... symmetry". Must we not suppose that if their symmetry is "never perfect" that snowflakes are always asymmetric?

We have seen that although Kepler retreated from his initial observation that snowflakes are "always" hexagonal, it became conventional for investigators after him to repeat that claim. This belief is sometimes based on more than (inaccurate) observation generalized to account for *all* snowflakes. Snowflakes, Nakaya and Libbrecht among others have suggested, are *necessarily* hexagonal because their structure is determined by the hexagonal molecular structure of water itself.[63] In 1966 however two of Nakaya's former colleagues at Hokkaido University, Choji Magono and Chung Woo Lee, both meteorologists, published a short paper which they tactfully declared "modified and supplemented" Nakaya's study. Their research, the two men were careful to say, had been undertaken with the "agreement" of Nakaya; and they added that they "would have liked to ask Dr. Nakaya's opinion" of their work but that unfortunately he died before its completion.

---

[62] Libbrecht 2006, p.12. (Libbrecht incorrectly states that Kepler dedicated his book on snowflakes to "his patron Emperor Rudolf II". In fact, the patron to whom Kepler dedicated the book was the imperial councilor, von Wackenfels.)

[63] So too Furukuwa 2007, pp.70-71. Comp. Mason (1992) that "the hexagonal symmetry of a snow crystal is a macroscopic, outward manifestation of the internal arrangement of the atoms in ice".

Actually, the two meteorologists' paper can be seen as a vigorous critique of Nakaya's book, and as such is an unusual departure from the deferential culture which (I am told) prevailed at that time in the Japanese academic world. Boldly, Magono and Lee declared that Nakaya's classification of snowflakes was "too simple". In particular, they criticized Nakaya's analyses of "unsymmetric, modified or rimed" snow crystals and stated bluntly: "In actual cases most of snow crystals are irregular, unsymmetric, modified or rimed". The typology they devised more than doubled the number identified by Nakaya.[64]

Magono and Lee's reference to "most" snowflakes can be taken to mean that *some* – though not all - snowflakes are symmetric.[65] However, there is no empirical evidence that snowflakes are ever shaped symmetrically. Nakaya claimed that he had observed bilaterally symmetric snowflakes "again and again" but of the more than five hundred photographs of snowflakes that he published in his book, he described only five as symmetric: and all of these are, without doubt, *asymmetric*. Not a single one of Nakaya's photographs is of a symmetric snowflake, and we must doubt whether he in fact ever saw even a single snowflake that was symmetric.

The same is true of the photographs that Libbrecht claimed were of symmetric snowflakes. Not one of them is symmetric; and their asymmetry is readily apparent to the naked eye. Equally, not a single symmetric snowflake is to be found in that remarkable collection of photographs taken by Bentley in Vermont.[66] (Nakaya thought that Bentley had doctored at least some of his photographs).

Thus it can be said, with considerable confidence, that on the basis of what the naked eye is able to perceive, without the assistance even of simple measuring instruments, *no photograph of a symmetric snowflake has ever been published, whether in scientific or popular works.*

What Wyman found regarding bees' cells is also true of snowflakes. There is no evidence that they are ever symmetric.

The underlying theme we have traced here is of a determination to establish that bees' cells and snowflakes – and beyond them, Nature's forms altogether – are shaped symmetrically. In pursuit of this goal men of great scientific eminence have ignored common sense and

---

[64] Magono 1966 - for example, types P2 b and c: plates 62-65. Magono and Lee were evidently unaware that Kepler later discovered that his "hexagonal" snowflakes in fact had *seven* branches.

[65] Magono and Lee do not explain what they mean by "modified" snowflakes, but it does not seem as if they are suggesting, as e.g. Hooke had done, that irregularly-shaped snowflakes were modified from their original symmetric shape.

[66] Bentley, 1961.

the rules of empirical evidence, with the result that palpable absurdities that would be the downfall of a freshman's essay have been acclaimed as important contributions to science.

Some scientists however have hinted that in a certain sense Nature's creations are simultaneously symmetric *and* asymmetric. Thus Darwin sought to distinguish the symmetric "typical form" of bees' cells (which he acknowledged "rarely if ever" exists) from the irregular shapes reported by Wyman. Nakaya, too, contrasted the "tendency" of snowflakes to be symmetric with their *actual* asymmetric form, and it is possible that Libbrecht had something like this in mind when he claimed that symmetry is "inherent" in snowflakes, even if it is seldom (we have shown in fact never) seen in them. An earlier anticipation of these remarks may perhaps be found in Kepler's notion that some snowflakes he observed conformed to "the plan of the Creator" while others were "abandoned by the Master Builder".[67]

The notion to which these men evidently allude was explored at some length by F. M. Jaeger, a Dutch professor of chemistry, in his *Lectures on the principle of symmetry and its application in all natural sciences*.[68] Jaeger acknowledged that he was strongly drawn to symmetric forms, and wrote of the "splendor and fascinating beauty" that he believed symmetry confers upon "a great number of living creatures" such as radiolaria, medusa, diatomae, corals, starfish and "innumerable flowers".

Nevertheless, Jaeger was led by his instincts as a scientist to ask a question that, for all its importance, many scientists have avoided. "How far", he wanted to know, "can we really speak of true 'symmetry' with respect to the geometrical properties of objects observed in nature?"

The question is very much to the point. Jaeger's answer to it however merely resurrected fallacies that had been repeated over and over again since Kepler's time.

In a section entitled "Observed disagreements between crystallographical and physical symmetry", Jaeger distinguished the ideal ("crystallographic") shape of a thing from its actual ("physical") shape. He likened the difference between them to a well-governed society in which most people are law-abiding but a minority "behave not as they should do".[69] In Jaeger's analogy the well-governed society is Nature, with its laws. Most forms obey Nature's laws, one of which is the re-

---

[67] In what appears to be much the same vein the psychologist Puffer (1905, p.10) declared that there is "a hidden symmetry" (she does not explain how she detected it) in some asymmetric forms.

[68] Jaeger 1917

[69] *ibid*, p.167.

quirement to have symmetric shapes. A minority however flout this law and adopt asymmetric shapes.

In another section Jaeger attempted to buttress this view with a different line of thought. He began by asking how it is that we are able to identify a particular object (an oak leaf, in his example) which we have not seen previously. His answer is that we have in our minds a construct of the *ideal* image of the oak leaf – the image, that is, of what the completely developed and perfect oak leaf looks like; and we instinctively use this image to recognize any actual oak leaf that appears before us.

This is an interesting, if not entirely original, hypothesis. Having stated it, however, Jaeger went on to declare that although Nature's forms as we see them are "never" symmetric –

> The one half of the oak-leaf appears never to be precisely the same as the other half; the alum-crystal never has twelve accurately equal angles, etc.

– in their ideal forms (which we never see) they are *always symmetric*.[70] This is a startling and highly dogmatic assertion. It reaches the reader unencumbered by explanation. We are merely told that the ideal form of a thing is always symmetric. That it is so Jaeger does not demonstrate; why it should be so he does not explain. We are handed a pronouncement, no more than that.[71] That this pronouncement is contradicted by some of his other utterances does not occur (it would seem) to Jaeger. If no symmetric shapes exist in the material world then surely nothing in it (to use his figure of speech) "behaves ...as it should do", leaving us either with a very strange view of reality or a very vulnerable understanding of it. Yet we have also learned from Jaeger of the joy he experiences in the "splendor and fascinating beauty" that, in the world of actual perceptions, symmetry confers upon everything from radiolaria to flowers. Surely, if symmetric forms do not exist neither can the beautiful symmetric natural forms that give him so much joy. There is not much to be gained, one suspects, from pursuing Jaeger's paradoxes further.

Yet there is an even more paradoxical construct which we should briefly note here. Symmetry, the British chemical scientist J. D. Bernal declared, "is attributable to all structures endowed with a struc-

---

[70] *ibid*, p.6.

[71] Jaeger (*ibid*, p.7) justifies this: "as regards living organisms, it can hardly be hoped within a measurable space of time to connect their intimate nature with the constant occurrence of their typical external form in any direct way". He claims however to have given "a rational explanation" of the two forms "in some cases" regarding crystals.

ture [!], and this holds true even if [a structure] is the negation of symmetry, asymmetry, where every part only resembles itself." Which is to say (if I understand Bernal correctly), that all structures that are structured are symmetric even when they are asymmetric... Bernal then went on to say that although the symmetry of crystals "had been assumed to be perfect", recent research has shown that "in a very large number of cases the crystal is only perfect ideally, whereas really it contained geometrical imperfections or singularities, known as dislocations, which play an essential part in crystal growth.... The dislocations are not an absence of symmetry but symmetry of a different order ... a perfect crystal could exist but it could never, as such, come into existence".[72]

These are extremely paradoxical remarks. They sound more like a Zen *koan* than a scientific statement. One wonders what kind of research could establish that crystals are "only perfect" – which is to say, symmetric – *ideally* but not actually. How do we know that perfect (=*symmetric*) crystals "could exist" but can never "come into existence"? What does that phrase even mean? And how can an asymmetric crystal be a symmetric crystal? My non-scientific mind, at least, boggles! "Imperfect symmetry" however is a solecism that we *can* classify. It is after all simply a reluctant way to refer to asymmetry. What we can take away from Bernals' remarks therefore is that symmetric crystals do not actually exist. All crystals, in other words, are asymmetric.

The perception (mistaken though it was) that Nature's artifacts are shaped symmetrically has often been used as evidence of transcendent forces at work.[73] For Darwin, the "perfection" he insisted on seeing in the structure of the bee's cell confirmed his notions about the purposeful evolution of the natural order of things. For Weyl, who anachronistically attributed the idea to Plato, "the mathematical laws governing Nature are the origins of symmetry in Nature" – all of whose forms, he went on to say, "are inherently symmetric".[74] The distin-

---

[72] Bernal 1955; other fallacies of Bernal (1937) include: "Symmetry is a character of nature anteceding any human construction. It is obvious in the flower, the starfish and the snowflake..."; "Something of our appreciation of symmetry must be inborn..."; and "The conscious apprehension and understanding of symmetry first [came] to our knowledge with the Greeks and their five regular solids"

[73] It seems important to emphasize again that although Kepler, Scoresby, Fontenelle and no doubt many others believed that the precise hexagonal shapes (as they thought of them) of snowflakes and bees' cells were the work of God's hand, they did not see those forms as symmetric. This distinction should be kept in mind in any study of symmetry.

[74] Weyl, op.cit., pp.7-8. Weyl did not explain what he meant by "inherently" symmetric.

guished physicist Leon Lederman, a Nobel prize-winner, held that the "perfect order and harmony" which underlies "everything in the universe" is affirmed by the symmetry of Nature's shapes "in the world around us".[75]

The facts presented here indicate that, however perfect the order and harmony of the universe may be, they do not require that Nature's artifacts have symmetric shapes. Indeed, the opposite is true, for those artifacts, as far as we can determine, are always asymmetric...[76]

But why is this? Why does Nature seem to choose only asymmetric forms? Why does she not create only symmetric forms, instead? Or both asymmetric and symmetric ones? The following observations may help in some degree to clarify these deep questions.

We can start by noting that the transformation of a symmetric to an asymmetric form, and the transformation of an asymmetric form to a symmetric one, are fundamentally different processes. In a symmetric shape every detail on the right half must be mirrored by every detail on the left half. For an asymmetric shape to be transformed into a symmetric one, therefore, a high level of precision is called for so that all the features on one half that do not mirror those on the other are altered to conform precisely to them.

By contrast, the creation of an asymmetric shape out of a symmetric one can be achieved merely by making any change at all, whether big or small, simple or complex, on the right (or left) half and not making exactly the same change, or the mirrored version of it, on the other half.

The one transformation, accordingly, requires highly specific changes to be made; the other transformation is accomplished merely by any change at all on one half of a shape that is not matched on the other half. A further distinction between the two processes is that because of the precision required, the creation of a symmetric from an

---

[75] Lederman, 2008, p.14. Lederman went on to say that "Humans, for thousands of years, have been drawn instinctively to equate symmetry to perfection. Ancient architects incorporated symmetries into designs and constructions. Whether it was an ancient Greek temple, a geometrical tomb of a pharaoh, or a medieval cathedral..." Having written so much nonsense he returned at one point to his role as Nobel prize-winning physicist and stated flatly (*ibid*, p.65): "There is no center about which everything turns in the universe." This is to say that the universe itself is asymmetric...

[76] Alexander, Neis, Alexander (2012, pp.204-5), in a particularly silly assertion, would have us believe that natural forms (as well as churches and the Parthenon) are symmetric, and that the reason for this is that "symmetries occur because there is no good reason for *asymmetries* to occur".

asymmetric form will only very rarely occur by chance – that is, unintentionally; whereas the creation of an asymmetric form may be either intentional or unintentional.

The passage of time, which is an integral part of Nature's scheme, unendingly subjects all material things to the processes of change. All forms are therefore ephemeral. A sapling grows from a seed and a tree grows from the sapling; branches extend from the tree's trunk and twigs from them; leaves and perhaps blossoms and fruit sprout and fall; eventually the tree decays and dies. At every instant of its existence the tree undergoes changes: its detritus too is subject to ceaseless change. The myriad interactions which lead to these successive changes will only in the very rarest instances give the tree a symmetric form. More typically – almost invariably – they will cause the transformation of an asymmetric form into another asymmetric form. And this is how it is, I dare say, with all the trees which you and I have ever seen.

But suppose, as is not *entirely* impossible, that at some stage the forces of growth or decay naturally cause a tree to acquire a symmetric shape. How long would it continue to retain its symmetry? After all, the passage of time during which the tree became symmetric does not cease now that the tree has become symmetric. Time will continue to pass and bring with it changes that will continue to affect the shape of the tree. Merely the smallest of these changes is likely to deprive this particular tree of its bizarre symmetry: and only the most random of coincidences would enable the tree to retain it. Miniscule as the likelihood of the tree becoming symmetric was in the first place, the likelihood that the forces of change will continue with each ephemeral transformation to create another symmetric form is virtually *nil*. The overwhelming odds are that it will return instead to an asymmetric configuration.

And all this is true in general and not only of trees, of course. Time causes change; arguably, time *is* change. It is a near certainty that naturally-occurring changes will preserve the asymmetry of a form and will make a form asymmetric again if – by a fluke – it happened to have acquired a symmetric shape. This is one of the reasons why Nature favors asymmetry. It is also perhaps why we should think of asymmetry and not of symmetry as rational. In a world without time and thus without change symmetry could be rational because it is consistent with the cessation of time. But in the world we inhabit, a world of time and therefore of change, symmetry is inherently vulnerable, unstable and even unpredictable (the odds against it being as great as they are). Whereas asymmetry survives almost every challenge.

A consideration having to do with our perception of a shape and not with its objective appearance is perhaps worth noting at this point. In the nature of things our glimpses of symmetry are necessarily transient and ephemeral. We are after all not often stationary and as we move our perspectives on things change, so that what appears to be symmetric from one position will – unless it is a perfect sphere – appear to be asymmetric from any other. If we stand anywhere on a line that is at an angle of 90 degrees to the precise center of the façade of the basilica of St Peter in the Vatican, for example, we will see an impeccably symmetric structure. Yet for all the care lavished on its symmetry – a roundel containing a clock on the upper right-hand corner of the façade for example is matched by an identical one in the identical position on the opposite corner – the moment we move to one side or another of that line, even if only by a single step, the façade no longer presents a symmetric view to us. Our perspective continues to be asymmetric no matter how many steps we take away from the line, and it is only by returning to any point on the line that we can recover the earlier symmetric view.

There are accordingly a vast number of possible asymmetric perspectives on a symmetric object but far fewer symmetric perspectives on it.[77] It is ironic perhaps that, for all the compulsive care lavished on the design and construction of symmetric buildings, their symmetry is only seldom visible to people who happen to be looking at them.[78]

We see from this that movement – a natural condition for us – is the friend of asymmetry and the enemy of symmetry. It is only in a world in which we never move in relation to the symmetric projection of every object around us that this would cease to be the case. Such a world is impossible to visualize and horrible to contemplate.

We saw earlier that the symmetry of material forms is, in an objective sense, an ephemeral condition; and now we have also established that in a specific but significant subjective sense symmetry is a *static* phenomenon. In both respects symmetry contravenes fundamental aspects of Nature, our inevitable movement in time and space.

We have already mentioned that the concept of symmetry is conjoined to the concept of simplicity. This brings symmetry into conflict with another fundamental aspect of Nature, too. I am referring to that most mysterious and wonderful penchant of Nature for variety. From the room in which I am writing I have a vast view across the up-

---

[77] Gandy (1805, pp.vii-viii) uses this as an argument for what we would now call asymmetric buildings: "Uniform buildings have but one point of view from whence their parts are corresponding; from every other point they fall into the picturesque by the change of perspective, which is an argument drawn from Nature, that the picturesque is the most beautiful…"

[78] For a challenging discussion of these issues, in the context of Doric architecture, see Duddy 2008.

per Sonoran desert of Arizona. In the distance I see several ranges of mountains, each with its own unique shapes; and closer in, reaching almost to my house, are boulder-strewn slopes on which an awesome variety of plants – cacti, trees, shrubs – grow in profusion: soon, Spring being almost at hand, many of these will adorn themselves with the luridly-colored blossoms characteristic of desert flora. A very large variety of birds, from hawks to hummingbirds, live here, as do insects and animals, many of them quite disagreeable to human beings, such as spiders, scorpions, rattlesnakes, javelinas, coyotes, Gila monsters, bobcats and mountain lions. And it is not only that each of these species is distinct from the others but that each animal, bird, tree, plant, boulder – everything out there - varies in size, shape and color from all the others of its own kind. On no two of the many saguaro, barrel, and other cacti I can see through my windows are the furrows and innumerable needles of their shells arranged in the same way. The configuration of twigs and branches on each of the Palo Verde trees I can also see, now swaying vivaciously in the wind, or the leaves and seed pods of the eucalyptus trees, or the fronds of the palms, each of them is distinctive and unique.

I understand, to be sure, that this variety reflects genetic differences and the effects of the immediate physical habitat, but it is not fully explained by them: and although the reasons for Nature's almost limitless variety are unclear we sense, I think, that it is an essential part of her scheme of things. And here too the juxtaposition of symmetry and asymmetry is an issue, for variety is well served by asymmetry and it is at odds with symmetry. In a symmetric shape the two halves mirror each other; an asymmetric shape with just one of those halves can have an unlimited variety of shapes (except one which is the mirror image of the other) on the other half.

Asymmetry therefore increases by a factor close to infinity Nature's ability to fill the universe with varied shapes. A universe of symmetric shapes would be far less varied and would contain much less information – and therefore be far less interesting and attractive to us – than the universe of asymmetric shapes we are fortunate enough to inhabit.[79] It would lack the "peculiarity", as Hogarth called it, "that leads the eye a wanton kind of chase, and from the pleasure that gives the mind, entitles it to the name of beautiful".[80]

Immune to the pleasure of this wanton chase are the two authors of a scholarly paper who in all solemnity intone their conclusion

---

[79] Lorand 2003-4.

[80] Hogarth 2007, p.33.

that we "prefer complex figures only when they are symmetric".[81] In their argument bilaterally symmetric shapes, being simpler than asymmetric ones, are more readily comprehensible to us *and are therefore preferable*! These authors, one may suppose, would rather gaze at the all-too-intelligible façade of the Seagrams building in New York than at the intricate patterns of hoar-frost on one of its windows or, perhaps, of a Jackson Pollock painting hanging inside on one of its walls. But they are surely in a very small minority. Or one hopes that they are.

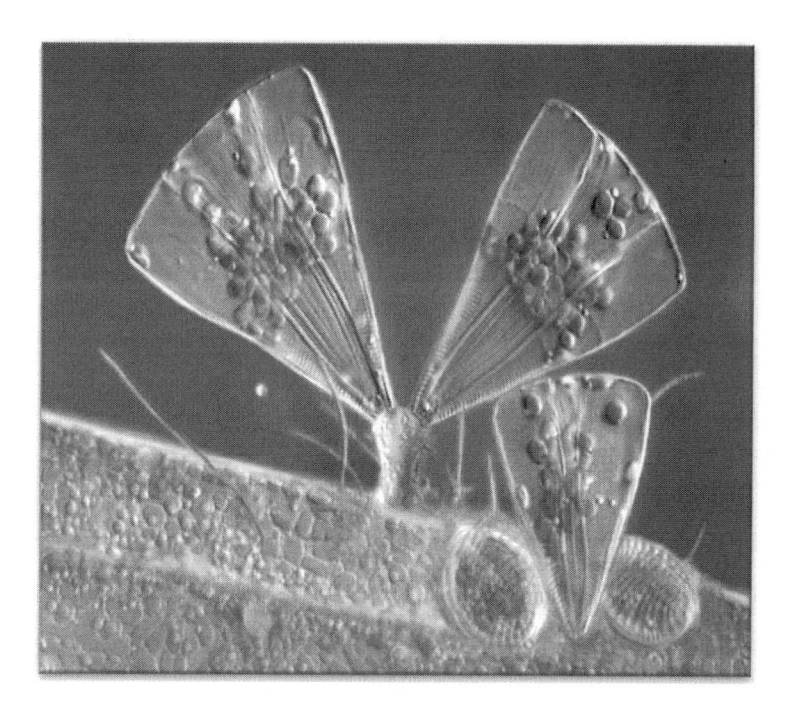

2.2 *Licmophora juegensii* on red alga[82]

---

[81] Eisenman and Gellens 1968. Comp. Montesquieu (in his "Essay on Taste", the section on "the pleasures of symmetry"): "*la raison que la symetrié plaît à l'âme, c'est qu'elle lui épargne de la peine, qu'elle la soulage, et qu'elle coupe pour ainsi dire l'ouvrage par la moitié*". ("The reason that symmetry pleases the mind is that it saves it trouble, that it gives it ease, that it cuts its work, so to speak, in half.")

[82] Wolfgang Bettighofer *Olympusscapes.com/gallery/2010/index*

2.3 Image of cosmic background radiation from the Big Bang

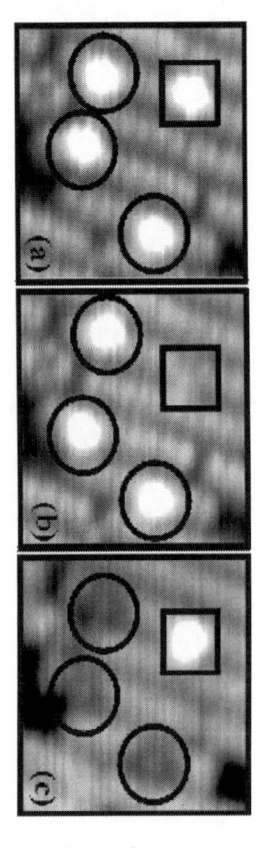

2.4 A series of 45 Å X 45 Å constant current (0.1 nA)
STM images of NBE molecules.[83]

---

[83] foresight.org/Conferences/MNT7/Papers/Hersam/index.html

2.5 Eagle Nebula, "Pillars of Creation" as seen by the Hubble Telescope

2.6 Olaus Magnus' illustrations of frost (upper left) and snowflakes (right).[84]

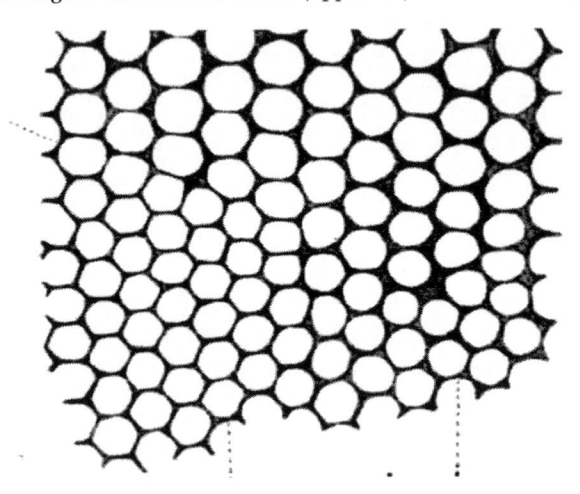

2.7 Portion of honeycomb as drawn by Wyman

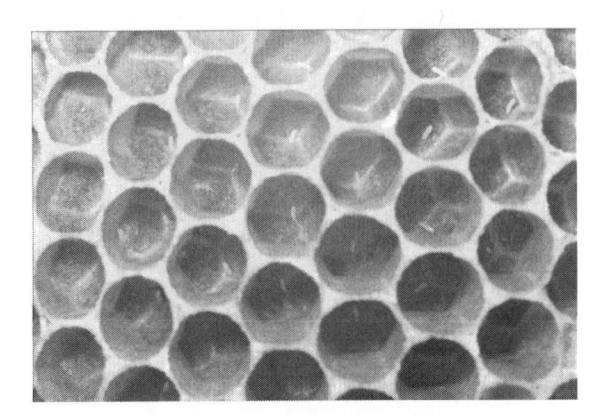

2.8 Photograph of bees' cells[85]

---

[84] Magnus 1996, Bk.1, cap. 22.

[85] casiochulrechner.de/de/teilnehmervektoria2008/andesgymnasiumschwabisch/gmuend/mathe_ist_alles.html

2.9 One of Weyl's purportedly symmetric snowflakes.[86]

2.10 Example of "especially precise sixfold symmetry"[87]

---

[86] Weyl 1955, *fig.* 38.
[87] Libbrecht 2006, p.14

SYMMETRY IN THE CLASSICAL WORLD

3.1 11th. cent BCE Gorgon from Rhodes
Source: Six, 1885

Note Three

> *"The Classical ideal was bilaterally symmetrical"*
> -Robert Evans (1995, p.199)

Statements to the effect that the ancient Greeks and Romans had a "passion for symmetry" have been bandied about for so long and with such great assurance that one might be forgiven for believing there is nothing more to be said on the subject.[1]

Several considerations suggest otherwise, however. Perhaps foremost among them is the fact that neither Classical Greek nor Latin had a word or phrase that denoted the mirroring of the right and left halves of a shape. How then, we must wonder, could people have expressed their "passion for symmetry" if they lacked any term for it? Are we perhaps to believe that their's was a love that dared not speak its name? Or is it more realistic to suppose that if people had no word or phrase for symmetry this was probably because they not only had no "passion" for it but were altogether ignorant of the concept?

To be sure, *symmetria* is a Classical Greek term and was later incorporated into Classical Latin. Its meaning in those tongues, however - something like "harmonious proportion" – was entirely different from the modern meaning of "symmetry" that in fact only dates back to the middle of the fifteenth century.[2]

Some modern scholars are evidently unaware of *symmetria*'s two different meanings. They make the mistake of assuming that

---

[1] Gardner 2005, p.102. Comp. the claim of Sturgis (1905, article on "symmetry") that the Ancients always required their buildings and other artifacts to be "perfectly symmetrical". The standard view of symmetry in the Classical world can be traced no further back than to the middle of the fifteenth century, when Leo Battista Alberti (1996, VI.3) declared that the Greeks and Romans unfailingly saw to it that the left and right halves of anything they made mirrored each other in the minutest detail . To this day restorers routinely defer to this doctrine when they replace missing parts of ancient statues (such as the right wing of the Winged Victory of Samothrace – see Landauro 2013) and monuments (such as certain reliefs on the Ara Pacis in Rome, for which cf. Iacopi 2008, pp.15, 24).

[2] See Note Six. The term's earliest recorded use in the modern sense is in the mid-15th century Latin *Commentarii* of Pius II (d.1464). At the end of the 15th century it occurs in Tuscan in *Hypnerotomachia Poliphili*.

when the word appears in a Classical Greek or Roman text it refers to the mirroring of the right and left halves of a shape – that it means "symmetry" in the modern sense of the word". Tavernor, for example, asserts that for Vitruvius *symmetria* "meant the mirroring of form across an axis, the modern reading of 'symmetry'".[3] In fact, Vitruvius used the word only in the Classical sense of "harmonious proportion" (or, more correctly, in his own idiosyncratic version of it). He did not use it for the mirroring of the two lateral halves of a form, a concept that all the available evidence indicates was unknown to him. The mere appearance of the word *symmetria* in a Classical text, accordingly, should not be taken as evidence that our modern concept of symmetry was known to the Greeks and Romans.

Symmetric shapes such as the square or equilateral triangle were of course known in Classical times, but there is no evidence that the Greeks and Romans recognized them as symmetric. Plato's solids, notably, are symmetric yet neither Plato, nor Euclid in his mathematical elucidation of them, appear to have been aware of their symmetry (a concept, as we have seen, that no word or phrase available to them denoted).[4]

Failure to recognize this distinction has led some modern scholars to interpret Greek notions about the cosmos in terms of a concept – symmetry – that the Greeks did not know. Kahn, for example, refers to the "all-pervading symmetry which is the stamp of Anaximander's thought" even though neither the term nor the concept appear in the few brief fragments of Anaximander's work that have come down to us.[5] Anachronistic references by modern scholars to the concept of

---

[3] Tavernor 1998, p.43. Others mistakenly attributing the modern concept of symmetry to Vitruvius include Lowic (1983); Eco (1986, pp.39-40); and Hart and Hicks (in Serlio 1996 vol. I, p.449 fn.72., p.83).

[4] The curious failure, as it strikes us nowadays, to recognize the symmetry of certain forms did not occur only in the ancient world. As we saw in the previous Note Kepler, and following him Descartes and many others, regarded snowflakes as regular hexagons but it was only at the beginning of the nineteenth century that those – allegedly – regular hexagons were first described as symmetric. It is also curious to note that although his much-acclaimed model of the façade of Santa Maria Novella in Florence is based on the square and a progression of halved squares, all the attention of R. Wittkower and his many followers (see Note Eight) is on the alleged *proportions* of this scheme, and not on its *symmetry*.

[5] Kahn (1960, p.90, echoed by Ferguson 2008, p.17). Anaximander had asked, "why after all should the world fall?" Kahn's answer was that "if the universe is symmetrical, there is no more reason for the earth to move down than up". This was *Kahn's* answer, of course, and not the one Anaximander gave. (We might add, too, that the few lines of Anaximander that survive do not warrant reference to *any* "all-pervading" characteristics of his thought.) In much the same vein Kahn

symmetry cannot, of course, be accepted as evidence that the concept was known to the ancient Greeks.

The lack of any philological or literary evidence of a "passion" for - or even merely knowledge of – symmetry in the Classical world is matched by a lack of material evidence, too. Nowhere is symmetry more obviously *not* present than in the design and decoration of Greek pots. About one hundred thousand vases and fragments of vases from all parts and periods of the ancient Greek world have been photographed and catalogued in the *Corpus Vasorum Antiquorum*.[6] My extensive sampling of the CVA images produced not one that I recognized as symmetric. In what follows, a small selection of such objects, arranged chronologically and including vessels from different parts of the Greek world, will illustrate the asymmetry that is a characteristic of these artifacts. (Because CVA images are generally of low resolution, the illustrations presented here are from other sources, although the objects themselves may also appear in CVA itself.)

- A Minoan vessel (*fig.* 3.2. Illustrations for this Note begin on p.78) of the "old Palatial period" (2100-1700 BCE), now in the museum of Heraklion, has a wonderfully vivacious floral or sunburst design.[7] The outline of the body of this vessel as seen in the photograph is asymmetric. The roundels from which the petals or rays emerge are irregular in shape and are well to the right of the vessel's center. The petals or rays on the right are noticeably shorter than those on the left and do not match the shapes of the ones opposite them.

- A vase (*fig.* 3.3) from the cemetery of ancient Thera, in the Cyclades, is dated between the 9th and 7th centuries BCE.[8] The handle on the right appears to be set higher than its opposite. The upper band contains a series of triangles, each of which is a different size; the triangle on the right is incomplete and, unlike the others, is not decorated internally. In the band below this one, two panels each differing in size, shape and interior decoration, flank stylized images of birds. The birds both face outwards but their sizes and shapes differ from each other; the roundel above each is placed to the right, i.e.. asymmetrically. In the lower band too the designs are markedly asymmetric. The

---

(p.79, fn.3) renders *Phaedo* 108e-109a as, "because its relationship is symmetrical it will remain unswervingly at rest." Neither the term nor the concept appear in the original text, a more reliable translation of which is that of Fowler, who uses the term "equipoise" where Kahn has "symmetry". For other examples the inappropriate use of "symmetry" see Kirk, Raven and Schofield 1983, pp.133, 136, referring to *Iliad* viii.13, and *Theogony*, 726.

[6] The *CVA* can now be accessed online at cvaonline.org/cva/default.htm

[7] en.wikipedia.org/wiki/File:AMI_-_Kamaresvase_2.jpg

[8] www.eidola.eu/images/1274

eight lozenges differ in size and as a group are not centered on the designs above them.

- Also from the geometric period is an 8th. century BCE prothesis vase (*fig.* 3.4) only a portion of which is shown in this image.[9] The meanders in the upper band face in the same direction; they do not, in other words, mirror each other across a central axis. The small rectangles in the checkered panel above the bed vary randomly in size and shape. The bed's leg on the left is shorter and thicker than the one on the right. The child-size mourner on the right is not matched by a similar figure on the left. The adult figure closest to the bier on the right is taller but narrower than its opposite number on the left. The two figures below the bier on the right are seated; those on the left are kneeling. The seated figures are flanked by vertical arrangements of an inverted "V"-like designs, those on the left by "M"-like ones. These "M"-like designs also flank the taller figures standing on both sides of the bier, but while there are 11 of these in each of the arrangements on the right, those on the left have 14, 15, 15 and 14, respectively.

- An amphora (*fig.* 3.5) from Euboea is dated *circa* 570-560 BCE. There are two lions on the vessel's neck. The middle point between them is far to the right of the center of the space between the handles, and the two circular patterns are not positioned one above the other (the dots in these patterns are arranged asymmetrically).Although both lions are resting on their haunches, the lion on the right has one foreleg well in front of the other, whereas the legs of the lion on the left seem to adjoin each other. The body of the lion on the right is considerably shorter than that of the other lion, and the dimensions and curves of their tails are quite different.

- An Attic neck amphora (*fig.* 3.6) is dated *circa* 540 BCE and attributed to Exekias. The eight scrolls in this design differ irregularly from each other in size, and are set at irregularly different heights; the top-right scroll has one less revolution than its opposite number. In each of the two pairs on the upper row the scrolls face away from each other. On the right-hand side the scrolls are extended from the upper to the lower pair by tendrils that curve in toward each other, thus ensuring that the directions of the lower scrolls mirror each other as well as those directly above them. On the left-hand side, however, the scrolls are extended in such a way that the tendrils follow approximately the same direction – i.e., they do not face each other as they do on the right – so that the scroll on the bottom right faces in the same direction as the scrolls beside and above it. The cluster on the lower

---

[9] Richter 1946, p.281, pl.400.

right is smaller but higher than the one on the lower left; it contains four leaves, while that on the left has three.

- A krater (*fig.* 3.7) from Apuleia is dated *circa* 330 to 320 BCE. The two decorative bands at the bottom of the vessel are not divided across a central axis, and therefore are asymmetric. The two pillars at the front of the pavilion differ from each other both in height and breadth; the two diagonal members of the pediment are of different lengths. The elaborate botanical arrays on the vessel's neck are arranged in a bilateral manner but without any attempt at making them symmetric. Note, for example, how the scroll-like tendril on the right is considerably higher up than the one on the left, and that while we see the former principally from within, we see the latter principally from without. The head on the vase's neck is shown asymmetrically in profile.

It is clear from merely the few examples presented here that the ancient Greeks did *not* insist on symmetric design for their pottery. This conclusion echoes that of R. M. Cook, a noted authority, who writes that "the neglect of exact symmetry" among Greek potters and their painters, "is undeniable".[10] In Cook's view, however, the prevalence of asymmetric design in Greek pottery does not reflect an aesthetic preference. Rather, he claims, it is accounted for by the fact that pots were regarded as "cheap product[s] not worth the laborious precision that was demanded in more expensive arts".[11]

Yet we also find abundant evidence of asymmetry in the "more expensive" artifacts of Greek civilization, as we can see from the following examples:

- A Picene or Samnite disc (*fig.* 3.8), dating from the 7th-6th centuries BCE, is a slightly irregular circle. On it are a pair of animals, a pair of dancing women (possibly Gorgons) and another of weird fish-like creatures in antithetical positions.[12] The woman on the right is shorter and set further off to one side of the disk than her companion, and her right arm is clearly much longer than the matching left arm of the other woman; each woman's arms are of drastically different lengths. The two facing animals (lions?) are also in an obviously bilateral arrangement but the body of the beast on the right is longer but lower than that of the other, and its eye is set farther back on the head. The beast on the left is closer to the edge of the disk than the one on the right.

---

[10] Cook 1972, p.28. Note Cook's pleonasm. As we pointed out in Note One, a shape is either symmetric or asymmetric; and there is no such thing as inexact symmetry.

[11] Cook 1972, p.28; comp. Vickers 1987.

[12] Mitten 1967, p.160.

- The bronze *mitra* or abdominal shield (*fig.* 3.9) in the next illustration is from sixth-century BCE Crete.[13] The bodies of the two sphinxes face each other, though their heads look out at the spectator. The bilateralism of this design is obvious. Nevertheless, the sphinx on the right has a longer body, and its tail has wider curves than the other; the mid-point between the two heads is to the left of the center of the field.
- A bronze Argive vase (*fig.*3.10) of the mid-fifth century BCE in the Metropolitan Museum of Art, New York, is inscribed on top of the mouth with the words, "One of the prizes from Argive Hera".[14] The disk attaching the right-side handle to the body of the vase is larger than that on the left. The figure on the rim is not centered on the vase but is closer to the right side of the rim and to the disk on the right. The disk on the left is closer to the edge of the rim than the disk on the right.

Asymmetric forms are commonly found in Greek sculpture, too, as will be apparent from the selection of illustrations that follows.[15] Given the asymmetry of the human body itself this should come as no surprise:
- The highly abstracted, one could almost say minimalist, Cycladic marble statues of women from the late third millennium BCE have among their characteristics heads with asymmetric lyre- or shield-like outlines; along with noses that are not centered on the face and heads that are not centered on the neck. The arms of full-length Cycladic statues of women are typically folded above the waist in a distinctive manner, as in *fig.*3.11, with one forearm directly above the other so that the upper portion of the higher arm is necessarily much shorter than the upper portion of the lower arm. This disparity is sometimes partly obscured by having one shoulder higher than the other. On the statue shown here the left breast is markedly lower than the other, and the shoulders differ in width.[16]
- A well-preserved statue (*fig.* 3.12) from the first half of the sixth century depicts a young man, *kouros.* His crown of locks hangs down asymmetrically over his forehead; there are eight waves of hair hanging

---

[13] *ibid*, p.50

[14] Metropolitan Museum of Art, New York; Purchase, Joseph Pulitzer Bequest, 1926 26.50

[15] One of those oblivious to this fact is Woodford (1988, pp. 41, 4), who refers to "the natural symmetry of the human body" and alleges that Greek sculptors "valued symmetry highly".

[16] Doumas 1983, p. 142, fig. 174.

down to his right shoulder but seven down to his left shoulder. His left eye, eyebrow and, even more so, his left ear, are higher than their counterparts on the right; although it is impossible to be sure from the photograph, it appears that his captivating smile, so characteristic of the *kouroi* statues, is crooked, with a more pronounced rise at the right than at the left corner. His left nipple is lower than its opposite number; his left shoulder is somewhat lower and much less broad than his right shoulder; and his right wrist, forearm and biceps are considerably thicker than those on his left.[17] His left testicle is lower than the one on the right.[18]

- Also from the sixth century BCE is an ivory head (*fig.* 3.13), about two-thirds the size of life, that was discovered under the Sacred Way of Delphi in 1939, and is said to represent Apollo.[19] The ear, eyebrow and eye on the left side of his head are noticeably higher than those on the right; the ear on the left appears to be thicker than the other; the eyes are slightly crossed; and the nose is bent to the left. The pupil of the right eye is partly concealed by the upper eyelid whereas the pupil of the left eye is not.

- The hair on the top of the famous Poseidon (or, as some believe, Zeus) of Artemision is arranged asymmetrically (*fig*.3.14a). The asymmetry of the statue's face, too, (*fig*.3.14b) is quite apparent – the right nostril, for instance, is considerably broader than the left; the shapes of the eyes are different, and the left eye and eyebrow are lower than the right. The strands of the beard do not mirror each other and obscure the lower part of the right (but not the left) cheek.

Turning our attention now to another type of "more expensive" Greek artifact we should note that although a number of sixth and fifth-century engraved gems have pronounced bilateral designs, none that are bilaterally *symmetric* appear in Boardman's standard work on the subject.[20] These include (*fig*.3.15; clockwise from the top left)[21]

---

[17] Beazley 1966, pl.29. Despite the evidence of this (and many other) statues Beazley (*ibid*, p.13) declared that sculptures of the Archaic period, and notably the *kouroi*, are symmetric. See, as other clear examples of asymmetric *kouroi*, Richter, 1946, figs.274 and 391, 394; 450,451.

[18] This being a topic on which McManus (2004; see also the literature cited there) has developed a particular expertise.

[19] Mattusch 1988, pp.177-178.

[20] Boardman 1968.

[21] *ibid*, figs. IV.68; I,22; IX,123; III.46 [found in Chiusi but, according to Boardman, *op.cit.*, p.33, probably not Etruscan]; III.48. The description of these gems' asym-

- The head of a cornelian Gorgon. Note the mirrored *direction* of the snakes heads but the asymmetry of their arrangement by both size and shape. The mouth is asymmetric.
- A cornelian scarab possibly from Cyprus, on which lions flank a sacred tree surmounted by a winged disk (the two wings of which are unequal in length). Note the different arrangements of their tails, and the much thicker forelegs of the beast on the right.
- A cornelian scarab showing a sphinx with two bodies: its asymmetries include the off-centered nose and mouth, and the tails, that on the right being taller and longer than the one on the left and having a different shape from it.
- Two cornelians, each with a winged Gorgon standing with outstretched arms: note the asymmetric arrangement of hair on top of the head of the creature on the left, and of the ribs of the wings of the creature on the right.

Perhaps nothing casts more dramatic doubt on Cook's idea that the Greeks created symmetric designs only in their "more expensive" artifacts than an exquisite seventh-century-BCE gold libation bowl (*fig*.3.16) at the Museum of Fine Arts in Boston.[22] The bowl is said to have been found at Olympia, and an inscription identifies it as the donation of the royal family of Heraclea. We can be certain therefore that this was not, by any standard, a cheap product; and we can be just as certain that it is an asymmetric one. The bowl's interior consists of nine elongated basins that radiate from a hub and give the rim of the bowl a scalloped shape. The bases of these basins are curves of the same size, a circumstance that makes the very different shapes of the basins themselves perplexing. The narrow troughs which separate the basins from each other are of unequal lengths, suggesting that the irregular configurations of the basins themselves were original. This possibility seems strengthened by the fact that the two concentric rings at the approximate center of the bowl are irregular in shape, and that the "mound" that they enclose is not centered on them. The various asymmetric features of this bowl therefore were almost certainly part of the original design and do not represent damage done in later times.

Asymmetric designs are commonly found in the art, architecture and decorative arts of Rome, too. Here are three examples from Rome's provinces:

---

metric features is not intended to be exhaustive and the alert reader will have no difficulty finding other asymmetric details as well.

[22] Museum of Fine Arts, Boston 21.1843.

- An Ionic capital (*fig*.3.17) of the fourth or fifth century CE is from the synagogue at Gamla, Israel.[23] The two scrolls wind in the same direction, which is to say they are asymmetric; and the scroll on the right is substantially larger than the other. The area between the scrolls is decorated with four ovals, that differ in size and shape from each other.
- A votive tablet (*fig*.3.18) from Pergamon, *circa* 200-250 CE, has the shape of an isosceles triangle (the lower side is shorter than the other two).[24] The figure on the lower right is set closer to the apex than the figure on the left; and none of the figures are centered on the large oval (which is lower than and to the left of the triangle's center). The upper figure is shown almost full length; the figure on the lower left is shown only down to just below her chiton, and the one on the lower right only down to her shins. The upper figure and the one on the right have markedly asymmetric shoulders. The figure on the left is centered on a line that bisects the bottom left-hand angle; the other two figures however are each off to one side of the bisecting line. The figure on the top has broader shoulders than either of the other two, while that on the right has a narrower waist. Thus although the shape of this object is that of a symmetric triangle and the disk inside it is a circle all the other features of its design are asymmetric.
- The plan (*fig*.3.19) of a large Roman structure – its function is unknown – recently excavated in England is entirely asymmetric:[25]

It is tempting to suppose that the asymmetry of artifacts like these reflects lower standards of craftsmanship that may have prevailed in the Roman provinces. In fact, asymmetric design is readily found even in the heart of the Roman empire in settings that are associated with wealth and power.

- Two murals now at the Archeological Museum in Naples were from Pompeii and are dated about 20-10 BCE (i.e., the so-called "Third Style" period).[26] Whether or not they are accurate representations of actual *villae marittimae* cannot be determined; but what is noteworthy for our purposes is that both the villas depict homes of wealthy persons and that they are both asymmetric. Thus, there are 14 columns on the right-hand wing of the villa in the first painting (*fig*.3.20), but 13 on

---

[23] Wilson Jones 2003, p.12, *fig*. 0.17.

[24] Staatliche Museen Berlin Antikenabteilung inv # 8612, from: Mitten and Doeringer (1967), p.310.

[25] news.yahoo.com/photos/mysterious-ancient-winged-structure-discovered-13-27331111-slideshow/ancient-rome-photo-1327331072.html

[26] Ward-Perkins 1978, p.118, #1.

the left-hand wing. The pillars on the right are shorter, and support a much taller architrave or cornice than those on the left. The lower, apparently enclosed, portion of the right-hand flank is lower than its equivalent on the other side, and no attempt is made to conceal the disparity between them on the central portion of the building. Moreover, the structure on the right appears to end in a façade of six columns, that on the left in a seemingly wider façade supported by four broad piers (or possibly pilasters).

In the second painting (*fig*.3.21) the columns to the right of the central portico appear to be narrower and more irregularly spaced than those on the left; there are 13 columns on the right but only 12 on the left, but the colonnade on the left is somewhat longer than the one on the right. Of the two pedimented flanking structures, the one on the left has taller columns but a lower architrave than the one on the right. Its overall height appears to be somewhat greater than that of the right-hand wing.

- The vessel in the British Museum now known as the Portland Vase (*fig*.3.22) was made in Rome during the first century of the Common Era. The entire outline of the vase – its bowl, neck, handles and rim – is asymmetric, and there is no hint of symmetry in the cameos that decorate it.

- The marble "Endymion" sarcophagus (*fig*.3.23) at the Metropolitan Museum of Art in New York dates from the later second or early third century, and was found near Rome.[27] The quality of the material and workmanship indicate that it was made for a person of wealth. The lower portion has a lion's head near each of its two sides but they do not represent an attempt at symmetry, the head on the right being somewhat smaller and perhaps further from the outside edge than the head on the left; and the manes of the two beasts are quite different from each other. The free and vivacious arrangement of figures and other elements of the design reflects a total indifference to symmetry. The entire ensemble on the lid is set well to the right of the midpoint of the sarcophagus. The arcade on the right side of the lid is lower than that on the left.

Asymmetric design was evidently acceptable, indeed, even in the highest circles of Rome itself, as we see from the following:

- Fig.3.24 shows the remains of decorations on the wall of a room in the *Palatina Domus* of the emperor Augustus.[28] Five horizontal lines extend from one side of the wall to the other. Except for the topmost,

---

[27] Endymion Sarcophagus MMA 47.100.4 Roman, c.190-210. McCann 1978, 39-41.

[28] Iacopi, 2008, p.15.

these lines are each connected to the one above them with a series of vertical lines, thus creating a set of frames. The horizontal and vertical lines are neatly drawn. It is difficult to tell how many of these frames are in the upper row; the middle row, which is by far the tallest, has five frames and the lower row has four. Each of the five frames in the middle row is of a different width. In the lower row the two frames at the right appear to be the same width (it is difficult to be sure exactly where the corner between the two walls runs), but the two frames to their left are each of a unique size. Of the vertical lines that delineate each frame in the upper and lower rows, several do not accurately bisect the middle row of frames. Clearly, then, the configuration of neatly-drawn vertical and horizontal lines (excluding of course the areas too damaged to allow a determination) is largely asymmetric. Perhaps it bears emphasizing that this decoration is on a wall in the palace of the great emperor Augustus, and not in the shack of a simple herdsman in a remote province of the Roman empire. Asymmetric design, we may infer from this example, was evidently acceptable at the very pinnacle of Roman power.

• The *Ara Pacis*, a ceremonial altar in honor of Augustus completed in the year 9, is a supreme expression of the power and wealth of Rome at the height of her greatness. Although the altar appears to be intact, or almost so, it suffered extensive damage over the course of the centuries and much of what we see now is in fact a modern reconstruction carried out in the 1930's under the aegis of the fascist government. Something of the spirit in which the reconstruction was carried out is conveyed by the statement in an official guide that "lost parts have been replaced with casts taken from corresponding originals symmetrically placed on the opposite sides".[29]

We have of course no reason to suppose that the "opposite sides" of the structure were originally part of a symmetric scheme. To the extent that portions of it have escaped modern reconstruction we can, in fact, infer that the original was *not* symmetrically designed. The two sides of the east face – that is, the structure on either side of the doorway – are not the same width as each other (the left is wider than the right) and their foliate friezes, though they appear to follow the same scheme, juxtaposed, are in fact substantially different and on different planes, and may have escaped the improving hand of Mussolini's reconstructionists. The asymmetry is particularly apparent in the two end pieces of the crowning slab (*fig.* 3.25) of the sacrificial table. One winged lion faces outward from each end. The tail of the beast in

---

[29] Rossini 2007, p.82. The author adds, "In the few cases when the decoration was missing on both ... sides, a new relief has been remodeled [sic]". It is probably safe to assume that this "remodeling" has been done symmetrically.

the right-hand photograph is not as high or long as the opposite one, and it has a rather different shape. The clear difference in the approximately triangular empty space between the tops of the animals' wings and the cornice also calls attention to the asymmetric design. The distance from the bottom of the tail to the corner of the mouth of the beast on the left is significantly greater than it is on the other (though the distance from the bottom of the tail to the peak of the breast bone is identical on both animals). The head of the beast on the right is narrower but taller than that of the beast on the left, and the arrangement of their manes is quite different. The botanical motifs that extend from the scrolls at the top, although they are similar in conception, are clearly different in execution.

- From a somewhat later period in the history of imperial Rome, the Arch of Constantine (*fig*.3.26) has a large heroic medallion set above the triumphal relief on its eastern side, one of several sculptures removed from older monuments by Constantine for his own arch. The rectangular recess into which this medallion is placed is not centered – it is further to the right than to the left.[30]

The physical evidence considered here does not *prove* that the Greeks and Romans never made things that were symmetrically shaped, but it convincingly establishes that they did not insist upon symmetric design. And this holds true, evidently, for both civilizations over the long span of their histories and in the vast regions over which they held sway, and it also holds true both for their common wares and for the most precious and prestigious artifacts they made. When the physical evidence is joined to the linguistic and literary evidence considered at the outset of this Note, the conclusion that the ancient Greeks and Romans did not *know* the concept of symmetry, or that, if they did know it they seldom if ever applied it to the shapes they made, becomes well-nigh inescapable. The view that they felt a "passion" for symmetry and always saw to it that the things they made were symmetrically-shaped is thus without foundation.

It is possible however that this conclusion may have to be modified by the evidence, which we have not yet considered, of Greek and Roman architecture. That evidence raises complicated issues and technical questions of their own and deserves to be considered separately. Before we turn to that task, however, we will address a problem that is implicit in the discussion up to this point.

---

[30] Bober and Rubinstein 2010, pl.182c. Desgodets (1682, pl.III, p.233) mistakenly draws the recess as precisely centered.

There is nothing ambiguous or elusive about the asymmetry of the artifacts at which we have looked here. Their asymmetry indeed is usually quite obvious to anyone who will look at them with unprejudiced eyes. Sometimes, to be sure, it can only be established by looking at an artifact closely, or perhaps by measuring a photograph of it with a ruler or divider, or a simple graphics software program: but after that has been done a person should be left in no doubt that what he has examined is indeed an asymmetric design.

The asymmetric artifacts at which we have been looking represent merely a tiny and more or less random sample of the many tens of thousands of artifacts that have survived from Classical times. Virtually every one of these artifacts, if it is sufficiently intact to make such a determination possible, is asymmetric.

Nevertheless, for more than five hundred years scholars have insisted that the concept of symmetry was known in the Classical world and that it was always meticulously employed in the shaping of every kind of material object.

If there are other accepted truths in scholarly circles that are as obviously mistaken but nevertheless as persistent as the myth of symmetry in ancient Greece and Rome I, for one, have yet to learn of them.[31]

It will be useful to look into this phenomenon more closely. We will do so in two stages. In this Note we will identify some of the procedures that lead people to avoid acknowledging the asymmetry of an object. Later, in Note Seven, we will examine the more fundamental problem of *why* the need arises to deny that a form is asymmetric.

What we find most commonly is people simply asserting – the scholarly *ex cathedra* pronouncement – that something is symmetric when it obviously is not. Usually (though as we will see, not always) there is no subterfuge involved. That is, the error is made in good faith by a person who failed to recognize that an object is asymmetric. And this is usually not because that person suffered from poor eyesight or some cognitive deficiency, or because the object's asymmetry is so muted as to be virtually invisible: but because the person's perceptions have been affected by the strong bias in our culture in favor of seeing asymmetric objects as symmetric. (The opposite error, of misperceiving symmetric shapes as asymmetric, is very rare.)

The mechanism that makes this possible is perhaps the one Festinger identified in his celebrated theory of cognitive dissonance.[32] Ac-

---

[31] Readers will have noted that the parallel here between the misperceptions of students of Classical art and architecture, on the one hand, and of the scientists whose ideas about Nature's forms we discussed in Note Two. This parallel is no coincidence. It is discussed more fully in Note Seven.

[32] Festinger, 1956.

cording to this theory, we sometimes alter our perceptions of the actual world in such a way that they do not conflict with the ideas or values that we already hold and wish to continue to hold. In the present context this suggests that under certain circumstances we assume that if an object before us was made in ancient Greece or Rome it must be symmetric – and therefore we see it as such. "I know that 'X' is a Classical artifact; I know that all Classical artifacts are symmetric; therefore I perceive 'X' as symmetric", is the syllogism that activates a person's defenses against cognitive dissonance.

Here are some instances of what are surely good-faith misperceptions of asymmetry by scholars. Ragghianti described the decoration of a Mycenaean *hydria* (*fig*.3.27) as "symmetrically and rigidly ordered".[33] Yet, not only the shape of the palm tree and the fronds growing out of it but even the jagged protrusions (remnants of former fronds) on either side of its trunk are markedly asymmetric. The two large plants that are growing up on either side of the base of the palm tree are asymmetric in themselves and in relation to each other. The motifs on either side of the trunk are also asymmetric, in themselves and in relation to each other.

Thus, immediately below the large fronds is a small pattern: that on the left has a cross-shaped figure within a quatrefoil frame; that

---

[33] Ragghianti 1979, p.46. Similarly, Jacobsthal (1925) who, referring to a black-figured amphora by Ezekias (BM210), writes – altogether incorrectly – that "the spirals roll in strictest symmetry"; or Hurwit (1977) who describes the hanging Kerkopes of a metope of Selinus Temple C as "symmetrical verticals", though neither figure is symmetric in itself or in relation to the other. See also Webster (1939) who claimed that one of the "great principles" of decoration in the early Geometric period of Greek pottery is that of symmetry. In Geometric pots, he stated, "the great structures and the minor parts within them are held together by the echoing of motives and figures symmetrically balanced". Yet the *tondo* from Knossos that Webster used to illustrate his analysis is obviously asymmetric. For the Byzantine period cf. Striker (1981, p.16), who refers to the "regular, bilaterally-symmetrical form" of the Myrelaion in Istanbul although his own drawings contradict this description. An example of cognitive dissonance in a more recent setting is given by Paret (1997, pp.87-93) in his discussion of a painting, "Frederick and His Troops at Hochkirch" by Adolph Menze. This work depicts Prussian soldiers as they rush to respond to a surprise attack by Austrian forces. The painting is thoroughly realistic and conveys the chaos of the moment, a scene very different from the accustomed view of Prussian soldiers acting in disciplined unison under the command of their officers. In a classic manifestation of the avoidance of cognitive dissonance Max Jordan, the Prussian director of the National Gallery in Berlin, where this picture hung, described it as showing "an infantry battalion at attention, firing by the numbers at the enemy". Almost certainly that is how Jordan actually saw the picture. He could not imagine Prussian soldiers in any other way, and so he saw what he expected and no doubt wanted to see.

on the right is a star-like design. Similarly, the motif that flows from the bottom of the handle on the left is entirely unlike the one that flows from the bottom of the handle on the right. Similar discrepancies can be discovered at many other points on the vase. Some of the juxtaposed elements moreover are not what some might think are incompetent versions of each other. Rather, they are entirely different designs, and this shows that there was no intention to make the decorations of this *hydria* symmetric. Indeed, although it seems likely that the vessel was thrown on a wheel, it is itself asymmetrically shaped.

The photograph's evidence that the *hydria* is asymmetric is incontestable and immediately obvious. Therefore, if Ms. Ragghianti had *intended* (for whatever reason) to mislead her readers into believing that the *hydria* is symmetric she would almost certainly not have included a photograph of it in her book. We must assume, rather, that she *expected* the vessel to be symmetric and that is how she saw it and – in good faith - described it!

What seems to be another instance of this dynamic at work can be seen in Weyl's description (in his classic work *Symmetry*) of the so-called "Praying Boy" statue in Berlin. This statue, Weyl wrote, is a "symbol [of] the great significance" that bilateral symmetry has "both for life and art".[34] However, the statue itself is certainly not symmetric. The boy's left hip juts sideways to support the weight that the right leg, bent at the knee, is not carrying; the two arms are not bent at the same angle; and the left shoulder seems noticeably broader than the right shoulder.

Could it be, however, that what we are seeing (and what Weyl may have had in mind) is a symmetrically-formed body whose stance makes it *seem* asymmetric – an asymmetric statue, in other words, of a symmetric body? In all available photographs perspectival distortions make it impossible to determine conclusively the contours of this statue. But a careful examination of a number of images establishes that (1) the curls on the boy's head are boldly asymmetric and (2) that the nipple on the left side of the body is lower than the other. These asymmetries alone are sufficient to disallow Weyl's description of the statue as an exemplar of bilateral symmetry.[35]

Nor are such unwitting misrepresentations only verbal. In Hopkins' report on the *Mithraeum* excavated at Dura Europos a photograph shows unambiguously that the steps lead up to the right-hand side of the recess in which the (conjectured) altar was housed.

---

[34] Weyl, *op.cit.*, p.6, fig.2. In his discussion of this object Weyl again reminds readers that the notion of bilateral symmetry has "a concrete precise meaning".

[35] I would also suggest, though somewhat less confidently, that the contours of the boy's lips appear to be asymmetric and that his right eye is lower than the left.

(*fig*.3.28)³⁶ On the facing page, however, the archeologist's *drawing* of the plan and elevation provide a central axis on which both altar and staircase are located. As if unconsciously acknowledging this error, his sketch has the staircase not quite centered on the altar but slightly to the left of center. Neither the artist, the author, nor the editors of the book appear to have noticed these discrepancies.

Yet there are also instances when the misrepresentation of an asymmetric form is done consciously, and may even be acknowledged as such. Drawings of Classical ruins made by Renaissance architects, writes Wilson Jones, "frequently 'correct' ... lapses of symmetry".³⁷ Serlio for example found the asymmetric placement of the windows of an ancient Roman gateway in Verona "very displeasing to the eye". Since, as he put it, "I could not bear such discordance", he presented readers of his *Third Book* with a drawing in which, as he disarmingly told them, "I placed [the windows] in an ordered way".³⁸ Serlio was not always so candid, however. Because he thought of the Pantheon as "the most beautiful ... and best-conceived" of all the buildings in ancient Rome, and as "an architectural exemplar", he did not voice his displeasure over the asymmetries of its interior but simply rendered them as symmetric in the drawing of it that he published in the *Third Book*.³⁹ In doing so he appears to have followed the example of Francesco di Giorgio (1439-1502) who also "corrected", without comment, the Pantheon's interior and depicted it as symmetric.⁴⁰ But for Antonio Sangallo (1484-1546) it was not enough to represent the Pantheon's

---

[36] Hopkins 1979, pp.204-5. Comp. the gentle comment of Seton Lloyd (1980, p.134) that the French archaeologist Victor Place, in his reconstructions of Sargon's palace, "occasionally assumed in the Assyrian architect a most un-oriental passion for symmetry".

[37] Wilson Jones 2003, p.2; Buddenseig 1971, p.266. The distinguished architectural historian James Ackerman (2002, p.201) has written that the revival of antiquity by Renaissance architects "became obligatory, but only so long as the ancient models did not break Renaissance rules". But this is not quite correct. What we see, rather, is that during the Renaissance the ancient models were altered – even if only on paper – to conform to, and in this way to validate, Renaissance rules. As Wilson Jones also noted, "The Renaissance conception of antiquity was a self-fulfilling myth: theory was projected onto ancient ruins, which in turn were used as evidence to justify the theory". An important exception to the "correction" of the asymmetry of Classical buildings during the Renaissance is to be found in the manifest asymmetry of Roman architectural elements in Mantegna's paintings in the Eremitani Chapel – see p.195, fn.108, *below*.

[38] Serlio 1996, Bk. III, 113v.

[39] *ibid*, Bk. III, 50 r & v.

[40] Giorgio 1967, v.II, p.412.

interior as symmetric in his drawings; he acknowledged its asymmetries by declaring, in no uncertain terms, that they were *una cosa perniciosissima* – "a most pernicious thing".[41]

These "corrections" were not always confined to paper. In the eighteenth century the attic drum on which the Pantheon's dome appears to rest was completely remodeled in an attempt to mute the asymmetry of the interior. This is the interior as we see it today, but for a small portion of the original scheme that was restored in the 1930's.[42] We have already noted how the "restoration" of the Ara Pacis in Rome imposed symmetric features that almost certainly were not on the original structure.

The conscious or unconscious transformation of asymmetric to symmetric shapes, whether in written or graphic representations or by the alteration of physical structures, is only part of the arsenal of those who wish to believe that Classical art and architecture were shaped by the "passion" for symmetry.

One tactic is to assert, dogmatically – i.e. without evidence – that the asymmetry of a shape as we see it today is the result of damage done to an artifact that originally was symmetric. The asymmetry of a building, for example, may be understood, not as reflecting the preferences of its builders but as an unintended consequence of acts of natural or human violence that caused the structure to lose its original symmetric form. We learn from one scholar, for example, that the asymmetry of the Pantheon's porch was brought about by "shocks from earthquakes combined with pressure from the surrounding earth deposited in the Middle Ages".[43] Similarly, the asymmetry of the curve

---

[41] Buddenseig 1971, p.26. The editors of Sangallo's drawings have this comment on his corrections of the asymmetry of Classical structures: "Everything seems impelled by a preordained ideology. The imagination of the observer is no longer stimulated. Instead, a uniform scheme has been imposed". Sangallo's drawing correcting the asymmetry of a gateway in Turin from the era of Augustus, along with an illustration showing the structure's actual design, is reproduced in Wilson Jones 2003, pl.3. Comp. Brown, 1983.

[42] The remodeling did not change the so-called "misalignment" of the dome's coffers with the details of the attic; the latter, now with heavily pedimented windows and framed panels, were aligned, rather, with the architectural details of the first level: Wilson Jones, 2003, p.190.

[43] Licht 1966, p.35. The difference between the largest and smallest intercolumniation on the Pantheon porch is over 6". A shock of the kind Licht refers to would almost certainly have displaced the columns equally. Yet the intercolumniations vary irregularly, making that hypothesis questionable. That the asymmetry of the intercolumniations was original and not the result of earthquakes or other events is also suggested by the irregular arrangement relative to the center of each capital of the dentelles at the base of the pediment, that are clustered as follows:

of the north edge of the Parthenon's stylobate is said to have been brought about by several factors, including earthquakes and the explosion in 1687 of ammunition that the barbaric Turks stored in the temple.[44] In much the same vein Penrose, having determined that the east edge of the Parthenon's stylobate was asymmetric in plan, declared this to be the result of later developments (he did not indicate what these were) and that the removal of a "trifling irregularity" in its present shape would bring about the "restoration" of the step's original "exact and symmetrical appearance".[45] Penrose describes the reasoning that led him to determine that asymmetric and other irregularities in the Parthenon were unintended in these words: "We may ... always suspect some disturbing cause to exist, when in quantities which tend to equality or some obvious proportion, a difference sensibly greater ... is ... found".[46] In other words: if a measurement is not what we expected we must always suspect that it is not the measurement that was originally intended!

Asymmetric forms are sometimes also explained as the unintended result of incompetence or carelessness. Perrault, for example, attributed the asymmetries of the Pantheon to a succession of poor decisions made by its architects.[47]

Others hold the builders and not the architect responsible. Confronted by the asymmetric distribution of the columns of Temple "C" at Selinus, Italy, Dinsmoor declared that the intercolumniations

---

8,6,7,7,6,6,7. Palladio noticed this irregularity in his drawing of the Pantheon façade but counted the dentelles incorrectly.

[44] Stevens, 1943.

[45] Penrose (1888, pp.29-30).

[46] *ibid.*, p.12,fn.

[47] Perrault (1993, p.157) criticized the coffering of the Pantheon's vault: "The squares in the coffers of the vault recede in steps, like hollow pyramids, and the center of the axes of the pyramids, rather than being near the center of the vault, is located at the center of the temple five feet above the pavement. This results in the axes not being perpendicular to the bases of the pyramids, which would have been necessary in order to maintain symmetry. This alteration makes the view of the hollow pyramids from the lower center of the temple the same as it would be if the viewer were lifted up to the center of the vault, with this point where all the axes of the coffers converge. However, as soon as one moves away from the center of the pavement the effect is destroyed, and one becomes aware of the obliqueness of these axes and of the defective symmetry of the pyramids, which is something much more disagreeable to the sight than if the orientation of the receding coffers had been straight, as it ought to be relative to the vault." Perrault (*ibid*, p.60) was baffled by the irregularities of the columns on the Pantheon's porch (none have the same circumferences) and evidently regarded this too as a shortcoming.

"were intended to be perfectly uniform" but that "carelessness of execution" caused them to be made irregular, instead.[48] He also suggested that variations in the width of the top step of the Parthenon "may have been the result of clerical error".[49] Robertson, too, accounted for the asymmetry and other irregularities of the Parthenon as "notable faults of execution".[50] Stevens offered six reasons, four of them having to do with human fallibility, why the north edge of the Parthenon's stylobate is, as he put it, "not quite a perfect curve".[51]

The "error" explanation is also offered for the asymmetry of Classical artifacts and works of art. For Cook, as we have seen, the asymmetry of Greek pots attests to the slapdash production methods employed by their makers. Pottery was "a cheap product", he wrote, that did not merit "the laborious precision demanded in more expensive arts", and one must not infer from its asymmetry that the Greeks saw any "virtue in imperfection".[52] For Richter "warped lips and

---

[48] Dinsmoor 1950, p. 62.

[49] *ibid*, p.80. Dinsmoor also declared (*ibid*, p.9) that the palace of Knossos "departs widely from the principles of symmetry and axiality", evidently implying thereby that those principles existed and were normative in Crete during the 16th or 17th century before the common era, with the palace representing a deviation from them.

[50] Robertson 1954, pp.116-7.

[51] Stevens 1943. In this paper Stevens both commends the "careful measurements" of the Parthenon taken by Balanos and declares that they could only have been "close approximations". The "error" explanation of asymmetry was also used by a distinguished archeologist of middle-eastern sites, Henry Frankfort (1969, pp.75-77). Frankfort wrote of Khorsabad and Sargon's palace there: "It is clear that the planners aimed at regularity and the frequent deviation from the right angle is due to imperfect methods of surveying. It is for instance characteristic of their love of symmetry that each side of the square should have two gates..." (Actually, only one side has two, or arguably three, gates). Frankfort acknowledged that the gates are placed asymmetrically but attributed this to the builders' "miscalculations". His explanation (p.76) of those alleged miscalculations - "In a country where paper, or even papyrus, was unknown there could not be measured drawings" - is very poor. Referring (p.48) to the plan of Gudea's citadel, Frankfort commented on "how awkwardly square elements are fitted in" but overlooks the fact that the entire plan is boldly asymmetric and that there is no reason to suppose that those elements really *were* intended to be square. (In fact, it is doubtful that there is a single square in the plan!) The superb finish on the statues of Gudea (note the precision with which the jewels [?] in his headband are formed and arranged) suggests that in his day craftsmanship was in fact of a very high standard.

[52] Cook 1972, p.28. Note Cook's tacit equation of "asymmetry" and "imperfection"!

sagged shoulders" on pots were "accidents or mistakes".[53] Winckelmann wrote of the asymmetric arrangements of Greek sculptures, such as the lopsidedness of an otherwise beautiful head of Venus, that they were caused by carelessness or incompetence.[54]

Most ingenious of all is the explanation that certain asymmetric configurations were not the result of poor design or craftsmanship but were intentionally and very carefully calculated *to make things look symmetric*.[55]

The French architect and architectural historian August Choisy, for one, argued that the asymmetrical curves he noted in the steps of the east stylobate of the Parthenon were created intentionally so as to correct an optical effect that would otherwise make the steps appear to be asymmetric.[56] Winckelmann declared that the inequality in the size of the feet in the Laocoon group and the longer rear leg of the Apollo Belvedere were perspectival devices calculated to compensate for "what might apparently be lost by the legs being drawn back". Schneider claimed that the asymmetry of the heads of Greek sculptures – which he stated was *"viel starker als in der Natur"*, surely an unprovable statement - was intended to convey the impression of symmetry when viewed from below.

The world of scholarship has treated these opinions generously, and I know of no instance in which someone has seen fit to ask what the evidence for them is. But that of course *is* the questions that these opinions beg. How, to take one example, did Dinsmoor know that the intercolumniations of Temple C "were intended to be perfectly

---

[53] Richter, op.cit. ad loc.

[54] Winckelmann 1968, p.265. "Incorrect drawing may also be observed in a head of Venus, which is a beautiful head in other respects, in the Villa Albani; the outline of it is the most beautiful that can be imagined, and the mouth is most lovely; but one eye is awry." Among other "errors" he records: a "beautiful rilievo in the Borghese villa has one arm that is too long; a laughing Leucothea in the Campidoglio has ears which should be parallel to the nose but fall below it".

[55] Schneider 1973, p.40. Similarly, Philipp 1999.

[56] Choisy (1996, v.I, p.419). On Choisy and his influence see the important paper of Etlin (1987). Choisy claimed that the asymmetric arrangement of the (allegedly symmetric) buildings on the Athenian Acropolis intentionally reflected Nature's own plan – *"ainsi procède la nature"* – whereby leaves, that he claimed are symmetric (*"les feuilles d'une plante sont symétriques"*) are on plants that are asymmetric. In actuality though neither leaves on plants nor the buildings on the Acropolis are symmetric! Comp. the thesis of Trachtenberg (1997, p.74) that the piazzi del Duomo and della Signoria in Florence were shaped asymmetrically in a way that was intended to create the impression that they are symmetric.

uniform"? Or, to take another example, how did Cook or Richter know that the "defects" of asymmetric Greek pots were regarded as such by the people who made and used them? The answer of course is that there is no evidence to support these statements. Penrose, as we have seen, insisted that an unexpected form must have originally looked like, or must have been intended to look like, what Penrose *expected* that it should have looked like! It could very well be that something like this preposterous solipsism inspires many attempts to explain away asymmetric designs as defective or unintended versions of symmetric designs.

Nor can one reasonably conclude from the fact that a building's present asymmetric shape is the result of acts of natural or manmade violence that its *original* shape was a symmetric one. Those episodes may well have replaced an earlier shape that was asymmetric. It can by no means be assumed that they caused a symmetric structure to become asymmetric.

The perspectival theory of Winckelmann and others is also inherently problematic. In particular, Schneider's account is called into question by the asymmetric arrangement of the hair on top of the head of the statue of "Poseidon" of Artemision.[57] The statue is about 6'9" tall and the top of its head would be invisible to anyone standing on the ground – all the more so if, as is probable, it was mounted on a plinth. Surely, the most plausible explanation of asymmetrically-shaped statues is that human bodies, along with all of Nature's shapes, are themselves asymmetrically shaped? And Choisy's explanation of the asymmetric curves on the Parthenon could only be valid for a single perspective on the structure, whose asymmetry would become evident again before one arrived at that point or as one moved away from it.

We will resume this discussion in Note Six, where we explore the motives that lead even reputable scholars to *avoid* acknowledging that a shape is asymmetric.

---

[57] Schneider (1973). See also Phillipp (1999).

Appendix: Is the Parthenon Symmetric?

When the 19th century historian James Fergusson declared that Greek temples "are perfectly symmetrical", so that "the one side exactly corresponds with the other" he was expressing an opinion about Classical architecture that has been widely held since the middle of the fifteenth century and remains a commonplace to this day.[58]

It is not at all easy to determine how valid this consensus is. Certainly, the challenge is far greater than the one we confronted in the main body of this Note, where we saw that it seldom requires more than a glance, merely, to decide if the decorative artifacts and works of art we looked at were symmetric. The conclusions we reached - that the Greeks and Romans did not require symmetry in the design of their works of art and their decorated artifacts, and indeed, that they did not use (indeed were almost certainly unaware of) the categories of symmetry and asymmetry when they made an object or looked at one made by someone else – are ones in which we can have a high degree of confidence. Not so with the architectural evidence, however, whose ambiguities preclude a conclusive determination of what if any role symmetry played in the design of buildings in ancient Greece and Rome.

To start with there is the difficulty of obtaining accurate measurements. Clearly, we cannot know if a building is asymmetric or symmetric unless we know its precise measurements. There are unfortunately almost no reliable measurements for any ancient Greek or Roman buildings. This holds true even with regard to the dimensions of that supreme achievement of Classical architecture, the Parthenon.

The Parthenon has been measured on several occasions during the past 350 years - it may indeed be the most frequently surveyed of all buildings – but unfortunately the quality of most surveys of it has been demonstrably poor, and there are good reasons to doubt the re-

---

[58] Fergusson 1849, pp.397-8. Fergusson was not consistent, however, for he also declared that symmetry is "a property which exists only in the imagination of the moderns", and that the Greeks were not guilty of such "absurdities", which he described (*ibid*, p.399) as "an invention of the Italian architects in the worst age of an attempted revival of Classical art"- an argument that anticipates a central theme of these Notes. Some historians regard both symmetric and asymmetric construction in the Classical world as intentional. Cf. Viollet-le-Duc, 1987 v. I, pp. 57-8, 88-9,103, 160, and 346.

liability of even the most recent of them. The first survey was carried out in the seventeenth century by the Englishman Francis Vernon, who reported back to the Royal Society in London that his measurements of the Parthenon were "exact to ½ foot": a degree of precision – or lack of it – that makes his measurements useless for most purposes.[59] The measurements carried out by Vernon's later contemporaries, Wheeler and Spon, were hardly more useful, being accurate, or so they claimed, to the inch in some instances and to the foot in others.[60]

By contrast, other surveyors made claims to accuracy that are not believable. Stuart and Revett, in the 18th century, declared that their measuring rod gave them results that were accurate to one-thousandth *of an inch*.[61] How far they fell short of such a standard is suggested by their failure to discover the *entasis* (or swelling) of the Parthenon's columns. A century later Penrose claimed that he had achieved "an exact delineation" of the Parthenon and that *his* measurements were accurate to one-thousandth of a foot (or about one-eightieth of an inch).[62] Nevertheless, he failed to discover, among other features, the curved elevations on the Parthenon's east front.

Troubling questions arise about the accuracy of more recent surveys, too. Dinsmoor and Balanos in the early decades of the twentieth century each declared that their measurements were accurate to within 1.0mm and in some instances to within 0.50mm, yet they usually differed about the length of anything that they both measured. For example, according to Dinsmoor the two flanks of the Parthenon's stylobate are the same length, as are the axial spacings of the external columns on the east and west fronts. Balanos on the other hand found that the two stylobate flanks differ from each other, with neither matching the length reported by Dinsmoor; he also found variations as large as 8cm., or about 3-1/8", in the axial spacings of the columns.[63] Again, in measuring the fourteen metopes on the Parthenon's east front Dinsmoor and Balanos agreed on the widths of only two; their

---

[59] Quoted Redford, 2002.

[60] Quoted Stuart 2008, v.II, pp.1-3.

[61] See for example such measurements as 30'8.834" in Stuart 2008, v.II,Pl.5. The introduction by Frank Salmon to this edition – i.e., a facsimile of the original *Antiquities of Athens* - offers a brief but useful critical survey of the methods employed by Stuart and Revett.

[62] Penrose 1888, p. *v*. An example (p.9) of Penrose's measurements is the diameter of "3.656 feet" that he gives for the naos columns.

[63] It is curious to note the report of Friedlaender (1969, p.92) that the Irish writer Frank Harris, who was no professional in art matters, mentioned in his *Autobiography* that he measured the intercolumniations of the Parthenon and found that they were unequal. (I have not found this passage in Harris' memoir.)

measurements of the other twelve differed from each other by between 2mm. and as much as 26mm. (or more than one inch).[64] Some of these differences significantly exceed the margins of error of one, or one-half, millimeter that each man claimed for his measurements.

In all probability Balanos' measurements of the Parthenon in the first decades of the twentieth century are the most reliable yet. They are, at any rate, the only ones in which advanced optical instruments were used and in which the work was carried out by trained engineers and surveyors.[65] The measurements were made over the course of thirty years, however, and there is no assurance that consistent procedures were employed during all phases of the work. Balanos' cursory description of his methods is all the more to be regretted, therefore.[66] But even if it is conceded that his measurements are superior to earlier ones the question of *how reliable* they are remains to be answered. That can only be done by a new survey using the extremely precise technologies available today. Unfortunately, no such survey is likely to be conducted in the foreseeable future.

Yet even if highly reliable measurements *were* to become available they would not resolve certain other crucial issues. In particular, they would do little and perhaps nothing to establish which dimensions of the Parthenon today reflect the intentions of its architects, and which reflect deviations from the original plans that may be attributable either to the workmen who built the structure or to natural and human acts of violence (earthquakes and, if nothing else, the detonation of the ammunition that the Turks had stored there) that the Parthenon has suffered over the course of two and a half millennia.

Nevertheless, there are certain measurements to which these reservations do not apply. One set consists of the heights of the peripteral columns that are still standing. Balanos found that they "vary erratically and obey no rules". Because it is highly unlikely that the

---

[64] Balanos' (1938, pl.6e) measurements of the metopes appear on the upper of the two rows below, and those of Dinsmoor (1950, pp.338-340) on the lower. Measurements are north to south, in meters; the two pairs of identical measurements are highlighted in bold type:

1.246 1.254 1.167 1.288 1.271 **1.271** 1.330 **1.317** 1.294 1.331 1.253 1.241 1.234 1.277

1.256 1.256 1.278 1.279 1.276 **1.271** 1.334 **1.317** 1.309 1.305 1.234 1.239 1.239 1.268

Dinsmoor's measurements at Bassai were not corroborated by Cooper (1996, pp.36, 230 fn.3), who found that his figures for certain columnar diameters erred by as much as 2cm, or more than ¾".

[65] Balanos 1938, p.53: "*un niveau Zeiss de grande precision*".

[66] Balanos says of his surveys merely that they conformed to "*la methode habituelle*". By contrast see the extremely detailed description of the procedures Cooper (1996, pp.36-42) used in surveying the temple of Apollo Bassitas.

heights of the columns would have altered over time we can be confident that these asymmetric variations were original. We cannot know, however, whether they reflect the architects' intentions or the workmen's indifference to (or inability to attain) a higher standard of precision.

Another asymmetric arrangement, also without doubt original, is that of the metopes on the east front. The metopes within each pair (counting outward from the center) differ in width by 13, 23, 40, 35, 26, 20 and 31 mm., respectively (*fig.*3.31).[67] No pair is symmetric, therefore, and the irregularities are not distributed consistently in the series of pairs. We can be confident that these measurements reflect the metopes' original dimensions and distribution, for the panels will not somehow have shrunk or expanded over time.[68]

Balanos' measurements of certain elevations on the east front of the Parthenon indicate the presence of symmetric arrangements.[69] His elevation γ is a line 30.870 meters in length that runs from the north to the south ends of the last step leading up to the stylobate. This elevation was measured at ten equidistant points with the following result (in meters; north to south; and with the middle of the series in bold type:)[70]

2.602 2.610 2.634 2.657 **2.667** **2.667** 2.655 2.636 2.610 2.602

---

[67] See upper row of figures, fn. 64, above. Balanos, pl.6.e. Balanos, for whatever reason, gave the widths of only 5 of the 15 triglyphs and of 4 of the 14 metopes on the west front – too few to determine whether their distribution by width was symmetric or not.

[68] Yeroulanou (1998) suggested that these metopes may have come from the earlier temple on the site. Perhaps so; but for our purposes this would mean only that the builders of *both* temples did not require the metopes to be of identical size or arranged symmetrically. In another structure on the Acropolis, the Pinakotheke of the northwest wing of the Propylaea, the asymmetric placement of door and windows has long caused architectural historians heartburn. The suggestion of Plommer (1960) that they were placed where they were in order to shield paintings from direct sunlight seems commonsensical and, at the very least, implies that symmetric arrangements were not compulsory.

[69] In what follows we will *assume* the accuracy of Balanos' measurements. We do so hesitantly and with full recognition that the reliability of those measurements remains unproven, and may well be doubted. It follows, of course, that conclusions drawn from his data are tentative.

[70] Balanos, Table 1. The fact that the 31-meter curve has been measured at 10 points is problematic. The "curve" as I have labeled it here is in fact a quasi-curve made up of ten equidistant points. We don't know why ten points were chosen – there is no reason to believe that the original builders used them when they made those curves – and it is possible that a larger number of points would have revealed a different, and perhaps even an asymmetric, curve instead.

Any two of these points that are equidistant from the center may be thought of as a pair. The measurements for the curve at elevation γ show that the points in each of three pairs are, to the nearest millimeter, the same length as each other; and that the points of each of the other two pairs differ in length by 2 mm. The ten points at elevation γ of the east stylobate of the Parthenon thus delineate an arc that deviates from exact symmetry by a total of 4mm. in its length of 30.87 meters (or 1/6th of an inch in 1215 inches). This can be expressed as a ratio of 1:7300.

Five other elevations on the east front are also in this sense symmetric arcs. They are elevation δ at the stylobate edge –

3.153   3.161   3.186   3.208   **3.218**   **3.218**   3.209   3.188   3.161   3.153

elevation ε at the innermost point of the column base –

3.182   3.203   3.224   **3.232**   **3.232**   3.223   3.202   3.182

elevation ζ at the base of the step leading up to the cella –

3.218   3.236   **3.241**   **3.241**   3.236   3.219

elevation η on the secos wall –

3.526   3.547   **3.558**   **3.558**   3.546   3.526

and elevation θ, also on the secos wall –

3.918   3.942   **3.952**   **3.951**   3.940   3.920

The deviation from a consistent curve of these elevations is 1 part in 10,600, 12,800, 19,400, 21,200, and 4700, respectively.[71] By virtually any standard these elevations, as measured by Balanos, are symmetric curves.[72]

Perhaps because they merely confirmed the prevailing assumption that Greek temples are symmetric, Balanos' measurements on the east front did not attract much attention. Balanos also surveyed the same elevations on the other three sides of the Parthenon and, as he reports, his measurements there *"m'a montré que ces courbes presentent une symmetrié parfait"*. He allowed himself the triumphant observation

---

[71] The *shape* of each arc is however different from that of the other five.

[72] Of the elevations Balanos found to be symmetric only the east stylobate edge – evidently, Balanos' elevation δ – had been measured previously, by Penrose, who found its curve to be asymmetric.

that he had thereby "disproved" theories that the curves of the Parthenon and other ancient monuments in general are "random".[73]

In a certain sense his elation was justified. The question of whether curves and other "deviations from ordinary rectilineal construction"[74] on the Parthenon and other Classical structures were intentional refinements has been debated since their discovery in the early nineteenth century. Captivating though such a possibility is, however, the evidence for it is not as compelling in every instance as it is for the more modest alternative, that proposes that these "deviations" are probably the result of indifference to, or of inability to attain, more precise standards of construction. But this uncertainty applies only to irregular shapes, for in the absence of unambiguous indications we simply do not know whether their irregularity was created intentionally or unintentionally.

The matter is quite different with regard to symmetric shapes. The creation of such shapes, that are symmetric to within one part in several thousand, must have been intentional, for it is impossible to believe that their precision was the result of happenstance. If this is true of a single symmetric curve it is all the more true of several curves that, like the six curved elevations on the Parthenon's east front, are in close proximity to one another but with each having its own shape. These curves can only have been created intentionally by skilled and disciplined masons working with detailed instructions and within the most exacting margins of error. Our assurance of this overrides otherwise reasonable objections that because the ancient Greeks (as far as is known) had no term for bilateral symmetry they could not have had the concept of it; or that we should not assume that they intended to create symmetric shapes unless we know why they wished to do so.

But this is not to say that Balanos was justified in claiming that all the elevations he measured were symmetric. Unfortunately, Balanos never indicated the standard he used for determining whether a shape is symmetric. To be sure, the deviations of the curves on the east-front elevations noted above are so slight that one need have no hesitation in designating those elevations as symmetric. The same elevations on the west front however, for all Balanos' claims that they are marked by *"une symmetrié parfait"*, tell a very different story (*fig*.3.30).

Counting outward from the center the discrepancies within each pair are 3,7,14,21,21; 6,6,13,21,20; 4,7,12,17; 7,1,9; 3,8,10; and

---

[73] Balanos pp.54-55: *"Ainsi la théorie qui formule que les courbes du Parthenon, et en général celles des monuments antiques, sont un effet du hasard ... est exclue"*. Balanos also claimed – though his reasoning for this is unclear - that this finding disproved the notion that the Parthenon's curves *"sont des courbes esthétiques"*.

[74] Penrose, 1888, p. v.

3,8,9mm., respectively. In no pair within any of these elevations do both points have the same measurement; in one pair there is a discrepancy of a mere 1mm; but the rest of the discrepancies are larger, and in most instances, substantially larger. As the table shows, the sum of all the discrepancies within each elevation of the west front is of an entirely different order of magnitude from the ones on the east front elevations:

Elevation	East Front (mm.)	West Front (mm.)
γ	4	66
δ	3	66
ε	2	40
ζ	1	17
η	1	21
θ	5	20

Balanos' claim that the elevations on the west front (and, insofar as they could be measured) on the two flanks are symmetric implies a notion of symmetry that is so loose as to be virtually without meaning. In point of fact, the discrepancies Balanos found fall into two categories. In one they are almost invariably either 2mm or less in a pair, while in the other they are considerably larger and also more erratic than that. The arrangements in which discrepancies are 2mm or less – or even non-existent – therefore seem qualitatively different from the rest; and it is on this basis that I call them "symmetric" and the ones where the discrepancies are greater, "asymmetric".[75]

But what about the other portions of the Parthenon? Some parts of the structure are too damaged to be measured. Other areas, where measurements could have been made, unfortunately were ignored, for whatever reason, by Balanos. In all, Balanos provided sufficient information to make a determination of symmetry on 106 parts of the Parthenon. They (including the features we have already noted) are listed here under the number of the table or plate in which they appear in his book; an asterisk identifies a feature as symmetric:

Table I (*various elevations of steps, stylobate, sub-basement of secos wall, entablature*) [n=20; *=7]
    East: β; γ*; δ*; ε*; ζ*; η*; θ*; ς; ο.

---

[75] It is very likely that the asymmetric forms were not made by the same craftsmen who made the symmetric ones. However, we cannot be completely certain that they did not regard *their own* work as symmetric. Possessed of inferior skills, they may have believed that the forms that I designate as asymmetric were in fact asymmetric, instead. With such an argument however – for all that it has validity – we descend further into the realm of *obscurum per obscurius*.

West: β; γ; δ; ε; ζ ; η; θ; ς; o; χ¹*; o1.
Table II (*various elevations of steps, stylobate, sub-basement of secos wall, entablature*) [n=9; *=0]
   North: β; γ; δ; ε; ζ ; η; θ; ς; o.
Table III (*various elevations of steps, stylobate, sub-basement of secos wall, entablature*) [n=9; *=0]
   South: β; γ; δ; ε; ζ ; η; θ; ς; o.
Folding Plate 2 (*north colonnade*) [n=4; *=0]
   Distance between capital centers
   Axial intercolumniations at base
   Height of abacus at center
   Height of abacus at ends
Folding Plate 3 (*general plan*) [n=18; *=1]
   West: two horizontal curves in plan
   West: projection of peristyle capitals
   West: projection of opisthodomos capitals
   East: two horizontal curves in plan
   South: two horizontal curves in plan
   North: two horizontal curves in plan
   West: intercolumniations at peristyle base
   East: intercolumniations at peristyle base
   South: intercolumniations at peristyle base
   North: intercolumniations at peristyle base
   West: opisthodomos intercolumniations
   East: opisthodomos intercolumniations
   Sum total of intercolumniations on flanks (=total lengths)[76]
   Sum total of intercolumniations on ends (=total widths)*[77]
Folding Plate 4 (*columnar dimensions*) [n=5; *=1]
   Entasis of column x'-22' (east-west)
   Entasis of column x'-22' (north-south)*[78]
   Entasis of column m'-12' (north-south[79]
   depths of flutes on north and south sides
   Entasis of a column of the pronaos
Folding Plate 5 (*interior façade of the opisthodomos entablature*) [n=3; *=0]

---

[76] North flank 69.466m vs South flank, 69.519mm, a difference of 53mm.

[77] East face 30.87m vs West face, 30.88, a difference of 1mm.

[78] Inclination of the outer profile on both sides is equal.

[79] Balanos refers to the "*cannelures symétriques*" on the south side of this column but this is unwarranted. The varying widths of the channels at each elevation – for instance, where the column is 1.687m. tall the channels vary between 0.032 and 0.137m. - are random and asymmetric. The depths of the channels on the north side of the column are more consistent with each other but here too their distribution by depth is asymmetric.

Abacus widths
Distance between abacus centers
Width of frieze panels
Folding Plate 6 (*interior of the west entablature*) [n=3; *=2]
Abacus widths *
Abacus heights*
Distance between abacus centers
Folding Plate 8 (*north colonnade*)[80] [n=2; *=0]
Intercolumnar distance at base
Distance between abacus centers
Folding Plate 10 (*east face*) [n=6; *=2]
Distance between triglyph centers
Width of [spaces for] metopes
Distance between abacus centers
Abacus widths*
Abacus heights*
Interaxial distance of columns at base
Folding Plate 11 (*east face, from interior*) [n=4; *=1]
Distance between abacus centers
Abacus widths*
Abacus heights
Interaxial distance of columns at base
Folding Plate I (*east and west face curves in elevation and plan*[81]) [n=11; *=5]
East: symmetric plans at 4 levels*****
East: asymmetric plans at 2 levels
West: symmetric plans at 3 levels
West: symmetric plans at 2 levels
Folding Plate II (*north flank in elevation and plan*) [n=7; *=0]
North: asymmetric plans at 7 levels
Folding Plate III (*south flanks in elevation and plan*) [n=5; *=0]
South: asymmetric plans at 5 levels

It can be seen from this table that, of the 106 parts of the Parthenon for which Balanos provided sufficient data to determine whether their shapes are symmetric or asymmetric, only 19 are symmetric. Of these, almost two-thirds – 12 – are on the east front; there, however, as already noted, numerous asymmetric arrangements are

---

[80] Despite the loss of columns on the north flank enough evidence remains on either side of the center to determine that the two measures given here could not have been symmetric.

[81] The elevations for Folding Plates I, II and III are provided in Table 1.

also to be found. The measurements Balanos provided do not concentrate on any particular portion or portions of the Parthenon's existing structure, which perhaps allows one a modest degree of confidence that additional measurements might not significantly change the relative distribution of symmetric and asymmetric arrangements from the one given here.

The examples of the metope widths and the columnar heights suggest that at least some of these asymmetries may have been part of the original structure. We can be confident too that the symmetric portions on the east front of the Parthenon and elsewhere, if Balanos did indeed measure them accurately, are original, for symmetric shapes are not created by accident.

It would seem, then, and this is a significant finding, that the Parthenon may have been built as a structure that was partly symmetric and largely asymmetric. Why this was so – and in particular, why the symmetric arrangements were concentrated on only a relatively few areas of the Parthenon and chiefly on the east front – is a puzzlement, and likely to remain so.

This finding, it cannot be over-emphasized, is a tentative one and cannot be confirmed until the Parthenon is surveyed, once again, but this time on the basis of established procedures and with the use of the highly precise surveying instruments and methods that are now readily available.

Also tentatively, I would put forward the suggestion that if symmetric features are indeed found to exist on the fabric of the Parthenon they may reflect the application of esoteric doctrines of the Pythagoreans or some other group. Assuredly, these few symmetric curves – *if indeed that is what they are!* - do not require us at this stage to suppose that the concept of symmetry was generally known in the Classical world and scrupulously applied in the making of things.

The predominant asymmetry of the Parthenon does not set it apart from other ancient Greek structures. There is no evidence, indeed, that any major ancient Greek buildings are entirely, or even largely, symmetric.[82] The plans of the Minoan palace at Gournia on Crete (*fig. 3.29*), for example, or those of Lerna in the Argolid, imply an utter indifference to symmetric design.[83] So does the temple of Apollo

---

[82] See the examples of asymmetric Greek construction, and a thoughtful analysis of some of the technical issues involved, in Goodyear 1912, chapter VI and appendix, pp.161-204.

[83] Soles 1991; Wiencke 2000,v.4, plan 24.

in Syracuse, the diameters of whose columns vary by as much as 12 inches.[84]

Another example is the Argive Heraion. The graphic restoration by Pfaff [85] shows a symmetric layout, but the actual state plan of the temple, and of its foundations, establish that the design was asymmetric. The perimeter foundations are asymmetric on both axes as indeed are the foundations of the cella, which are not parallel; the extension at the south end is not centered on the temple foundation. From the aerial photograph it is easy to tell that the foundation walls are not parallel – a feature that the "state plan" does not state quite fully enough. In another example, the windows of the East Building of the sanctuary of Apollo Hylates at Kourion are asymmetrically arranged. Noting this, Scranton adds rather curiously that this is "perhaps of no great significance".[86] The Temple "C" at Selinus is another example of asymmetry. According to Dinsmoor while most of its columns have sixteen flutes, three on the east front and two on the west front have twenty, and these columns are not arranged symmetrically in the rows of columns of which they are a part.[87]

On the other hand, two well-documented buildings from the same century as the Parthenon are reported by twentieth-century surveyors to have a small number of symmetric areas, but are predominantly asymmetric.

According to Koch horizontal curves on all four sides of the stylobate of the Theseum (or Hephaiston) in Athens are asymmetric, as are the cella walls and the geisons, and, on the west front, the curvature in plan of the columns and the distribution by height of the abaci; while on the other hand the arrangement of metopes, triglyphs and the intercolumniations throughout the structure is symmetric.[88] According to another investigator, Korres, the orthostates of this structure are also symmetric.[89] These findings are reported without information about how they were obtained: and they too must be confirmed before any firm conclusions are drawn from them. Cooper, whose measurements are possibly the most reliable ever made of an ancient Greek structure,

---

[84] Lawrence (1967, p.169), without a word of explanation and rather unpersuasively, attributed these variations to the builders' "incompetence".

[85] Pfaff (2003, v.1, fig.84).

[86] Scranton, 1967.

[87] Dinsmoor 1950, p.80.

[88] Koch 1955, figs. 31 p.171, 34 p.172, 40 p.176. Koch gives the plan of the columns and the height of abaci only for the west front.

[89] Korres 1999, p.93.

has described in detail the complicated layering of the stylobate of the temple of Apollo Bassitas that combines both symmetric and asymmetric arrangements; he also found a few minor parts of the temple's superstructure that are symmetric.[90] His measurements show that the spacing of the flanking columns measured at their bases (*fig*.3.32) is asymmetric, and that the heights of the columns also vary asymmetrically (*fig*.3.33).

Naturally, there is not much that we can confidently infer about the intentions of builders who lived twenty-five hundred years ago and who left behind no written texts that might have explained their work to us.[91] When the intentions we wish to understand concern a phenomenon – symmetry – for which they had no word, and when the evidence that we can obtain by studying a few ruined buildings is both scant and ambiguous, our problems are greatly compounded. Despite these difficulties however the facts reviewed here establish that the standard view – held for over five centuries - of Greek architecture as symmetric is clearly invalid. Even the most exemplary of Greek buildings, the Parthenon, has at most only a few symmetric portions; the greater part of the structure is asymmetric.

It should not be supposed that all the asymmetries that have been detected in the Parthenon are the result of later acts of natural or human violence. That may be true of some of the structure's asymmetries, but I am inclined to think - bearing in mind the asymmetric arrangement, undoubtedly original, of the height of the peripteral columns or of the width of the metopes - that it is likely that the "irregularities" of many portions of the temple are original and were regarded (to the extent that they were so much as noted) as acceptable. Unfortunately, we cannot know whether they represent deviations, caused by workmen's carelessness or incompetence, from the architects' plans

---

[90] Cooper, v.1, pp.164-183. Cooper writes that the crowning course of the tympanum is "a single symmetric block", (p. 251) and that the east entrance may have been symmetric p. 211. He also determined with his naked eye (for they were too small to be measured with a micrometer) that two of the six types of cyma reversa moldings on the pteroma coffers are symmetric (p. 365). Cooper also described (p. 185) the corner intercolumniations as "symmetric", though the other intercolumniations are not distributed symmetrically. His drawing of the north end (pl.20) indicates that the widths of the metopes and triglyphs follow a regular distribution, but as he only gives measurements for the right-hand side of the structure we cannot infer that the distribution is symmetric.

[91] According to Tobin (1981) the "spatial symmetry" of Doric temples, which he takes for an established fact, "was always subordinated to architectural ends". Unfortunately, he failed to disclose both how he knew this and what those "architectural ends" were.

It has been suggested that the Parthenon's asymmetries were created intentionally, as part of a subtle aesthetic scheme. Penrose had this to say on the subject: "It has often been noticed that the works of Nature, although usually their tendency is to be symmetrical, are seldom absolutely so; and when, in architecture, exact symmetry does prevail, a dry effect is not infrequently produced". The Greeks, Penrose went on to say, produced with "extreme care and refinement" the "charm which is sometimes the result ... of irregularity of design or even of workmanship".[92]

Explanations like these of the asymmetries of the Parthenon and other Greek temples is less convincing than the notion that those asymmetries were unplanned and no doubt even unrecognized, and that they manifest the deep but not necessarily conscious sympathy for the asymmetry of Nature's forms that is a mainspring of all great design.

Obviously, asymmetric shapes cannot be created intentionally by people who have no concept of symmetry. More often than not, one suspects, asymmetric shapes are created unawares, by default, without deliberate intent. Symmetric shapes by contrast are created when, for whatever reason, there is a deliberate decision that the two lateral halves of a design are to mirror each other.[93]

If the measurements that I have utilized here are accurate – and I cannot stress sufficiently that we do not know whether they *are* accurate – then it seems highly probable that the concept of symmetry did indeed exist in ancient Greece and perhaps Rome but was applied in the construction of buildings on only a very limited basis. The lack of linguistic and literary evidence suggests that it would have been an esoteric concept known only to a small number of people.

This conclusion could be refuted – or confirmed and enlarged – if measurements of unquestionable reliability are made of the Parthenon and other ancient structures. As things now stand, however, our only certain evidence comes from the non-architectural sources we considered at the outset of this Note. And they give us the confidence to say that the ancient Greeks and Romans did not require that sym-

---

[92] Penrose 1888, pp.11-12. Goodyear (1912, pp.205-6) quotes the German historian Michaelis who like Penrose also attributes the "fascinating effect" of the Parthenon to the "considerable variations of width; the heights of the columns; the widths of the abaci, of the triglyphs and metopes".

[93] Michaelis, (quoted Goodyear 1912, pp.205-6,) similarly argues for the *un*intentionality of the Parthenon's asymmetric portions that, as he writes, are "mostly so complicated, and of such various characters in the different parts of the building that have been compared, that it is difficult to consider them intentional".

metric arrangements in their works of art and their decorated objects and that this was probably because they were unaware of the concepts of and asymmetry. Albeit with some hesitation, we may well apply this conclusion to the architecture of the ancient Greeks and Romans, too.[94]

---

[94] For a further discussion, with valuable examples, of asymmetric Greek construction and a thoughtful analysis of the technical issues involved, cf. Goodyear 1912, chapter VI and appendix, pp.161-204.

3.2 Minoan vessel, c. 2100-1700 BCE

3.3 Vase from Thera, c.9th – 7th century BCE

3.4 Detail of 8th-century BCE prosthesis vase

SYMMETRY IN THE CLASSICAL WORLD 80

3.5 Detail of Euboean amphora, c.570-560 BCE

3.6 Attic amphora, attrib. to Exekias, c.540 BCE.

3.7 Krater, Apuleia, *c.* 330-320 BCE

3.8 Picene or Samnite disc c. 7th-6th centuries, BCE

3.9 *Mitra* from Crete, 6th. cent. BCE

3.10 Argive vase 5th cent. BCE

3.11 Female, Cyclades, 3rd millennium BCE

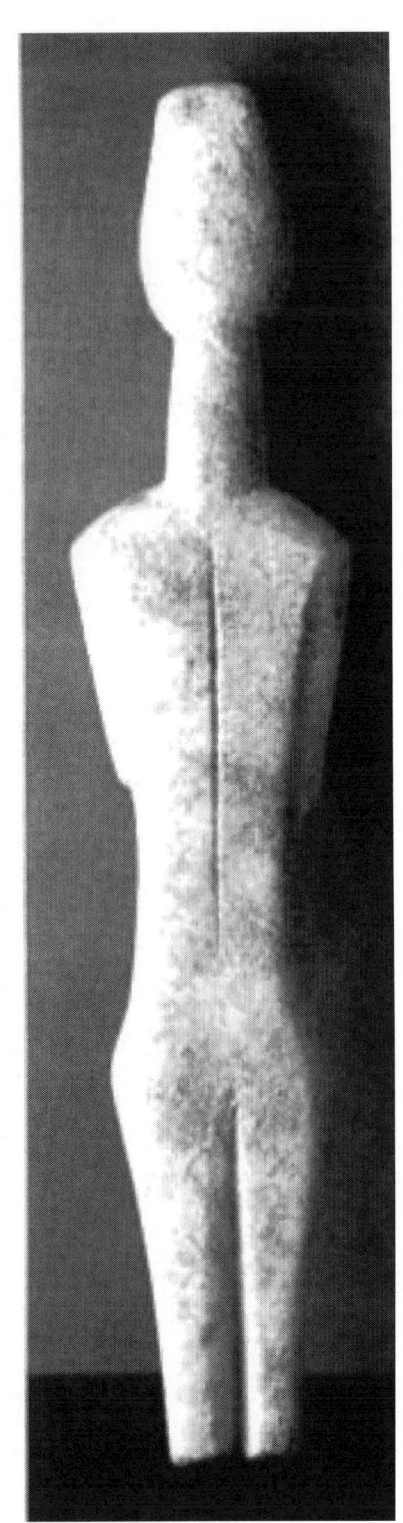

THE SYMMETRY NORM AND THE ASYMMETRIC UNIVERSE

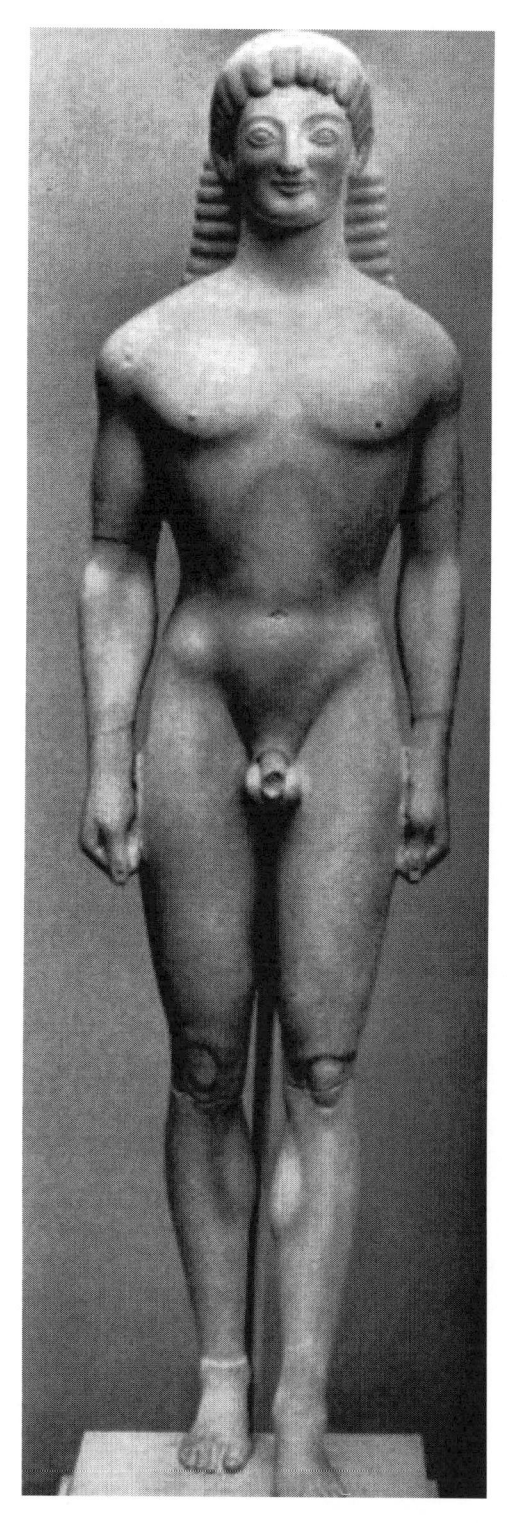

3.12 *Kouros*, 6th cent. BCE

3.13 Delphi, head of Apollo (?) 6th cent. BCE

3.14a and b, Poseidon (?) of Artemision

THE SYMMETRY NORM AND THE ASYMMETRIC UNIVERSE   87

3.15   Engraved gems, 6th–5th century BCE

SYMMETRY IN THE CLASSICAL WORLD 88

3.16 Gold libation bowl, Olympia, 7th cent. BCE

3.17 Capital from synagogue in Gamla, Israel, 4th-5th century C.E.

3.18 Votive tablet, Pergamon, c.200-250 CE

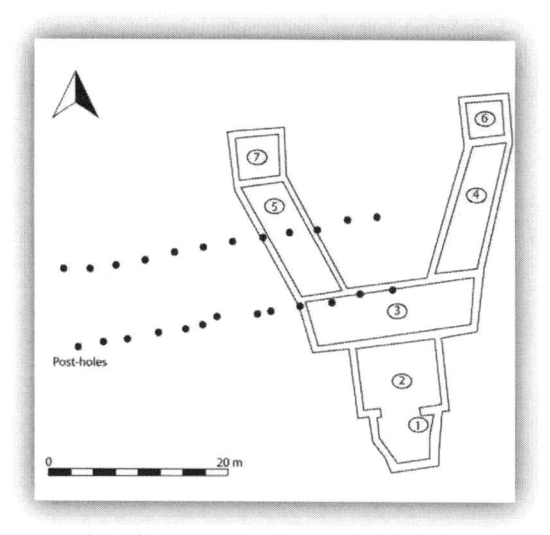

3.19 Plan of unidentified Roman structure, England

3.20 (above); 3.21 (below): murals of villas, Pompeii, *c.* 20-10 BCE

3.22 The Portland Vase

SYMMETRY IN THE CLASSICAL WORLD 92

3.23 The Endymion Sarcophagus. Rome, 2nd-3rd century CE

3.24 Mural, Rome, *Palatina Domus*.

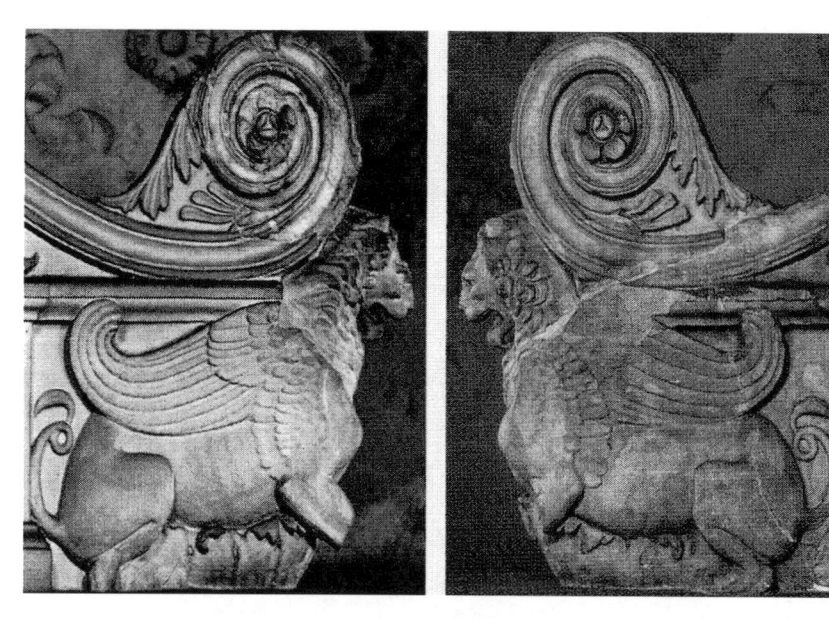

THE SYMMETRY NORM AND THE ASYMMETRIC UNIVERSE 93

3.25 Rome, *Ara Pacis*. Details of outer ends of sacrificial table.

3.26 Rome, Arch of Constantine (east side)

3.27 Ragghianti's "symmetrically and rigidly ordered" *hydria*.

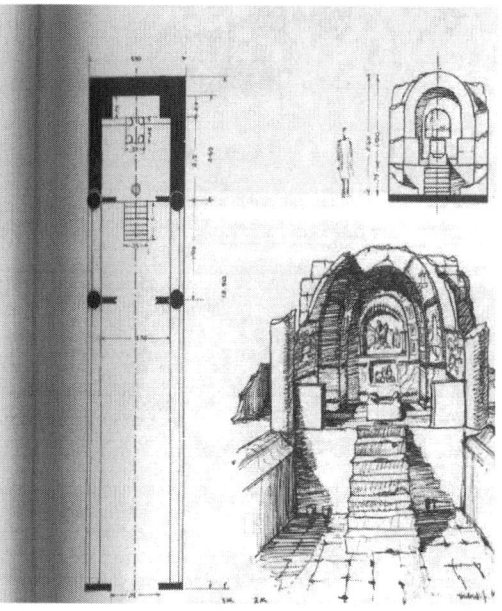

3.28 Dura Europos *Mithraeum*

3.29 Crete: Aerial view of Minoan palace complex
(*Source:* Soles, 1991)

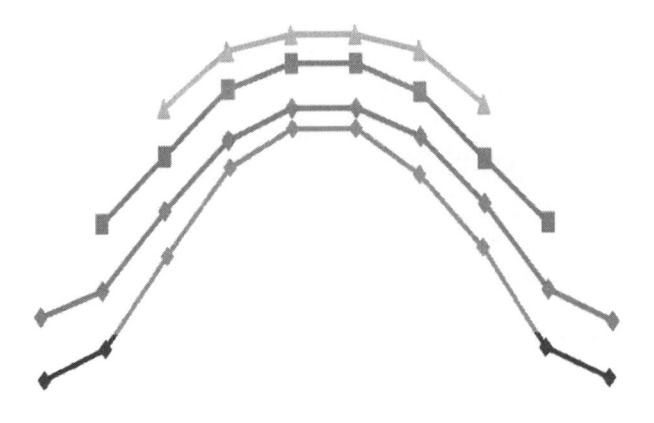

Parthenon east stylobate elevations gamma to zeta (after Balanos)

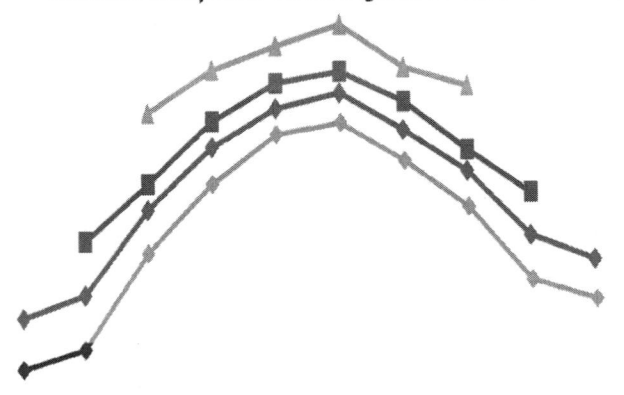

Parthenon west stylobate elevations gamma to zeta (after Balanos)

3.30 Parthenon stylobate elevations

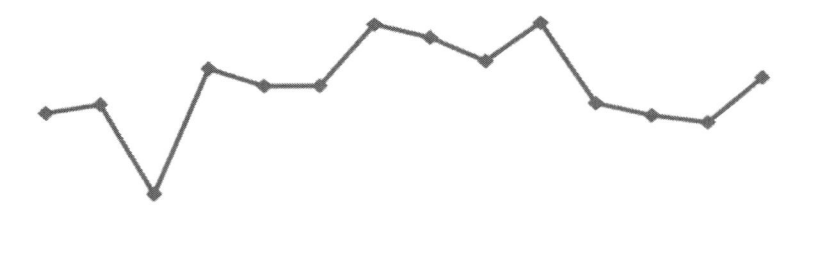

3.31 Parthenon east front metope widths (north to south) after Balanos

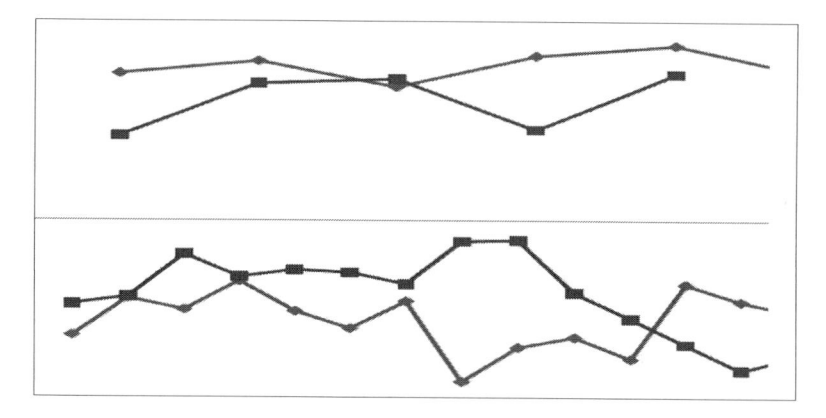

**3.32 Column offsets, Temple of Apollo Bassitas:
north and south flanks (upper); east and west flanks (lower).**[95]

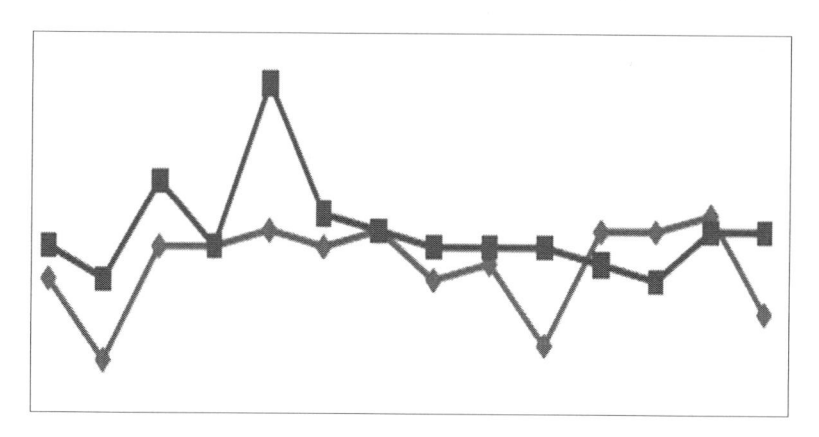

3.33 Column heights, east and west flanks, of the Temple of Apollo Bassitas.[96]

---

[95] Cooper, *ibid*, v.1, 186. The variations among these offsets are not as apparent in Cooper's drawing of them in *ibid* v.4, pl.16.

[96] Graphed from data in Cooper, *op.cit.*, v.1, 230.

THE QUESTION OF MEDIEVAL SYMMETRY

4.1 Chartres Cathedral

Note Four

> *"The confusion and messiness of Chartres"*
> - John James (1982, p.21)

The concept of symmetry was unknown in the Middle Ages. This is sometimes questioned by people who suggest that medieval eyes would have accepted as symmetric shapes that we today, with our ability to measure and perhaps to see more accurately, would regard as asymmetric.[1] Whatever merit this suggestion may have, it cannot account for medieval structures such as the west front of the 13th century cathedral of St Lo (*frontispiece*). The building was destroyed during the Allied landings in Normandy in 1944, but as we can see from old photographs its façade was so pervasively asymmetric that it is impossible to find *any* detail at all on one lateral half that is mirrored on the other. Note, for example, the different height, width and design of the two side portals – and the blatantly off-set position of the central doorway; note the different designs and dimensions of the two great flanking windows on the second level; and note, too, the entirely different designs and sizes of the two towers and their spires. It is impossible to believe, of course, that the men who built this asymmetric structure were so inept, or suffered from such defective eyesight, that they thought that they were duplicating the details of one side on the other and that they had placed the main portal on the façade's central axis.

Nor is asymmetric design limited to relatively obscure provincial buildings.[2] The two towers of the great cathedral of Chartres (*fig*.4.1) were built more or less concurrently but do not at all resemble one another; no one will think that they were intended to be identical. Not just their shape but their dimensions, too, are different, for the left-hand side of the facade, from the ground to the top of the steeple, is perhaps 15% narrower than the other side, though its steeple is taller. The flanks of the façade moreover - the bases of the towers - are designed quite differently. We can be sure that these differences are the result of bold and magnificent – *and certainly conscious* - decisions by the builders. Assuredly, they did not arise because the builders attempted, but failed,

---

[1] In fact it is not unusual, even today, to find people perceiving an asymmetric object as symmetric. But that, as I suggested in Note Three, may be because they prefer, or are culturally conditioned to expect, to see things as symmetric (particularly if those things are considered attractive).

[2] Goodyear (1905) has assembled an interesting selection of examples of medieval architectural asymmetry.

to duplicate a single design: let alone because they could not see any difference between the two sides.

There are however those who infer that a design of such "confusion and messiness" as the west face of Chartres must have emerged from an uneasy and reluctant accommodation to contingencies that are unknown to us today.[3] In this view, the two towers and their spires were built at different times and reflect different tastes, and the builders of the later tower were willing to put up with "messiness" if as a result at least *one* tower and spire was consistent with their taste.[4] This is on the face of it a plausible explanation – but only until we notice that the window above the right-hand portal is rather narrower (and perhaps lower) than that above the left-hand portal and – even more startlingly – that the great rose window of the façade is not centered on the same axis as the middle window or in the rectangle in which it is contained. I have no explanation for these irregularities, but the point to make now is that they tell us that the asymmetry of the west front of the cathedral must have been built into the structure virtually from the very outset and was not the result of later contingencies. (If Simson is correct in believing that the construction of the two towers took place more or less concurrently in the middle of the 12th century, their asymmetry was not the result of unavoidable contingencies but may have been freely chosen.[5])

The asymmetry of the great façade of Notre Dame in Paris, which makes no attempt at concealing itself, also cannot possibly have been inadvertent (*fig*.4.2) or the awkward result of later decisions. Even the casual observer must notice that the two flanking portals of the façade are quite different from one another. The portal on the left is wider and shorter than the one on the right and it is contained in a sharply-angled recess, which the other is not. Moreover, while there are eight kings lining the arcade above the left-hand portal there are only seven in the arcade above the portal on the right. This indeed is a clue for those who have not yet detected it that *the entire left side* of the façade, from the base to the top of the tower, is wider – by about 15% - than the façade's right-

---

[3] James, *op.cit.*

[4] Lovejoy (1960b, p.146) argues that the asymmetry of Gothic cathedrals "was partly due to the historical accident that few ... were completed in accordance with the original design". Weyl (1952, p.16) seems to echo this explanation when he suggested that there are "historical reasons" why the towers of Chartres are different from one another. (Unfortunately, Weyl did not disclose what, in his opinion, those reasons may have been.) Whether or not this view is correct may be debated, but the relevant point is surely that if people had thought it important for Chartres' two towers to look alike they would have built one as the facsimile of the other. That they did not do so shows that, at the least, they had no objection to having the façade flanked by two obviously different towers.

[5] Simson 1962, p.148.

hand side. These are variations that must have been built into the structure from the outset. Their meaning, alas, is unknown to us today.[6]

There are still a number of important asymmetric medieval churches in Italy. The remarkable unfinished façade of the Fiesole Badia (fig.4.3) is one of the most memorable. A rectangle of elaborate dark-green and white marble geometric patterns is superimposed asymmetrically (it is much further to the left of the structure) on an unfinished brick wall. The two large panels on either side of the doorway – the one on the right is both wider and taller than the other - are each framed with a band of a continuous (thus asymmetric) design that differs from one side to the next. Rectangular panels set into the three white marble compartments on either side are all of different patterns (I have not determined whether they are symmetric). In the left-hand panel the two flanking compartments are of different widths. The linear designs in the three flanking semicircles in the band above the doorway are asymmetric in themselves and also in the relation of one semicircle to the other; as are the arrangements of vertical lines above this arcade. The vertical bands of the upper row, too, are asymmetric both within and between each panel.

The modernization of the medieval interior of Santa Maria Assunta, the cathedral of Padua, was completed in the middle of the eighteenth century and no trace of the earlier fabric survives. The cathedral's façade, however (fig.4.4), which probably dates back to the twelfth century, was not rebuilt. It is markedly asymmetric. Its two shoulders are set at visibly different heights, and the wall of the central section that reaches up to the pitched roof is much taller on the right than on the left. The door on the left is taller and wider than that on the right, and further from the center door. The structure attached to the cathedral is its baptistery (fig.4.4a), also of the twelfth century. Its porch is asymmetric and is sited asymmetrically on the main body of the building. Both drums are sited asymmetrically in relation to the structures on which they rest.

The shoulders of Ancona's 12th-13th century cathedral (fig.4.5) differ in length and angle, as do the two pitches of the porch roof. The side windows on the lower level are not equally distant from the outside cor-

---

[6] Other medieval French churches with asymmetric facades include St Etienne, Caen, the cathedrals of Coutances and Amiens, and the great church of the royal abbey of St Denis. Crosby (1987, p.174) acknowledges that early engravings indicate that the design of St Denis' north tower "was not the same as that of the south tower". Nevertheless, his reconstruction of the façade shows the towers as identical, "on the assumption that [the...] master mason intended to build twin towers"! Crosby gives no explanation for why he made this thoroughly dubious "assumption". He acknowledges however (pp.176; 177-179) that "the major vertical axis of the central portal is not in exact alignment with the axis of the upper rose window, and the north side is slightly narrower than the southern". (The discrepancy between the widths of the two sides is 30cm., or just under 12 inches.)

ners of the structure (that on the left is closer in). As can readily be seen from the photograph, the porch is well off the center axis of the circular window.

Another example of asymmetric architecture in medieval Italy is the exquisite little oratory in Pisa known as Santa Maria della Spina, completed in the fourteenth century and still in a splendid state of preservation (*fig*.4.6). At first glance this oratory appears to be an unambiguously symmetric structure. But that is only at first glance. Closer inspection reveals that the "half" on the left is significantly narrower than the other "half" – as are its doorway and the two arches that surmount it; the lintel above the doorway on the right is substantially taller than its opposite. The roundel above the left portal is a trifoliate design; that above the left appears to be a single circle. The pediment above the right door is taller than the other; it is surmounted by a square inset decorative panel; while that above the left is surmounted by a circular one. The rose windows within each pediment are of different designs. The pillars of the lower aedicule on the left are different from those on the right; and the two aedicules on the right are substantially taller than those on the left. All in all, what appears at first sight to be a symmetric structure soon shows itself to the objective observer to be pervasively *asymmetric*, instead. The interior of the chapel, too, is asymmetric.

The Basilica of St Mark in Venice, completed during the thirteenth century, is a treasury of asymmetric design.[7] What I would point out here, because less well-known, are the asymmetries of the great and lovely piazza in which it is set. The plan of the piazza (*fig*.4.7) is asymmetric; the axis of the basilica itself is at a very different angle from that of the piazza;[8] the tall campanile rises from a seemingly arbitrary spot near the mouth of the piazza and is not centered on or aligned with any point around it. The piazzetta that leads to the lagoon is also asymmetric; note the position of the two columns toward the water. The façade of the doge's palace – Ruskin called it "the first building" of the world – also has more asymmetries than are usually noted. Particularly fascinating, and I think particularly enlivening, is the fact that the diagonal lines and rows of rectangles on it, composed of different-colored bricks, are often not set straight and are not always continued on a straight line when intersected by a window.[9]

---

[7] See the foldout plates, with elevations of the basilica, in Samonà *et al* (1977); and Goodyear (1905, pp.88-107 and the foldout plan) for detailed measurements of the basilica's interior.

[8] Some paintings correct this axial "error", for example the view of P. San Marco attributed to Giambattista Cimaroli (late 18th century), published in the Winter, 2012 edition of *Bonham's Magazine*.

[9] Palladio had hoped to replace the existing palace with a neo-Classical structure. Fortunately, his ambition was thwarted.

In Italy today however there are also numerous medieval churches whose facades are symmetric. Virtually without exception these are not their original facades.[10] From the late fifteenth to the late nineteenth centuries Italian churches were re-faced in order to "correct" – as it was thought – their asymmetric design and other alleged flaws.[11] I have not discovered a single rebuilt façade that is asymmetric.[12]

Two of the greatest churches in Florence are among the many in that city whose facades were refashioned. Far from being authentic, as people often seem to assume, the symmetric confections of ineffable vulgarity that are the present facades of the church of Santa Croce and of Santa Maria del Fiore, the Florence cathedral, are nineteenth-century travesties. Fortunately, we have illustrations that show what the facades looked like in their unaltered states. The church of Santa Croce is shown in a painting (*fig.*4.8) by Giovanni Signorini, dated 1846, that documents the asymmetry of its original appearance. The buttress-like devices on either side of the circular window are different in width, and the portal on the right is lower as well as closer to the outer edge of the façade than the portal on the left. The arch enclosing the main portal seems not to be centered on the great circular window above it. That window, most stri-

---

[10] Some medieval churches, such as San Miniato in Florence and the cathedrals of Venice, Pisa and Siena, or the Badia of Fiesole (*fig.*5.1) have facades that are encrusted with asymmetric designs, sometimes multi-coloured, in marble; some also have mosaic murals. I know of no asymmetric façade of this type that was demolished, a circumstance that suggests that these facades' decorative value may have trumped their asymmetry. Indeed, it would seem that the decorative scheme on the façade of Santa Maria Novella in Florence may actually have been *extended* during the work done on it in the fifteenth century (see Note Eight). The façade of the old St Peter's in the Vatican was surmounted by Giotto's mosaic *Navicella*, some surviving fragments of which are now in the Renaissance basilica. It is not a counter-example of the point made here, for the destruction of the façade was part of the demolition of the entire old basilica. The marble-and mosaic-encrusted façade of Orvieto's cathedral is symmetric, but it is a very rare and possibly unique exception.

[10] Nathaniel Hawthorne (1874, entry for October 2, 1858) noted that the Florentines and Romans "have obliterated, as far as they could, all the interest of their medieval structures by covering them with stucco, so that they have quite lost their character, and affect the spectator with no reverential idea of age." He did not recognize, however, that transforming asymmetric features, or concealing them, was a large part of the motivation for making these changes. That this was so may be seen from the fact that the building of the new façade of the Florence Duomo was accompanied by the moving of windows and tombs in the cathedral's interior to create a symmetric distribution.

[12] Among the many designs submitted for a new façade proposed for San Petronio in Bologna were two – by Baldassare Peruzzi (c.1521) and by Giulio Romano and Cristoforo Lombardo (1546) – that are clearly asymmetric (Wittkower 1974a, pls.98, 99). I can offer no explanation of this remarkable circumstance. The old façade has never, in fact, been replaced.

kingly, is not centered on the wall in which it is placed but is closer to the right. *Fig*.4.8a shows the symmetric façade, completed in 1863, that replaced it.[13]

The asymmetries of Santa Maria del Fiore were even more striking. They are recorded in the drawing made by Bernadino Poccetti in about 1585, shortly before the façade was demolished (*fig*.4.9).[14] The drawing, which is almost certainly an accurate depiction of the structure, shows that the two flanking portals are of different designs and dimensions; that the tall recesses that rise from either side of the main portal are not centered on the great oval window nor on the point where the façade meets the peak of the roof. Those recesses moreover are of unequal height, the one on the right being lower than the other. Most obviously, the two oval side windows are set at markedly different heights on the façade.

In decorative details of "uncorrected" medieval churches we can find innumerable instances of asymmetric design. The asymmetry is typically unselfconscious. One interesting example are the black-and-white bands on the great piers of the nave of S. Maria Assunta, the Siena cathedral (*fig*.4.10).[15] The left and right piers nearest the entrance have 23 and 22 such bands; the next pairs 21 and 22; 22 and 22; 20 and 21; and 21 and 22, respectively. Only one facing pair of piers thus has the same number of bands. The bands on these piers also vary perceptibly in height.[16]

The façade of the Siena baptistery has a number of more or less square frames recessed into its lower walls, each containing a small carving. *Fig*.4.11 shows one of these frames, in which it can be seen that although three sides of the frame each have eight dentelles, the fourth

---

[13] The story, no doubt apocryphal, persists that the prominent Star of David on the façade reflects the Jewish antecedents of the façade's architect, Niccolo Matas of Ancona.

[14] Businani 1993, p.95. The original drawing is in the archives of the *Opera* of the cathedral.

[15] On the cathedral's façade the "misalignment" of the piers framing the central portal with those of the piers framing the rose window, although not an asymmetry, has been a source of consternation for art historians. Gillerman (1999) suggests that it is offset by "a heavy emphasis on axial symmetry" of the overall façade but, in fact, the façade, and the exterior generally, of this great cathedral is asymmetric. Gillerman adds, however, and I think quite correctly, that the "misalignment" would not have seemed anomalous to people in the Middle Ages.

[16] We may mention here the finding of Hiscock (2002, p.107 and fig.4.1) that in the transepts of Norwich Cathedral "the wall-piers dividing each part into three bays only face each other imprecisely... The south transept overall is shorter than the north". Hiscock used electronic means to measure the cathedral, so that his results can be considered more than usually reliable.

side has nine. The lion's head in the frame, moreover, is set markedly off-center, and its mane and facial features are asymmetric.[17]

No less remarkable as evidence of an easy-going acceptance of the irregularities that we now regard as asymmetric is the famous 12th century "tree of life" mosaic in the apse of the church of San Clemente in Rome (*fig*.4.12).[18] The left arm of the crucifix (and indeed Jesus' right arm) is visibly shorter than its opposite; the scrolled vines on the left are higher than those on the right; the curve of the vines enclosing the two standing figures differ in shape from each other; and the cloud-like shapes above the crucifix are all asymmetric in shape and in their relationship across the central axis.

The medieval panels of the main door of S. Zeno in Verona are unabashedly irregular in their relation to each other. None of the panels themselves (*fig*.4.13) have symmetric designs and many differ in size and the angles at which they are set. The overall effect is of a slightly crazy patchwork quilt(*fig*.4.14). Leisinger suggests that some of the panels may have been a added at a later date, though their designs, too, are asymmetric.[19]

Figs. 4.15 and 4.16 show two lunettes above doorways leading into Santa Maria della Pieve in Arezzo. In *fig*.4.15, the reliefs of the lunette and the scroll below it are asymmetric. More strikingly, the doorway and its frame, along with the lunette above it are not centered on the wider arch in which they are contained. *Fig*.4.16 shows another doorway into the Pieve. The carvings on the lunette are boldly asymmetric; the doorway and the circular window above it are not centered on each other.

Asymmetric design is common in medieval book arts, too. *Fig* 4.17 shows a Hebrew prayer book for Yom Kippur from 13th-century Germany. The design of the titlepage is strongly bilateral, but almost every detail on the one side differs from that on the other side. For instance, the mythical (?) beasts at the bottom of the page are quite different from each other: note the differences in the set of the two heads, or the lengths of the bodies. The chevrons on the columns, by the same token, resemble each other but their dimensions are different; and the same can be said of the architectural details that surmount the arch. In the crennelated

---

[17] Comp. the lion head reliefs on the reverse of the North Doors of the Florence Baptistery, Pope-Hennessy 1991, pp.45-46.

[18] See Lloyd 1986 for a useful discussion of the date of the apse. The arms of medieval crucifices are frequently asymmetric. Brink (1978) documents a difference of 4 cm. in the arms of the Santa Croce Cimabue crucifix.

[19] Leisinger 1957, introductory section, "Verona". The bronze doors have now been placed inside for their protection; the wooden doors that were substituted for them have frames that are evidently supposed to recall the bronze panels of the original door but they are arranged symmetrically.

structure on the right, for example, we see one more arch than we see on the equivalent structure on the left.

Fig.4.18 shows a leaf from an early 15th-century Parisian Book of Hours that had once belonged to Sir Edward Burne-Jones.[20] The design is asymmetric throughout. The exquisite bed of flowers is of course asymmetric; the panel set into it is well off-center; the three-sided frame that encloses the illustration and the text is asymmetric: note, for example, the different sizes (and in fact different colors, too, though that is not apparent from the illustration used here) of the opposing sections.

From a somewhat earlier period, *fig.*4.19 shows the rear cover of the ninth-century Ashburnham Gospels, one of the greatest treasures of the Pierpont Morgan Library in New York City. This sumptuous work is asymmetric throughout and manifests complete indifference to symmetric design. Even the three visible cruciform arms of the halo of the Jesus (?) figures facing the center panel are asymmetric. So too are the four sections into which the cover is divided, and all the intricate designs within them.

Finally, we must also attest to the asymmetry of secular medieval architecture. The glorious Chateau de Chambord (*fig.*4.20) may be regarded as the last magnificent efflorescence of medieval French architecture, the close of a period that had earlier produced the marvels of Chartres and Notre Dame. Construction of this palace was begun in 1519, well before Serlio brought the Italian Renaissance's new aesthetic of symmetry to France. An observer must spend many minutes in order to comprehend the intricate asymmetries of the façade, and especially of the playful roof line (*fig.*4.21).

Another example of medieval asymmetric design is the awesome Palazzo Vecchio in Florence, also known as the Palazzo della Signoria (*fig.*4.22). Most obviously, the immense tower is not centered on the structure, and the fenestration is distributed unevenly on the principal façade.

There is abundant evidence, as we have by now seen, that medieval builders and craftsmen were in general indifferent to what we think of as symmetric design. Stendhal recognized this but surely overstated the matter when he wrote that "There is no exact measurement, no symmetry, in medieval buildings ... if there are arches in a straight line, the breadths are rarely equal", *etc.*, *etc.*[21] For in France and elsewhere there are numerous medieval structures that *are* symmetric. Examples of them include the main facades of the cathedrals at Laon (completed c. 1225); Salisbury (completed c.1320); or Orvieto (much of it completed by c. 1350).

---

[20] www.bonhams.com/auctions/21845/lot/9/

[21] Stendhal 1962, p.255.

These structures however do *not* attest to a knowledge of the concept of symmetry in medieval times. The use of the terms "asymmetric" and "symmetric" in a medieval context is anachronistic: no one who lived in those times knew those words, in our understanding of them, or the concepts for which they stand. The fact that *we* can identify medieval designs as being either the one or the other this does not mean that people in the Middle Ages also saw them as such; almost certainly they did not. A case in point is the ground plan of the Palazzo Vecchio. It is a quite irregular shape, and definitely not symmetric. But for the Florentine chronicler Villani (d.1348) the problem with its design was not that it was irregular or that it was asymmetric but that it was not square. As Villani expressed it, it was *una granda diffalta di non farlo quadrato* – "a big mistake not to have made it square".[22] Designing the plan of a building "on the square" (*ad quadratum*) or its elevation on the equilateral or isosceles triangle (*ad triangulum*) was an important principle of medieval architecture, albeit one that is not always evident in the actual structure of a building.[23] As a principle of *proportion* based on regular geometric forms it led to designs that we regard as symmetric. But, to repeat, there is no evidence that the men who designed and built structures *ad quadratum* or *ad triangulum* intended to create – or even recognized that they were creating – symmetric shapes.[24] The very detailed discussions during the late fourteenth century of *ad triangulum* issues in the design of the cathedral in Milan, notably, include no reference to the symmetry that

---

[22] *Cronica*, Lib.VIII, cap.26. Villani did not however comment on the many asymmetric features of the building's elevations, including the design of its principal facade. Two centuries later Vasari (in the *Life* of Michelozzo) would also criticize the Palazzo della Signoria for its irregular design "built out of square" and with "unequal columns in the courtyard", but although he too did not refer to these irregularities as asymmetric, we know that he regarded symmetry as an essential element of good architecture. On the other hand a modern scholar, Goldthwaite, did not see that the palazzo's design is asymmetric. He declared (1993, p.181) instead that the structure "has been called [he does not say by whom] one of the most important buildings in the history of Italian architecture for the influence of its … symmetrical façade … on the evolution of domestic architecture in the Renaissance"!

[23] For an overview of the issues regarding *ad quadratum* see Wu 2002 and Shelby 1972.

[24] For Christian Platonists in the middle ages the square was "the geometrical representation of the Godhead and as such the source of all aesthetic perfection"- Simson 1962, p.49; similarly Hiscock 2000, p.39. But there is no evidence that the *symmetry* of the square was thought of as an aspect of its perfection (or even that it was detected). Similarly, outlines of one-half of the north transept portal and rose window for the Clermont Cathedral, evidently intended as templates for stone masons, have been found incised on a flat roof of the structure (Davis, 2002). The use of these templates *recto* and *verso* as it were would have resulted in structures that are symmetric. But it seems more plausible that this was a device to ensure accuracy and the equal distribution of loads, rather than a method to create symmetric structures.

would result from the application of this principle.[25] We must therefore regard the symmetry of medieval architecture and decorative work, where it occurs, as unintentional and unacknowledged - an unwitting consequence of the geometric principles that were sometimes employed by their designers.[26] It is not evidence that the concept of symmetry existed in medieval times.[27]

But few ideas ever spring forth into the world fully formed, and one supposes that the concept of symmetry probably had its roots in trends that were gathering momentum in the late Middle Ages. A hint of them, possibly, may be found in the suddenly relentless and self-conscious symmetry of buildings (*fig*.4.22) in the paintings of Giotto (d.1337) and Taddeo Gaddi (d.1366) whom Villani likened to Vitruvius.[28]

---

[25] Ackerman 1991, pp.211-268; and Wittkower 1974a, pp.17-65. In Note Three we saw that although the ancient Greeks knew shapes that are symmetric there is no reason for us to suppose that *they* recognized those shapes' symmetry. Plato's solids, notably, are symmetric but neither he, nor Euclid in his mathematical elucidation of them, seemed to have been aware of that.

[26] It is difficult to accept the claim of Crisp (1924, p.18), even on the basis of the material he himself presents, that medieval gardens "were ... symmetrical". Some medieval gardens, as Crisp himself acknowledged (p.15), consisted of little more than an untended space enclosed by a wattle fence; others were made up of "a picturesque confusion of roses, hawthorns and honeysuckles mixed with fruit-trees and shrubs, all growing in wild profusion" (p.27); others again were like the garden whose "lawn of exceedingly fine grass, of so deep a green as to seem almost black [was] dotted all over with possibly a thousand kinds of gaily-colored flowers" in which Boccaccio (1972, p.252) sets part of *The Decameron's* third day. There is no evidence that "paths of unusual width, all as straight as arrows" that crisscrossed and surrounded this garden "were ... symmetrical". On the other hand in medieval times there were apparently also gardens "nigh broad as wide and every angle duly squared", like the one we read of in the 13th century *Roman de la Rose*. Whether they reflected the geometric principles of medieval architecture, views about the design of the Garden of Eden (Prest 1981) or the desire for efficient tending and harvesting of the plants - often herbs - that grew in them is unclear. But we cannot infer that they were designed to be, or were regarded as, symmetric.

[27] That *ad quadratum* was not associated with bilateral symmetry can also be seen from the fact that in a section about the proportions of a gateway captioned "...*La Symmetria dilla Magna Porta*" Colonna (1499, c4) declared, "*la principale regula peculiare al'architecto è quadratura*". In this passage Colonna clearly intended *simmetria* in the traditional meaning of harmonious proportions, that is attained (in his view) by obeying architecture's supreme imperative of *ad quadratum* ("quadratura"). For him, therefore, building on the square was a way to ensure that a structure's proportions would be harmonious. He nowhere associated it with bilateral symmetry, though he used *simmetria* in this sense as frequently as he used it in the older sense of "harmonious proportion" (see Note Seven).

[28] Ladis (2008) states that for Giotto "symmetry [was] an aesthetic imperative ... a guiding ideal in every sense". Since the concept of symmetry had not yet been for-

Another hint, perhaps, could be the warning of Lorenzo Maitani (d.1330), when he was in charge of the construction of Siena's cathedral, that if a proposed extension of the choir were carried out the dome would no longer be centered on the crossing of the nave and the transept, as it ought rationally – *rationaliter* – to be. [29] The impetus for these ideas came in all likelihood from the *ad quadratum* and *ad triangulum* precepts, but it may well be that those precepts also provided some movement toward the concept of symmetry, itself.

Yet (to anticipate) it was not from them that the concept of symmetry emerged. It seems rather than the principal impetus behind this new concept was the need for an ordered and immediately comprehensible visual environment. This need, as I will suggest in Note Six, was engendered by the terrible depredations of the Black Death of 1348-1350, and the long succession of lesser (but still appallingly deadly) plagues that followed in its wake.

---

mulated, this statement is anachronistic. It is also incorrect in a more direct sense, for the Arena chapel, from which Ladis claims to have derived his insight, is not arranged symmetrically – compare, for example, the two banks of angels, or saints, on either side of the Last Judgment. Indeed, Giotto seems on occasion to have gone out of his way to create what we think of as asymmetries – see for example the intentionally crossed eyes of both Madonna and Child in his Ognissanti Madonna, and in his St. Peter Enthroned in the Vatican. On the asymmetry of the Baroncelli Polyptich cf. McManus (2005 pp.163-5), and comp. Caglioti (1992 pp.112-113), who writes that crossed eyes were "intentionally introduced" by the Byzantines, though he does not offer any suggestion as to what that intention may have been. The building depicted on the counter-façade of the upper basilica in Assisi (if that is by Giotto) is asymmetric, as is the roundel containing the Dove. Note for instance the 6 dentelles on the right edge of the pediment on the left versus 7 on the other edge. None of this is to deny, of course, the appearance of symmetric design in some of Giotto's work; rather, I mention this to dismiss Ladis' overstatement about symmetry being an "imperative" that Giotto obeyed..

[29] Norman 1995, vol. II, p.142; and comp. Burns 1971 and Onians 1992.

4.2 Paris, Notre Dame

4.3 Fiesole, the Badia.

4.4 Padua, Santa Maria Assunta

4.4a Padua, Santa Maria Assunta, baptistry

THE SYMMETRY NORM AND THE ASYMMETRIC UNIVERSE   113

4.5 Ancona Cathedral

4.6 Pisa, Santa Maria della Spina

4.7 Venice, Plan of Piazza San Marco

THE QUESTION OF MEDIEVAL SYMMETRY 116

4.8 Santa Croce, Florence. Above, the medieval facade as it was in 1846 (Detail from Giovanni Signorini, *Il Carnevale di Firenze*)

4.8a The facade of Santa Croce today

4.9 Florence, Santa Maria del Fiore. Poccetti's drawing.

4.10 Siena cathedral, nave
(first pair of piers only partly visible)

4.11 Siena Baptistery carving

4.12 Rome, San Clemente: apse mosaic

THE SYMMETRY NORM AND THE ASYMMETRIC UNIVERSE *121*

**4.13 Verona, San Zenobia, door panel.
(St. Zeno driving out the devil.)**

4.14 Verona, San Zenobia, door.

4.15 Arezzo, Santa Maria della Pieve.

4.16 Arezzo, Santa Maria della Pieve

4.17 13th-century Hebrew prayer book from Germany

4.18 Leaf from early 15th. century, Paris, Book of Hours

4.19 Rear cover of Ashburnham Gospels, c.800

4.20 Chateau de Chambord

4.21 Chateau de Chambord, roof line

4.22 Florence, Palazzo Vecchio.

4.22 Giotto's symmetric architecture

THE ASYMMETRY OF PRIMITIVE ART

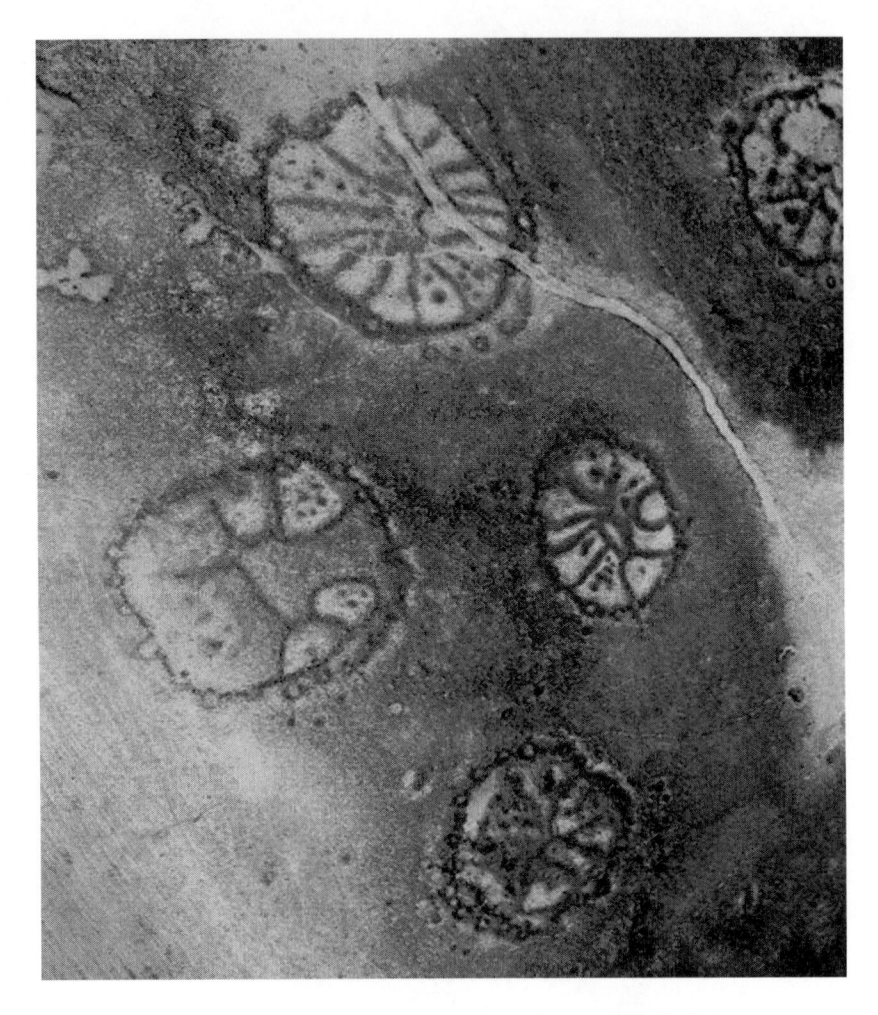

5.1 Aerial view of giant stone structures in Azraq Oasis, Iraq[1]

---

[1] *news.yahoo.com/visible-only-above-mystifying-nazca-lines-discovered-mideast-0114306688.html*.

Note Five

According to Franz Boas, artisans who have attained "technical perfection" or a "high degree of mechanical skill" are found very widely in primitive cultures. Work done by Indian joiners and carvers in the regions north of the Puget Sound, for example, "rivals that of our very best craftsmen" in the civilized world.[1] In a remarkable passage Boas declared, indeed, that "the appreciation of the aesthetic value of technical perfection is not confined to civilized man. It is manifested in the forms of manufactured objects of all primitive people that are not contaminated by the pernicious effects of our civilization and its machine-made wares... In the households of the natives we do not find slovenly work, except when a rapid makeshift has to be made. Patience and careful execution characterize most of their products. Direct questioning of natives and their criticism of their own work also shows their appreciation of technical perfection... Slovenly work does not occur in an untouched primitive culture."[2]

For Boas bilateral symmetry represented "perfection of form".[3] According to him craftsmen and craftswomen in primitive cultures generally possess the skill needed to give their artifacts symmetric form. Symmetric design, he then went on to say, is one of the "characteristic features" of "the art of all times and all peoples". It is "one of the most ancient and most fundamental characteristics of all art ... a common characteristic of art the world over".[4]

Asymmetric designs, on the other hand, were regarded by Boas as aberrations. They are found only quite rarely, he claimed, either when primitive people have not acquired the skill needed to make

---

1 ibid, p.12.

2 *ibid*, pp.19-20; 352.

[3] In this passage he referred, rather obscurely, to bilateral symmetry as the only "true" symmetry.

[4] Boas 1955, pp.32, 49. Fifty years before the publication of *Primitive Art* Allen (1879) had made a similar point, claiming that "A savage ... makes his arrowheads and his club bilaterally symmetrical with an amount of care that puts to the blush his civilised companions". Thus the myths of the primitive craftsman's high standard of precision and his preference for symmetry were evidently not invented by Boas (and possibly not by Allen, either).

things symmetric, or when – as in the case of the unequal halves of the image of a killer-whale's tail on a Tlingit blanket – the artisan happens to have made "a mistake".[5]

Although artisans in primitive cultures are led by their appreciation of the aesthetic value of technical perfection to give symmetric shape to their work, Boas did not believe that their preference for symmetry has a doctrinal basis. Rather, he supposed that there is something inherent in the way things are made that causes them to acquire symmetric form. "Symmetry" he stated, "results from the process of manufacture" of such objects as coiled pottery and coiled baskets.[6] Another, more important, source of symmetric design however, indeed one of its "fundamental determinants" is, Boas declared, the symmetry of animal forms. In particular "the symmetry of the human body" - one consequence of which is the symmetric motions of our arms and legs[7] – engenders in all humans "the feeling of symmetry", and this leads us naturally to create artifacts that are symmetric.[8]

I am not aware that Boas' ideas regarding the alleged preference for symmetric design in primitive cultures have been challenged, but there are certain fundamental objections to them that ought to be set down. Most obviously our bodies (and Nature's forms in general) are *not* symmetric. They therefore could not be the inspiration that leads people to make symmetric objects.

How, one also wants to know, is the "feeling of symmetry" consistent with our pleasure in making and looking at asymmetric forms – at landscapes, for example, or paintings of them? Moreover, if "the feeling of symmetry" arises naturally it is surely a paradox that we must first acquire highly specialized skills before we can create artifacts that are symmetric. Boas meets this latter objection by arguing that "a feeling for symmetry may exist without the ability of perfect execution". Both the Bushmen and the inhabitants of Tierra del Fuego, he claimed, have "the intent to give [symmetric] form" to their artifacts

---

[5] *ibid*, p.230, fig.234. Comp. Reichard (1922) who declared that the asymmetry of a beaded design was "doubtless due to the fact that the maker ... misjudged her distance".

[6] *ibid*, p. 34. Boas also claimed that the use of two-handed implements such as the bowdrill resulted in symmetric forms.

[7] "Symmetrical motions of the arms and hands are physiologically determined ... I am inclined to consider this condition as one of the fundamental determinants, in importance equal to the view of the symmetry of the human body and that of animals; not that the designs are made by the right and left hand, rather that the sensation of the motions of right and left lead to the feeling of symmetry" *ibid*, pp.33-34.

[8] *ibid*, p.33.

but lack the ability to do so.⁹ Boas did not indicate the evidence for these bold statements, and so one wonders how he learned of that "intent" and of that "feeling for symmetry" on the part people who lack the ability to make (and probably even to describe) artifacts that are symmetric. Might it not be more plausible to see in their artifacts evidence, if anything, of an innate feeling for *asymmetry* instead? Indeed, why do we assume that the creators of those artifacts gave any thought at all to whether they should make things that are either symmetric or asymmetric? Perhaps this question, this choice, did not occur to them! It seems significant that neither Boas nor any other anthropologist has ever reported finding words or expressions that denote "symmetry" or "asymmetry" in the cultures they studied.

One of Boas' claims was that "the tribes of Tierra del Fuego decorate their faces and bodies with designs, many of which are symmetrical".[10] This is a puzzling statement, in part because we have already seen him declare that the Fuegans lacked the technical skills needed to create symmetric designs. If as it now appears they *did* in fact possess those skills, we must wonder why they did not employ them in *all* of their artifacts rather than only in "many" of their bodily decorations. Setting this concern aside for the moment, Boas' association of the impulse to create symmetric shapes with the purported symmetry of the human body and its movements makes instances of body ornamentation of especial interest for our purposes here.

Yet when we look at the drawing that Boas used to illustrate the symmetry of Fuegan facial painting – he referred to it as a "series of symmetrically arranged dots running from ear to ear across the nose" - we can at once see that the dots are in fact arranged *asymmetrically* (*fig*.5.2).[11] (The painted board from Tierra del Fuego that he described as "symmetrically decorated" is also *not* symmetrically decorated.[12]) The Andaman Islanders too, Boas wrote, "like to decorate their bodies with symmetrical patterns", but the photograph with which he illustrated this statement (*fig*.5.3) also shows decorations that are asymmetrically arranged. The striations on both arms for example do not converge on a central axis but run in the same direction and are therefore asymmetric. Further, the more or less central dark line is flanked on one but not on the other side by a broad, light-colored band, and the band that runs vertically down from the woman's right shoulder to her waist is matched only very imperfectly on the left side

---

⁹ *ibid*, p.24.

[10] ibid, p.23.

[11] *ibid*, p.32.

[12] *ibid*, p.3 and fig.7, p.23.

of her body. These features probably reflect conscious aesthetic decisions; and we have no grounds for supposing that they manifest a lack of technical skill.[13]

In *Primitive Art* Boas documented his claims about symmetry with numerous illustrations of purportedly symmetric designs, yet in every instance these illustrations show objects that are asymmetric. Boas' statements, for example, that "many of the designs of the Australian aborigines are symmetrical" and that "in paleolithic painting geometrical forms occur that exhibit bilateral symmetry" are contradicted by the objects with which he illustrated these claims, for they are all unambiguously asymmetric.[14]

The same mischaracterization occurs in the description of a slate Haida dish carved with the representation of a sea-monster (*fig*.5.4). Boas rather strangely remarks of this object that although its design "appears asymmetrical", in fact it "is perfectly symmetrical".[15] As even a casual observer can see, however, the design is an asymmetric one. Note for example the differences between the two eyes, or between the two nostrils.

Boas also specifically identified as symmetric decorated boxes from British Columbia; Kaffir neckrests; Melanesian shields and paddles; painted rawhides of the Sauk and Fox Indians; and prehistoric Peruvian heraldic devices: yet it is easy to see from his illustrations of these artifacts in *Primitive Art* that all of them are asymmetric. Other objects illustrated in the book, though not directly identified by Boas symmetric, are also appropriate as a test of his contention that symmetry is a characteristic of primitive art. They include the painting on a Haida box; the decorations of Kwakiutl house fronts; a Haida painting representing a dog-fish;[16] an Arapaho pouch-painting; and the woven pouches from British Columbia.[17] All of these objects are asymmetric. So is the arrangement of beaded thongs on Thompson Indian leggings, that do not follow the palindromic abcba | abcba progression Boas de-

---

[13] *ibid*, p.32 and pl.II. Comp. the remark of Alsop (1982, pp.30-31) about the "*brilliantly skillful* [my emphasis] and idiosyncratic use of asymmetry" that characterizes the body-painting of the southeastern Nuba.

[14] *ibid, p*.32. That this error continues to be made by modern anthropologists is attested by Sutton, 1988, in whose important study of Aboriginal art the Lake Eyre toas (p.62; fig 89); the Lumarluma bark painting from Arnhem Land (p.66; fig.99); and another untitled bark painting, also from Arnhem Land (p.69; fig.96), are described as symmetric but are in fact quite obviously asymmetric.

[15] *ibid,* p.246, fig.258.

[16] This is the same painting that Adam (1936) described as having "two symmetrical profiles".

[17] Boas 1955 *figs*. 246-248; 232; 151a; Pl.VII.

scribed but an asymmetric 6.6.7.6|6|6.6.6.8 pattern.[18] Another of Boas' illustrations is reproduced in *fig*.5.5.[19] It shows a Congolese mask, intricately decorated in geometric patterns, not one of which is symmetric in itself or with its nominal opposite. The bottom corners for example each have a triangle. That on the left is much larger than the one on the right, but the larger one contains 4 horizontal lines within it whereas the smaller one has 6. Note too the completely different set, shape and size of the two eyes. How Boas could have thought that this remarkable artifact upheld his claim that primitive art is symmetric is perplexing.

An even more curious instance of Boas' misperception is the painting on the edge of a Tlingit blanket representing a killer-whale. According to Boas the asymmetry of the two tail-halves on one side of the blanket was the result of a mistake made by the artisan.[20] In fact, the mistake was by Boas, who declared that the design he reproduced in the book was "repeated" on the other side of the blanket "but with symmetrical tails". A photograph of that other side (fig.5.6), kindly taken for me by a member of the Amerian Museum of Natural History staff, shows that both halves of the blanket are asymmetric - in themselves as well as in relation to each other!

In fact, not one of the 15 plates and 308 text figures that Boas included in *Primitive Art* shows an object that is symmetric. Contrary to Boas' descriptions and the analyses he built upon them, these illustrations document the *asymmetry* of primitive art, not its symmetry.

In other publications Boas wrote at length about the designs of blankets made by Chilkat women on the northwest coast of the United States. The production of these blankets began with the weaver's husband, who sketched on a wooden board the general concept and principal feature's of the blanket's design. The weaver transferred to her loom some, though not necessarily all, elements of the pattern drawn by her husband, and then filled in (evidently as she saw fit) the areas for which no designs had been indicated on the board. Remarkably, a number of these pattern boards have survived, and in some instances it is even possible to match a board to the blanket that was derived from it.

Boas misunderstood the nature and function of the pattern boards. In the note that he contributed to Emmon's exhaustive study of Chilkat blankets he declared that the boards show "only one part of the whole middle pattern and one wing ... the other side being sym-

---

[18] *ibid*, fig.16, p.29.

[19] *Ibid*, fig.64, p.70.

[20] *ibid*, p.230, fig.234.

metrical with the one shown on the pattern board".[21] Later anthropologists echoed this claim.[22] However, the design on pattern boards is not usually limited to either the right or left half but typically extends from one side to between one-eighth and one-half of the other side: *and the extension is not the mirror image of the equivalent area on the other side of the central axis.* We do not know why the design extends across the center – no researcher appears to have investigated this question – but that the extension does not reflect the other side completely dispels the notion that the design of Chilkat blankets was intended to be symmetric. Nor indeed are any symmetrically-woven Chilkat blankets known.

*Fig.*5.7a shows the pattern board that appears in Emmons' study as *fig.*576. The design extends beyond the central axis into the left half of the board. It can readily be seen that the details on the left differ in size, shape and spacing from their equivalents on the right side. Thus, the eyebrow in each pair differs asymmetrically from the other, as does the eye in each pair; and the nostrils are not centered on the mouth and teeth below them. *A fortiori* this also holds true of the blanket – Emmons' *fig.*575 – whose design was apparently derived from this pattern board (*fig.*5.7b). It should be noted that the asymmetries of the blanket itself are not copies of those on the pattern board. Different as the uppermost pair of eyes and eyebrows on the blanket are from each other, for example, they are different from their equivalents on the pattern board. Indeed, the layers above and below the principal face are rather more closely aligned on the blanket than they are on the pattern board. Moreover, details (such as the peaks in the white spaces above the eyebrows of the lower face) that are original to the blanket, and were not derived from the pattern board, are also asymmetric. Some of the asymmetries of the blanket accordingly are not attributable to the designer of the pattern board but are the invention of the

---

[21] Boas 1907, pp.188-189. He claimed that the symmetry is achieved by using a reversible bark stencil, and that this technique is also used to obtain symmetry in painted designs. No such stencils exist in ethnographic collections, as far as I have been able to determine, and no other reference to them exists in the literature. The point of course is moot, for the blanket designs are asymmetric and so the technique described by Boas could not have been used on them.

[22] Crawford (1978) writes: "Since the design is bilaterally symmetrical, the pattern board need show only half of the design". Comp. Holm (1965, pp.84-85): "The principles of splitting and of representing the whole animal naturally leads to bilateral symmetry". But what if the sides of the animal that has been "split" are not symmetric? Holm concedes that "there are to be sure many examples of asymmetric design" but then states that the principle of bilateral symmetry holds for many of the individual design units such as the ovoid eyes that "are essentially symmetrical within themselves". However, "essentially symmetrical" is a euphemism for "asymmetric"!

weaver herself. We conclude that the pattern board and the blanket, while strongly bilateral (or, in the case of the board, strongly suggestive of bilaterality) are – each in its idiosyncratic way – *bilaterally asymmetric*.

One anthropologist has made a point of emphasizing the avoidance of symmetry in the work of potters in the culture she studied. The decorative designs on Zuni pots, according to Ruth Bunzel, are characterized by their "very marked lack" of bilateral – or as she preferred to call it, "duplicating" – symmetry:

> To paint a bird or animal with two heads in order to preserve the symmetry of the design would be utterly foreign to Zuni taste. This applies to the geometrical patterns as well as the representative. The "steps" designs which could so easily be made symmetrical without destroying their character are never so drawn. There seems to be a careful avoidance of this particular type of symmetry, in spite of the fact that the parts of the design are carefully balanced. This lack of duplicating symmetry extends also to the arrangement of the motives. There is no feeling that the designs on any field must be arranged with reference to an imaginary center line. The decorative importance of this principle is most apparent in the treatment of deer and sunflower designs. An artist trained in our traditions would certainly treat these motives differently. He would turn the two deer in each horizontal field either towards one another or away from one another, dividing the field into two halves, each of which mirrors the other, and bringing the two deer on each side of the sunflower into the same relationship with it... However the Zuni artist... turns all his deer with their heads to the right... The lack in Zuni design of the particular kind of symmetry which we expect in our own decorative art, but which is by no means common to other styles, does not mean that Zuni designs are not constructed without a careful balancing of the various units.[23]

---

[23] Bunzel 1929, pp.28-29. Bunzel adds that in Zuni pottery "the whole jar is symmetrically laid out" but seems to imply by this merely that it is shaped symmetrically on a potter's wheel. Regrettably, Bunzel never discussed *why* the Zuni eschew symmetric decorations. When Dillingham (1992, pp.85-86) asked an Acoma or Laguna potter "what makes a pot beautiful?" she replied, "the overall shape of

Bunzel stands alone, however, in her recognition of asymmetric design in primitive art. Most anthropologists seem instead to follow Boas in his view of the near-universal occurrence of symmetric design, and to account for this by alleged universal characteristics of the human and other natural forms. Anna O. Shepard, for example, attributed what she saw as the prevalence of symmetric design in primitive art to the fact that "bilateral symmetry is most conspicuous in nature and, above all, it is expressed in the human body".[24] Dorothy K. Washburn, who has written extensively on the subject, agreed with Shepard. "Just as symmetry has been found to underlie the structure of the natural world", she wrote, "so too, by extension, do humans use the property of symmetry in their perception of the world".[25] It is these influences, she explained, that established symmetry as one of the "universal properties of form" and account for the fact that "most designs produced by most societies are symmetrical".[26] A similar point was made by the ethno-mathematician Slavik Jablan, who claimed that symmetry "has been present from the earliest time in all that has been done by man", a circumstance that he explained as "the reflection in human artifacts" of "the symmetry existing in Nature".[27]

Views, like these, about the universality of symmetric design are very often reflected in anthropologists' descriptions of the artifacts of specific cultures they study. Examples include Fewkes, in an important study of prehistoric Hopi pottery, who says of a pot in one of his photographs that "the vessel is symmetrical"; and of another, that its "form is regular and symmetrical".[28] Adam tells us that the Haida

---

the jar ... symmetry in motion". Unfortunately he did not ask her to elaborate on her statement which, in truth, evokes the college seminar room more than the native pueblo. Comp. the observation of the writer Zora Neal Thurston, (Hurston, 1983, p.54) that "Asymmetry is a definite feature of Negro art... the sculpture and the carvings are full of this ... lack of symmetry". It is unclear whether she was referring to African art or to the art of African-Americans.

[24] Shepard 1948, pp.221, 231. Shepard quoted approvingly the opinion of Puffer (1905, p.10) that an asymmetric arrangement can only be pleasing if it has a "hidden symmetry". Puffer does not tell us, unfortunately, how we are to detect this hidden asymmetry. Could it be that if we find an asymmetric design attractive that must be because a symmetric design is hidden in it?!

[25] Washburn 1995, p.525.

[26] Washburn 1999; Washburn and Crowe 1988, p.33.

[27] Jablan 1955, p.4. Michelis (1955) states that humans have an "innate sense of symmetry".

[28] Fewkes 1895, p.651; plate CXIX, a and c.

painting of a dog-fish (*fig.*5.8) is "symmetrical".[29] Mainzer, pointing to a sand painting, remarks that he is "astonished" by the symmetry of Navajo artifacts.[30] Mokhopadhyay refers to the symmetry of the decorations on Tlingit baskets, and Patkau declares that "symmetry of design is very important" to the Nlaka'pamux as they decorate their baskets.[31] Crawford states that the design of Chilkat blankets "is bilaterally symmetrical"; Holm, that asymmetric designs in Northwest Coast nevertheless uphold "the principle of bilateral symmetry" because their component parts are "essentially symmetrical within themselves".[32] Reichard states that in the work of artists in the Admiralty Islands "the feeling for symmetry [a Boas-ian phrase] ... is very pronounced" and attributes the few designs she recognizes as asymmetric "to poor technique rather than to the artist's taste".[33] She finds that the Solomon Islanders too show a "liking for symmetry" in all their work.[34]

None of these descriptions is supported by the illustrations that accompany them. One can readily see that Fewkes' two pots are asymmetric; that Adam's Haida painting of a dog-fish (*fig.*5.8) is asymmetric; that Mainzer's sand painting (an example as he thought of the "astonishing" symmetry of Navajo work) is asymmetric; and the same is true of the baskets described by Mokhopadhyay and by Patkau; of the Chilkat blankets Crawford refers to; and of *all* the artifacts that Holm illustrates in his *Northwest Coast Indian Art*. Similarly, the photographs published by Reichard clearly show that all the works she described as symmetric are asymmetric.[35]

Asymmetry, it would appear, is indeed one of the most pervasive characteristics of primitive art. Any collection of primitive art confirms this. One such collection is Torbrügge's *Prehistoric European Art*.[36]

---

[29] Adam 1936.

[30] Mainzer 1996, p.16.

[31] Mokhopadhyay,2009; Petkau n..d..

[32] Crawford 1978; Holm, 1965, pp. 84-5.

[33] Reichard 1933, p.148.

[34] *ibid*, p. 118.

[35] eg pl. cxxvi, nos.492, 493; pl.xxiv, no.69. Remarkably, Reichard *ibid*, p.149 acknowledges that among the Tami and the Massim designs are characterized by "the avoidance of symmetry... The better a composition is conceived and the more carefully it is carried out the more likely it is to be asymmetrical, and this always with the preservation of perfect balance". It would have been hoping for too much to expect that this observation would lead anthropologists - including Boas himself, to whom Reichard dedicated her work - to reconsider their assumptions about symmetry and asymmetry in primitive art.

[36] Torbrügge, 1968

This work contains 350 illustrations of artifacts; my selection here is made at random from among them except insofar as certain photographs do not allow us (because of the camera angle) to determine whether or not the objects they show are symmetric:

- A terracotta bowl of the 6th or 7th century BCE from Dietldorf, Germany (*fig*.5.9) has an erratic figure, like a six-pointed star, at its center.[37] The twelve sets of lines that describe the outline of the star vary markedly in length, and range from 8 lines on one side to 5 on another; the paired limbs of two of the tree-like figures branching out from the center are not aligned with each other, and vary erratically in the numbers of roundels along their lengths (in one pair the arms have 9 and 12 such figures); the triangular patterns on the circumference are of different sizes; the abstract human figures are not the same size or placed at equal distances from each other (the one near the top has two thumbs on its right hand). Not a single feature of this complex design appears to be part of a symmetric configuration.

- The voluptuous "Venus of Vestonice" (*fig*.5.10) has vast pendulous breasts of unequal size that are not centered on her body; a head and perhaps shoulders that are asymmetric; eyes that are set at varying angles, differ from each other in length, and are not equidistant from the center of the face. The shapes and sizes of her two hips do not match each other; and the oval of her navel is irregular and is not at the center of her stomach.[38].

- The two highly-stylized female ivory idols from Dolni (*fig*.5.11, overleaf)) are both asymmetric. The legs of the figure on the left are not equally thick, and the torso is on a different axis from the legs. The lower torso of the idol on the right is quite irregularly shaped; her breasts differ notably from each other in size and shape.[39]

- The rock drawings in Skavberg, Norway (*fig*.5.12) show two human figures. The outlines of their bodies and heads as well as the shapes and lengths of their arms and legs are markedly asymmetric.[40]

- The decorations of a female idol (*fig*.5.13) from Cucuteni-Baiceni in Romania are asymmetric; so is the shape of her body. Note, for example the discrepancy in shape and size of her two shoulders; the marked difference between the outline of the two sides of her head; and the un-matching positions of her eyes.[41]

---

[37] *ibid*.fig 10, p.11.

[38] *ibid*, p.1 5

[39] *ibid*, p.26.

[40] *ibid*, p.56.

[41] *ibid*, p.65.

- The design of a bronze belt-hook (*fig.*5.14) from Hoelzelsau, Austria, is strongly bilateral in emphasis but no less strongly asymmetric: in the two bird-like heads flanking the human figure, for example, the eye of that on the left is placed near the bottom of the head and of the other near the top. The bird on the right has a longer beak than the other and its neck protrudes much further beyond the curve of the buckle than that of the bird on the right. The left-hand portion of the cross-bar at the top of the hook is longer and appears to be broader than its opposite on the right.[42]

- The exquisite sinuous forms on a bronze mirror from Desborough, England (*fig.*5.15) are asymmetric in themselves and do not mirror each other on either side of the central axis of the design; both the handle and the frame are asymmetric.[43]

A random selection from among the 570 photographs of artifacts in Sydow's *Kunst der Naturvölker und der Vorzeit* also shows the prevalence of asymmetric design.[44]

- The remarkable tribal house in Togoland (*fig.*5.16) is made up of a cluster of cylindrical towers, each evidently of different height, circumference and shape; the oval entrance to the structure is irregularly-shaped and not placed on the central axis of the cylinder in which it is set.[45]

- A bronze statue of a king from Benin (*fig.*5.17) is flanked by two attendants, one of whom is notably shorter than the other. The object that the king holds in one hand is different from that in the other. His nose and mouth are not centered on the face, though the eyes are. However, the left eye is smaller than, but has a pupil that is both larger and lower than, his right eye. The left nostril is smaller than the right. On the pedestal the arms holding what appears to be a bush are of different sizes.[46]

- The decorative edge of the "dance-cap" from the Cameroons (*fig.*5.18) alternates three rows of black and white beads (they are described as pearls) that slope in the same direction along the entire perimeter without regard to a central axis. A triangle with similar bands of beads reaches up from the front of the cap; its left and right sides are of unequal lengths. The bird's head at the apex of this triangle points

---

[42] *ibid*, p.191.

[43] *ibid*, p.222.

[44] Sydow, 1932.

[45] *ibid*, p. 131. Cf. also the complex of buildings from the northern Cameroons, p.132.

[46] *ibid*, p.139.

asymmetrically to the left. The three other pairs of birds on the cap either point toward or away from each other but they are asymmetric in their size, shape and location on the cap.[47]

- The prominent geometric designs of a dance mask from the Bena Lulua of the Congo ((fig.5.19) are asymmetric. The left-half of the mouth and the left eye are lower than their opposites; the axis implied by the bottoms of the two "V"- shaped designs on the forehead veers sharply away from the middle of the mask; the three black-and-brown stripes reaching down from the left eye extend much lower than those on the right side of the face. The arrangement of black triangles above each eyebrow is different, as is the arrangement of triangles on either side of the upper lip. Thus, the row of triangles on the upper right lip contains four triangles and ends at the corner of the mouth, whereas the row on the upper left lip contains at least six triangles and extends to the edge of the jaw.[48]

- A pavilion-like structure housing the graves of the family of a Borneo rajah ((fig.5.20) has elaborate bow-like projections on either side of the roof that are different in size and shape from each other; asymmetrically-placed carved birds on the ridge of the roof; and two large panels contain mythical, dragon-like beasts that both face away from the center but are unlike each other.[49]

- Reliefs in the entrance chamber of tombs in Croizard, in the Petit Morin valley of the Marne (France) are exquisitely stylized images of a woman and a man ((fig.5.21). The heads are not centered on the bodies of these figures, nor the noses on their faces; the curved lines that possibly indicate the man's beard extend much further on his left cheek than they do on the other side. The woman's breasts are not centered on the same axis as her face.[50]

- The elaborate decorations of a 7th-century silver buckle from Fonnaas in Norway (fig.5.22) have a strong bilateral quality but are asymmetric throughout. To take just one area of the design: the face at the bottom of the object is set well to the left of the central axis but the nose on this face is far to the right; the eyes and the curves above them are also asymmetric. The motifs that border the buckle immediately above the face are different in both size and scale.

The examples given here do not preclude the possibility that symmetric designs are to be found in some works of primitive art. Indeed, I have found a few myself. One is a headhunter's wooden shield

---

[47] *ibid*, p.155.

[48] *ibid*, plate VI, opp. p.176

[49] *ibid*, p.293.

[50] *ibid*, p.475.

from northwest Borneo, that is particularly noteworthy for having an outline that is symmetric while the interior decorations are asymmetric, including a floral pattern that straddles the clearly-delineated central entirely different. axis.[51]

Also paradoxical is the fact that symmetric designs recur with some frequency in the woven straps, bands and pouches of the Huichol Indians of northwest Mexico, but not in other objects made by Huichol artisans.[52] Possibly, the symmetry of the woven work is brought about by the tight and even spacing of warps on their looms. But this explanation is challenged by the fact that Navajo blanket designs seem to be symmetric as often as they are asymmetric, even when they are from the same period. A mid-19th century serape blanket in the Arizona State Museum has three rows of rectangles in its middle that are asymmetrically aligned with each other on both vertical and horizontal axes; the rectangles within any of these rows vary asymmetrically in shape and size.[53] By contrast another serape blanket from the same period, in which the basic diamond shapes of the design are linked together to create a web-like overlay, is symmetric.[54]

We should not infer from such designs, however, that the artisans who made these objects possessed the concept of symmetry. On the other hand, in view of the fact that symmetric forms are almost never created inadvertently, it seems most unlikely that the creators of these artifacts did not intend to make them (as we would now say) symmetric. Symmetry then, although very rare in works of primitive art, is clearly not non-existent. Its occurrence poses a very interesting problem. Unfortunately, this is a problem that remains unrecognized by anthropologists, who are trained to believe that primitive art is naturally and almost invariably symmetric.

In conclusion it is worth speculating briefly about why Boas insisted that almost all works of primitive art are symmetric.

Boas was born to a cultured liberal Jewish family in Minden, Germany. The pervasive anti-Semitism of German academic life and his distaste for the rising tide of Prussian nationalism prompted him to

---

[51] Sydow, *op.cit.*, p. 308.

[52] Powell 2010 fig 4.19, p.62. Although the design of the fabric in 4.23, p.63, is symmetric, it is used asymmetrically on the pouch. Most Huichol artifacts have the marked asymmetry of e.g. the decorated votive bowls shown in fig.3.9, p.39.

[53] Kallenberg 1972, pl.16, p.38. Comp. also pl.37, p.62; pl.39, p.64; pl.47, p.72; pl.49, p.74; pl.61, p.87.

[54] *ibid*, pl.17, p.39. Scholars have not accounted for, in fact appear not to have recognized, the fact that both symmetric and asymmetric designs are commonly found in these blankets.

leave his native land after he completed his doctoral studies. He settled in the United States and before long was appointed assistant curator of ethnology at the American Museum of Natural History in New York City, as well as head of the new anthropology department at Columbia University.[55] In Germany Boas had worked under Adolf Bastian, the ethnographer – and a specialist in primitive art – who was an early advocate of the belief that people in all human cultures have essentially the same intellectual capacity. This was a radical idea at a time when the theory of evolution readily lent itself to concepts of racial superiority and inferiority. It reinforced the liberal and idealist values with which Boas had grown up at home, and would play a profound role in shaping his work as America's leading anthropologist. Boas' claim that the precision routinely achieved by artisans in primitive tribes was no less than that of "our very best craftsmen" in modern advanced societies is not borne out by any facts adduced by Boas himself – indeed it is on the face of it a preposterous claim! - but it reflects his *desire* to affirm the equality of all branches of the human family.[56] From a purely humanitarian standpoint that desire is no doubt a commendable one; but it led Boas, the scholar, to the cognitive errors – the misperceptions, the spurious reasoning – noted here. In Note Two I had suggested that the misperception that snowflakes and bees' cells are symmetric may have reflected a belief – arrived at on *a priori* grounds that are scientifically invalid: yet none the less influential down the generations for that – in the order and rationality of Nature and its Creator. A similarly *a priori* conviction, now in the equal capacity of all cultures, seems to have shaped Boas' work.[57]

Boas acknowledged that he was still "undecided" about whether his analysis sufficiently accounted for the symmetry (as he

---

[55] Boas' influence would be spread by a number of his former students who themselves went on to establish anthropology programs at American universities. Among his most prominent students were Alfred L. Kroeber, Margaret Mead and Ruth Benedict.

[56] "... no trace of a lower mental organization is found in any of the extant races of man... the mental processes of man are the same everywhere, regardless of race and culture, and regardless of the apparent absurdity of beliefs and customs" - Boas 1955, p.1. The unequal distribution of intelligence in different parts of the human family is now widely documented, even if still not always acknowledged.

[57] See the interesting comments on Boas by Gombrich (2002,p.269ff.). Gombrich who had earlier declared that "Primitive art, on the whole, is an art of rigid symmetries" (Gombrich 1966, p.94), joined Boas in questioning the notion of "primitive", and the idea that there is a continuum of artistic development from primitive to advanced. Whatever the merits of Gombrich's position, it is indisputable that Boas failed to offer any evidence of the concept of symmetry or of symmetric design in the cultures about which he wrote in *Primitive Art.* Nor do we find any such evidence in Gombrich's works.

saw it) of primitive art around the world.[58] He did not indicate however which were the aspects of his work that he thought were open to doubt, and there is no suggestion in his writings that he ever reconsidered his notion that primitive art is symmetric.

Boas' contributions to the study of symmetry and asymmetry, it must be said, are far from unimportant. His focus on the technical skills needed to create symmetric design was a valuable original insight that, unfortunately, neither anthropologists nor art historians have explored. Nor should we dismiss Boas' notion that the forms we make are unconsciously inspired by Nature's own forms, including the forms of the human body. However, if these are indeed the prototypes that shape the work of the artisan in a primitive society, we must not lose sight of the fact that natural forms, including our bodies, are asymmetric. As such, it is possible that they are part of the reason why primitive cultures (and until not all that long ago, our own civilization) almost invariably made things that are asymmetric.

---

[58] Boas 1955, p.34.

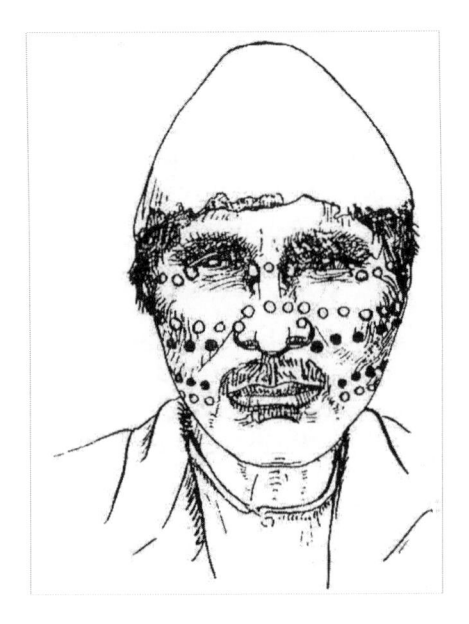

5.2 "Symmetric" Fuegan facial painting

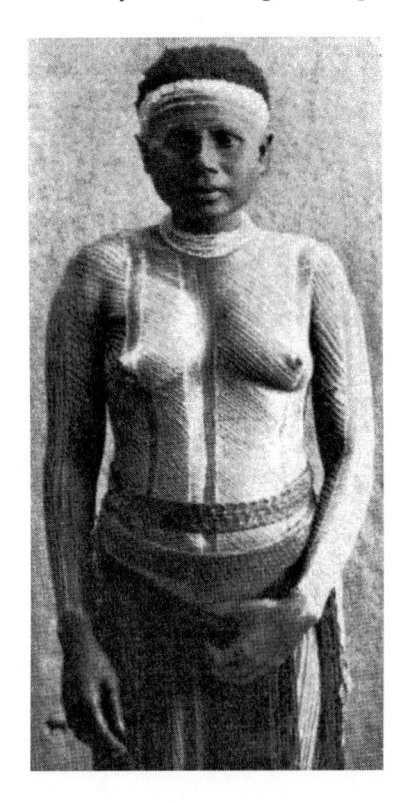

5.3 Andaman Islander with allegedly symmetric body decorations

5.4 Haida dish, described by Boas (1955, p.246) as "perfectly symmetrical"

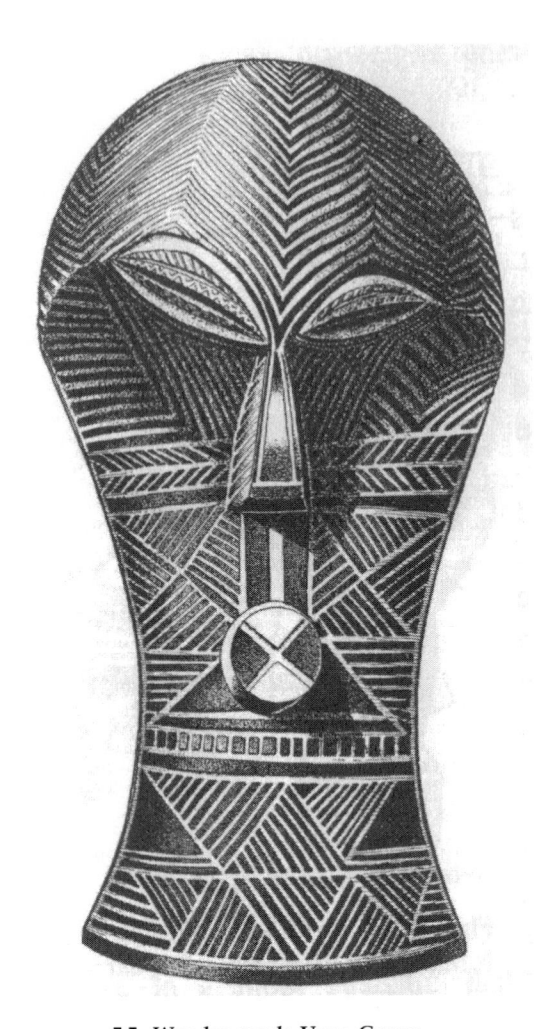

5.5 Wooden mask, Urua, Congo.

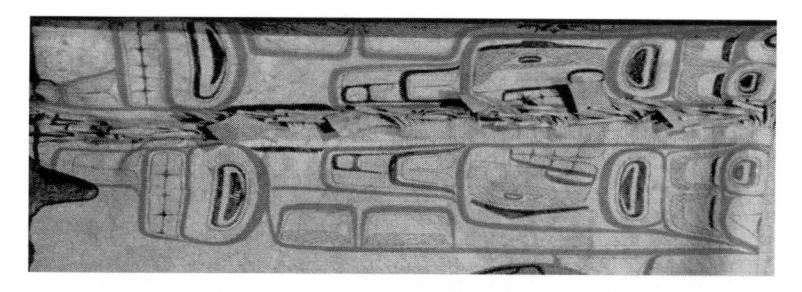

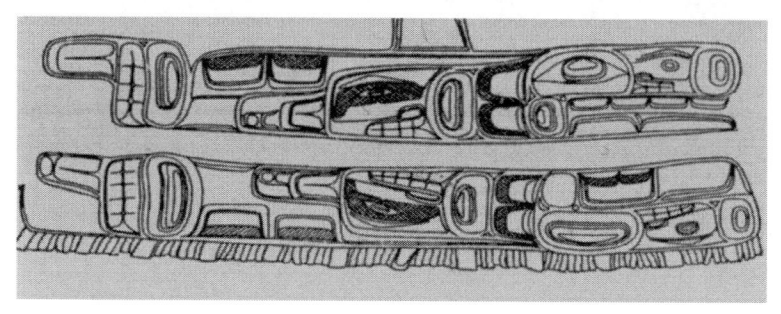

THE SYMMETRY NORM AND THE ASYMMETRIC UNIVERSE 147

5.6 The two halves of a Tlingit blanket American Museum of Natural History E-1502. Upper illustration is from Boas 1955, p.230, fig.234; lower, an American Museum of Natural History photograph

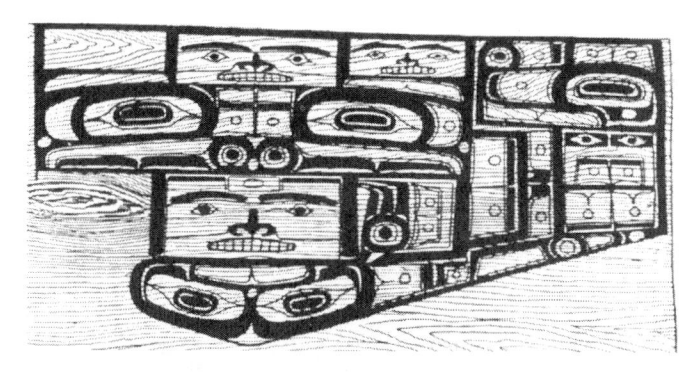

5,7a (upper) and 5.7b (lower). Chilkat pattern board and blanket based on it.

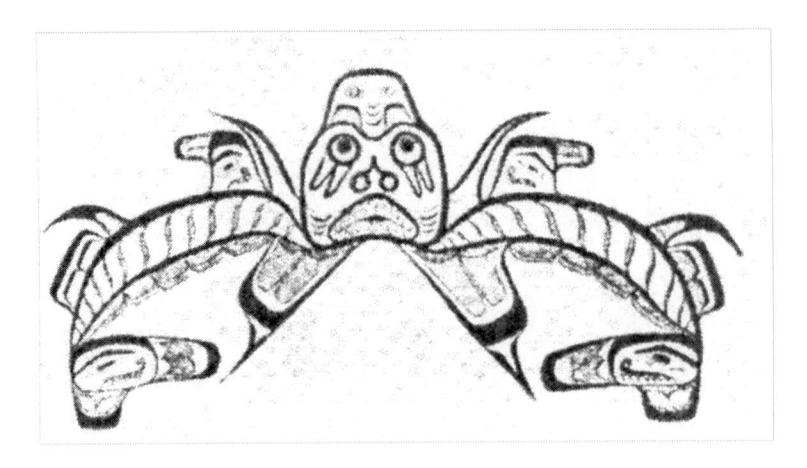

5.8 Haida Dog-Fish painting

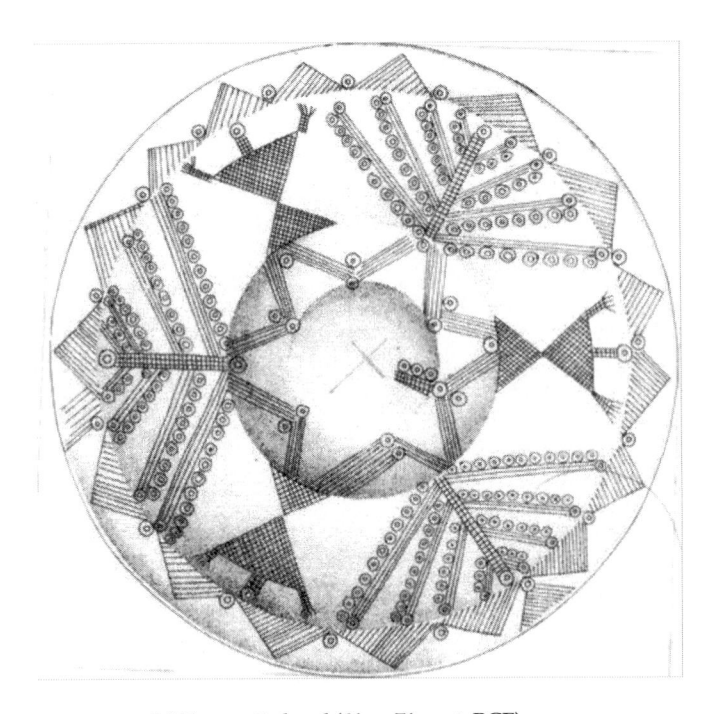

5.9 Terracotta bowl (6th or 7th cent. BCE)

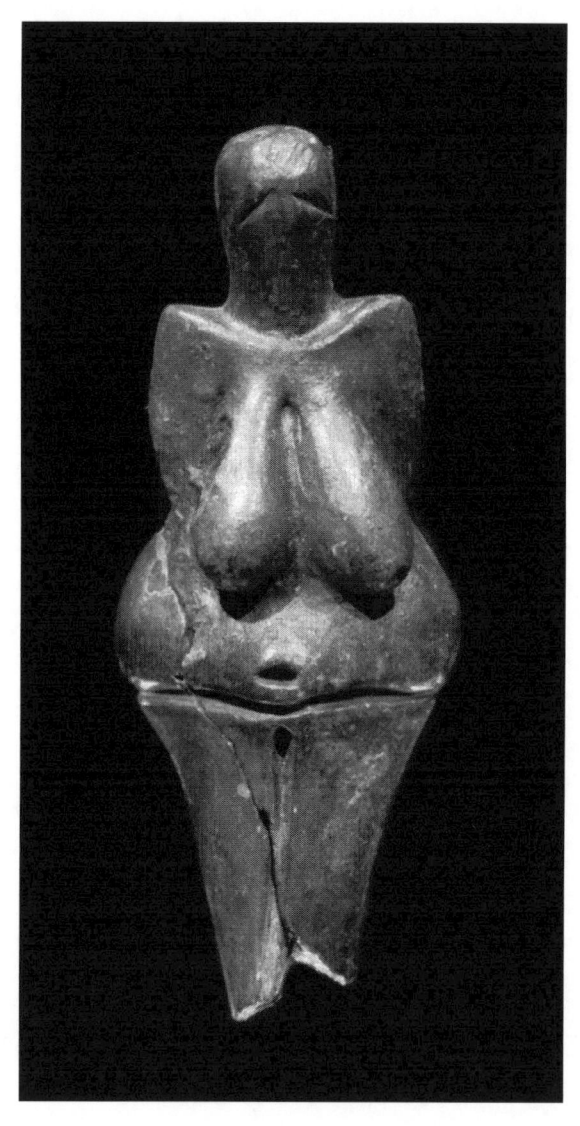

THE SYMMETRY NORM AND THE ASYMMETRIC UNIVERSE 149

5.10 Venus of Vestonice

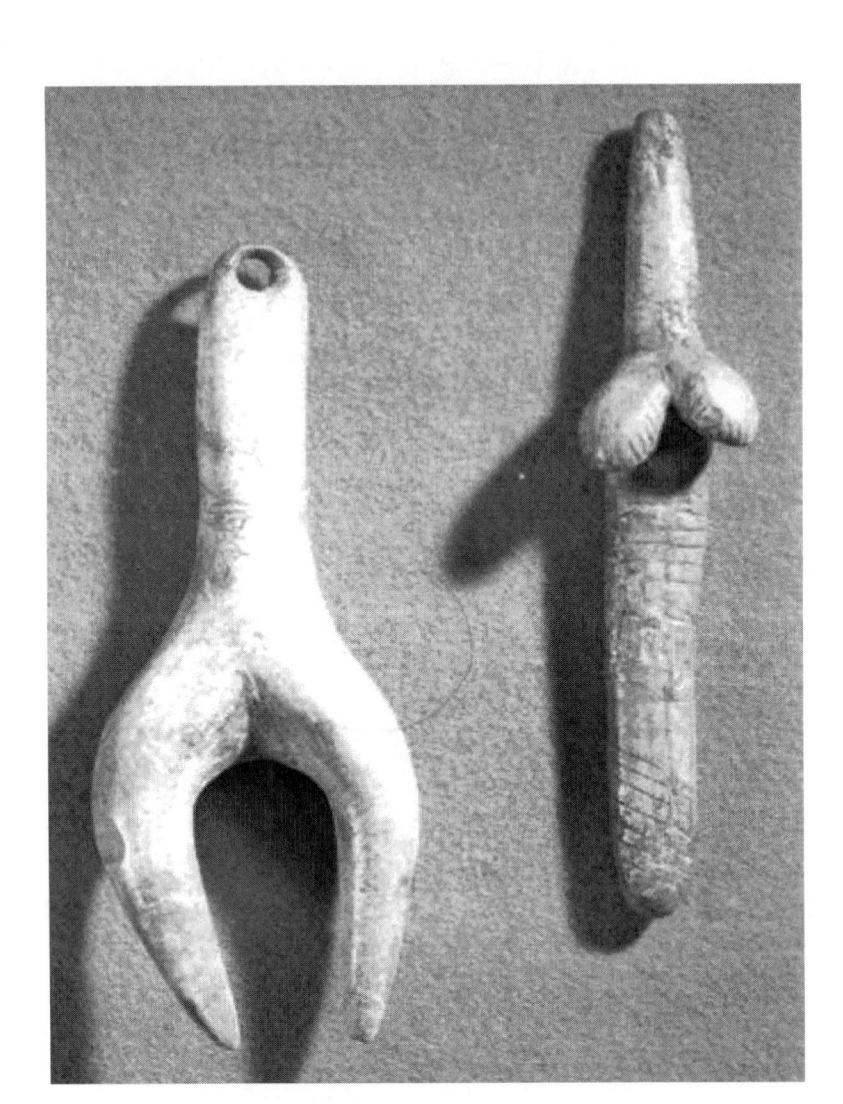

5.11 Female ivory idols from Dolni

THE SYMMETRY NORM AND THE ASYMMETRIC UNIVERSE   151

5.12 Rock drawings in Skavberg

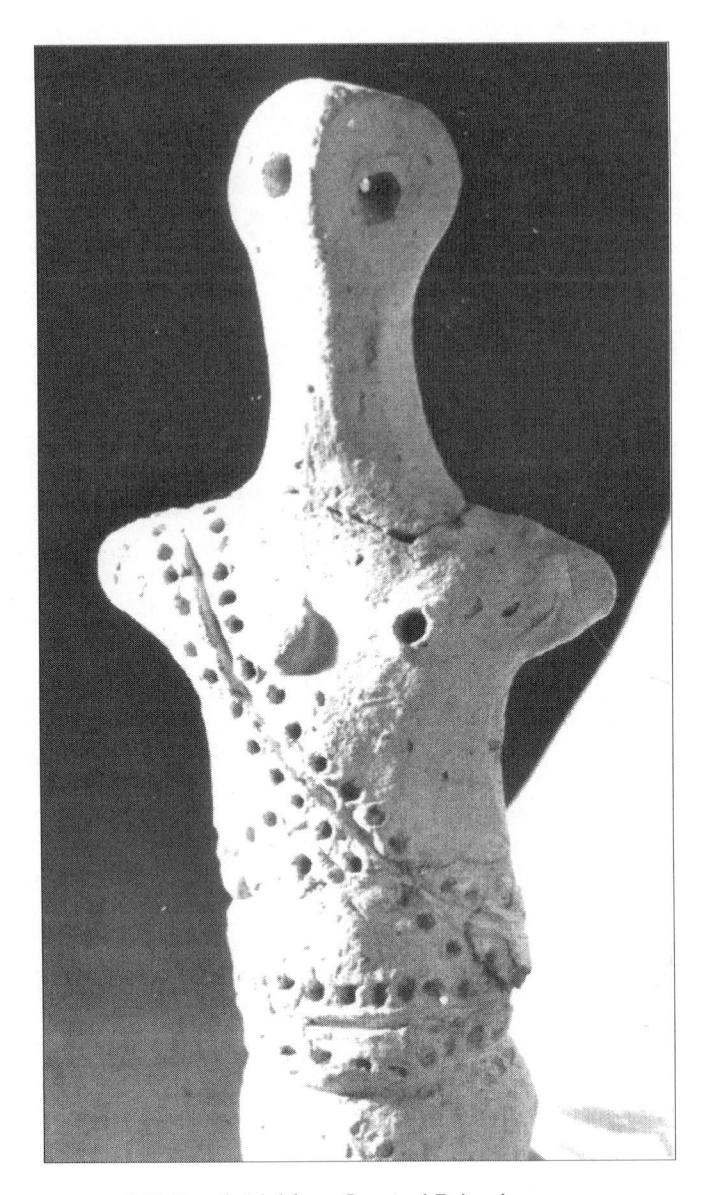

5.13 Female idol from Cucuteni-Baiceni

5.14 Bronze belt-hook from Hoelzelsau

THE ASYMMETRY OF PRIMITIVE ART   154

5.15 Bronze mirror from Desborough

5.16 Tribal house in Togoland

THE ASYMMETRY OF PRIMITIVE ART   156

5.17 Bronze king and attendants, Benin

5.18 Dance cap, Cameroons

5.19 Congo dance mask

THE ASYMMETRY OF PRIMITIVE ART 158

5.20 Royal graves, Borneo

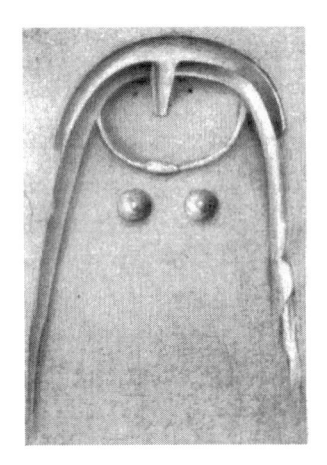

6.21 Tomb reliefs, Croizard

5.22 Silver buckle, Fornass

THE HISTORY OF THE CONCEPT OF SYMMETRY

6.1 Serlio: the "miser's" house renovated

Note Six

> *"[Symmetry is] an invention of the Italian architects at the worst age of the attempted revival of Classical art"*
> – James Fergusson (1849, p.399)

There are some who claim that the concept of symmetry has been known in all cultures since the earliest times – indeed, that it is an inherent part of human consciousness. This opinion is certainly mistaken. There can be little doubt that in fact the concept of symmetry originated in the fifteenth century, at the dawn of the Renaissance in Italy.

On the other hand, we do *not* know who first discovered this concept, or what the train of ideas and circumstances was that led to its discovery.[1] Our ignorance in this regard is particularly regrettable

---

[1] I know of only three writers who have gone some way toward recognizing that the concept had specific and perhaps identifiable origins. The German poet Goethe attributed it to a reborn appreciation, both of Nature's loveliness and of the forms of Classical architecture, that he thought had emerged in the thirteenth century. (*"Als aber in dreizehnten Jahrhundert das Gefühl an Wahrheit und Lieblichkeit der Natur wieder aufwachte, so ergriffen die an den Byzantinern gerühmten Verdienste, die symmetrische Komposition ... Prächtige Gebäude des Altertums standen Jahrhunderte von ihren Augen..."* - Goethe 1963, p.96.) Bernard Berenson (1953, p.163), for his part, suggested that during the early years of the Renaissance a "tropism of pattern" (by which he meant a certain weariness with the medieval idiom) led "by automatic reaction toward ... symmetrical design..." The discovery of Antiquity, Berenson added, "helped to accelerate this process by lighting the way and cheering with examples of successful effort". Berenson seems here to echo the broader point of Burckhardt (1985, p.26) that "In Florence, at a time of high prosperity, the feeling first gained ground that the great art of the 13th and 14th centuries had expended its vital force and something new must come". (Cole [1973, pp.231-234] more convincingly places this revival in the middle of the fourteenth century.) On the other hand the historian Richard Goldthwaite (1993, p.180) has attributed the emergence of symmetric design in architecture to a desire at the beginning of the fourteenth century "to heighten and refine the physical presence of the city". This desire, he claims, brought "a genuine urban aesthetic into focus" that "consisted in [*sic*] the organizing principles of spaciousness, regularity, orthogonality, symmetry and centrality". These speculations are not satisfactory. Goethe and Goldthwaite place the origin of the concept of symmetry two and one hundred years too early; and Goethe's assumption that Nature's forms, and those of Classical architecture, are symmetric is also incorrect. For its part, Berenson's "auto-

because the many irrational but persistent fallacies that, as we have seen, are tied to the concept (such as the belief that Nature's forms are symmetric) probably can only be understood by reference to its origins.

Lacking solid evidence, accordingly, we must either ignore the very important question of how the concept of symmetry was discovered or else give ourselves permission to speculate about its origins. I opt here for the latter, and will do so by attempting to relate the concept to certain events that importantly mark the period in which it originated and then became entrenched. Correlation, of course, as any dime-store sage will point out, does not prove causation. I hope to minimize this potential pitfall by taking as my guide the insight of the brilliant psychologist Karen Machover that symmetry is a device that offers "protection against a menacing environment".[2] As we will presently see, the environment in which the concept of symmetry made its first appearance and then, with remarkable speed, came to be almost universally accepted, was an environment of immense and perhaps even unprecedented danger.

I shall propose, accordingly, that the concept of symmetry arose from people's need to cope with this very dangerous environment.

No data, unfortunately, attest to a causal connection between the former and the latter, and it would be wrong to pretend that the hypothesis linking them is anything less than a highly speculative one. Nevertheless, I hope that readers will find some merit in it.

---

matic reaction" is an empty concept, as is Goldthwaite's "heightening and refining the physical presence of a city". Neither explains why, out of almost endless possibilities, that of symmetry was chosen. We may digress here to note the interesting insight of Rochberg (1997), that the concept of symmetry first appeared in fifteenth-century Italian polyphony's "self-enclosure ... self-imitation". We may further digress bynoting that, contrary to Goldthwaite's suggestion, symmetric design is not a panacea for urban problems; and creates its own ills. Sir Joshua Reynolds (1997, p.243) had this to say about Wren's plans for rebuilding London: "If the city [of London] had been [re]built on the regular plan of Sir Christopher Wren, the effect might have been, as we know it is in some new parts of the town, rather unpleasing; the uniformity might have produced weariness, and a slight degree of disgust" – those being precisely the sentiments evoked in people of refinement by another attempt to create "a genuine urban aesthetic", the Rue de Castiglione in Paris, built in 1802 (*fig.7.5*). John Gwynn, Reynolds' contemporary, complained in his *English Architecture, or the Public Buildings of London and Westminster* (1758; quoted McCarthy 1987, p.13) of "a dull sameness" in modern buildings. Gwynn did not however not admire the "unrestrained licentiousness" that he discerned in London's medieval structures.

[2] Machover 1949, pp.87-8.

We will begin by noting that the concept of symmetry did not emerge gradually as the outcome of a prolonged evolution. It appeared, rather, quite suddenly and unexpectedly, and as a drastic and discontinuous shift in taste. This shift occurred during the transition from the Middle Ages to the Renaissance, broadly speaking, and it is in the contrast between the aesthetics of the two periods that its character can most readily be discerned.

The aesthetic of the Middle Ages mirrored the almost endless visual variety and complexity of Nature's own – invariably asymmetric – forms. It is exemplified by the richly elaborated textures of the Gothic cathedrals of Chartres and Paris (*figs.* 4.1 and 4.2), and by the "picturesque confusion of roses, hawthorns and honeysuckle mixed with fruit-trees and shrubs, all growing in wild profusion" found in many medieval gardens (*fig.* 6.2).[3]

By contrast, the aesthetic of the Renaissance was an *anti*-naturalistic one of symmetry and simplicity of form.[4] It is exemplified by the vacuous appearance of such structures as the Villa Saraceni (*fig.*6.3), designed by Palladio, and the Palazzo Farnese, which is partly the work of Michelangelo (*fig.*6.4).

It is also manifested in the formal gardens of the Renaissance (*figs.* 6.5, 6.6, 6.7). Laid out on a vast scale and in precise, spare, symmetric and immediately-comprehended geometric forms, these gardens were characterized by "extreme simplicity" and "sameness".[5] No pleasing intricacy or artful wildness, as Pope might have said, ever perplexed the scene in the Renaissance garden. No chaos was permitted to "shimmer through its veil of order" (Novalis).

The change from the medieval aesthetic to that of the Renaissance is cast in vivid relief by the contrast between a passage in *The Divine Comedy* and a drawing to illustrate that very passage that Botticelli made about one hundred and fifty years later. In a brief but evocative phrase Dante had described a forest as "*spessa e viva*" – dense and

---

[3] Crisp 1924, p.27. Comp. Boccaccio 1972, p.252. Renaissance theorists, remarks Panofsky (1955, p.182), regarded Gothic architecture as a "naturalistic" style that originated in the imitation of living trees. Comp. Dante's view (*Paradiso* XIII, 76-79) of the irregularity of Nature's forms: "*ma la natura la dà sempre scema, similemente operando a l'artista ch'a l'abito de l'arte ha man che trema*" (i.e. Nature resembles the artist who knows his art but has a hand that trembles).

[4] In his famous essay, "The First Page of Giorgio Vasari's' *Libro*'", Panofsky (*op.cit.*) identifies certain instances in which "Gothic" elements were incorporated in Renaissance designs, but these are not characteristic of Renaissance architecture as a whole and do not invalidate my generalizations about the contrast between the two periods.

[5] Walpole 1995, pp.25-29.

living.⁶ Botticelli's illustration of it however shows merely a sparse and barren arrangement of a few forlorn, largely leafless, trees (*fig.6.8*). It is a forest with nothing of the "*spessa e viva*" about it. Indeed, if it resembles a forest at all it is one in which only a very few trees are still standing after it has been ravaged by a devastating fire or blight. Ruskin might well have had this very drawing in mind when he commented on "the expiring naturalism of the Gothic school" with these words: "Autumn came, - the leaves were shed, - and the eye was directed to the extremities of the delicate branches. *The Renaissance frosts came, and all perished!*"⁷

The intellectual foundation of the Renaissance's new aesthetic was laid by theorists who dismissed the rich complexities of medieval design as "barbaric", "confusing" and "irrational".⁸ Instead, they equated beauty with forms that are simple enough to be comprehended the moment one first sees them. "Anything that impedes the sight in any way", declared Filarete (c.1400-c.1469), "is not as beautiful as that which leads the eye and does not restrain it"⁹. He explained that this was what made him prefer the circle to other forms, for when one looks at a circular shape "the eye, or, better the sight, quickly encompasses the circumference at first glance". By contrast, Filarete continued, the pointed arch "departs from perfection" because "the eye does not run along it as it does on the circle" but "must pause a little at the pointed part". For his part, Leon Battista Alberti (1406-1472), Filarete's slightly younger contemporary, thought it most disagreeable when variety leads to "discord and difference". Indeed, he found the sight of varied objects acceptable only when they were viewed from so far away that they came to "conform and agree with each other" – that is, when their differences were no longer apparent!¹⁰ Somewhat later Bernini (1598-1680) wrote in much the same vein that "When at the first instant the eye meets a form that satisfies by its contour and fills

---

[6] *Purgatorio*, cant. XXVIII, 2.

[7] *Stones of Venice*, Ruskin 1903-12, v. XI, p. 22. (The italics are Ruskin's).

[8] Instances include the opinion of Vasari (1908, p.38) that "German" (i.e. Gothic) architecture was "*mostruosi e barbari ....confusione o disordine*"; and Bramante's of it as "beyond all natural reason" - *fuori d'ogni ragione naturale* (quoted Germann 1973, p.29). Comp. Michelangelo's view (Hollando 2006, pp.46-6) that the densely naturalistic landscapes of Flemish painters were "done without reason...without care in selecting or rejecting". Michelangelo added that Flemish paintings are (in Hollando's Portuguese text) "*sem simetria nem proporção*". (The distinction between these two terms awaits clarification.)

[9] Filarete 1965, 59*v*.

[10] Alberti 1966a, I.9.

the beholder with admiration then the aim of art has been fulfilled".[11] Remarkable indeed that an instantly satisfying contour – just a contour! - without even regard for what might be contained within it, and requiring (*and inviting*) no further contemplation and exploration than takes place at the first sight of it, was thought sufficient to fulfill the aim of art.[12]

The Renaissance preference for visual simplicity was rationalized by the argument that the forms Nature creates are themselves always simple, and that it is these forms that provide us with our templates of Beauty. Alberti voiced this thought in *De re aedificatoria* when he wrote of the "moderate" character of Nature's forms, and the importance of imitating it in the design of buildings.[13] A century later Palladio referred to "the simplicity which appears in things created by Nature", and urged that churches be built on a circular plan, "as that alone … is simple, uniform, equal".[14]

---

[11] Quoted Wittkower 1974, p.54. Bernini's Vatican colonnade meets this criterion: but one may doubt whether it "fulfills the aim of art".

[12] The preference for designs that reduce Nature's forms to the point where they become comprehended instantly proved remarkably long-lived, so that we find a late 19th-century English garden historian (Blomfield 1892, p.54) arguing in favor of the "extreme simplicity" of the formal garden that "There is no difficulty in grasping the principles of a garden laid out in an equal number of rectangular plots. Everything is straightforward and logical; you are not bored with hopeless attempts to master the bearings of the garden".

[13] *Modestiam naturae imitari",* Alberti (I.9)

[14] Palladio 1570, p.51 (Bk.I, chap. XX): "*quella semplicità, che nella cose da lei [la Natura] create*". The fallacy that Nature's forms can be pared down to a few simple and symmetric figures has enjoyed a very long life, indeed. "*Tout dans le nature*" Cezanne declared (quoted Clark 1949, p.137), "*se modèle selon la sphère, le cône et le cylindre*": everything in Nature is modeled like the sphere, the cone and the cylinder". In the twentieth century Corbusier showed himself in this regard a child of the Renaissance when he extolled "the great primary forms" that are "distinct… without ambiguity" as the central principle of his architecture. Even more unattractive is Mies van der Rohe's ethic of "less is more" which – if we allow ourselves to overlook Mies' enthusiastic sojourn in the world of Adolf Hitler – can also be seen as a sentiment whose ultimate origin is in the Renaissance. The American architect Robert Venturi has remarked that van der Rohe's "less is more" can only be accomplished "at the risk of separating architecture from the experience of life and the needs of society". He added: "Where simplicity cannot work, simpleness results. Blatant simplification means bland architecture. Less is a bore … I like complexity and contradiction in architecture… I like elements which are hybrid rather than 'pure', compromising rather than 'clean', distorted rather than 'straightforward', ambiguous rather than 'articulated', perverse as well as personal, accommodating rather than excluding, redundant rather than simple, vestigial as well as innovating, inconsistent and equivocal rather than di-

The requirement that forms be simple was accompanied by the further requirement that they be symmetric. Here too Nature's creations were alleged to be the prototype that all good design must emulate. "It is of the essence of Nature (*tam ex natura est*)", Alberti declared in *De re aedificatoria*, "that things on the right should correspond in every respect to those on the left (*ut dextra sinistris omni parilitate correspondeant*)": and he then went on to claim that nothing can be beautiful until its lateral halves, too, correspond in every respect.[15]

The more or less simultaneous appearance of these two new standards was not a coincidence, for symmetry, by limiting a form's complexity to that of one of its halves, is itself a simplifying device. It was this attribute, indeed, that provided Montesquieu with one of his principal arguments in favor of symmetric design which, he said, "pleases the mind by the ease with which it allows it to embrace the whole object immediately".[16]

We should be clear that these ideas were not mere intellectual playthings. They were, rather, basic elements of a comprehensive, radical and highly successful program for reshaping the physical appearance of civilized Europe. The triumph of this program is nowhere more apparent than in the design of the Renaissance garden. There, the gardener's traditional task of sympathetically facilitating the manifestation of Nature's inherent beauty was subordinated to – in fact, largely abandoned in favor of - the revolutionary agenda of symmetry and simplicity.[17]

Nature's forms of course are not symmetric and they are not simple. They encompass, rather, an almost unlimited range of shapes,

---

rect and clear. I am for messy vitality over obvious unity..." (Venturi 1977, pp.16-17.) Unfortunately, these preferences are not always apparent in the buildings that Venturi designed. (See also Havens, 1953.)

[15] Alberti 1966, IX,7. An early statement combining the criteria of symmetry and visual simplicity is Alberti's dictum (quoted Thacker 1979, p. 95) that trees "ought to be planted in rows exactly even and answering to one another exactly upon straight lines".

[16] ..."*qui plait a l'âme par la facilitité qu'elle lui donne d'embrasser d'abord tout l'objet*" (Montesquieu 1825, p.616). Montesquieu continued: "The reason that symmetry pleases the mind is that it saves it trouble, that it gives it ease, that it cuts its work, so to speak, in half" ("*la raison que la symetrié plaît à l'âme, c'est qu'elle lui épargne de la peine, qu'elle la soulage, et qu'elle coupe pour ainsi dire l'ouvrage par la moitié*".)

[17] To be sure, it is not that beauty was excluded from the Renaissance garden but that its beauty was regarded as the creation of Man and not of Nature. Charles Cotton, referring to the loveliness that he saw in the gardens of Chatsworth, said it was achieved "[de]spite Nature" and not with her help. The severing of the age-old connection between Nature and Beauty is indeed the *ultima ratio* of at least some elements of Renaissance aesthetics.

colors and textures: and they do so, as we saw in Note Two, not incidentally or accidentally, but out of their very essence.

It was these facts that Renaissance horticulturists set out to negate. In their gardens they *forced* Nature into forms that are intrinsically alien to her. They concealed her variety, complexity and asymmetry beneath a *burqa* of inauthentic, man-made simplification.

The attitude of Renaissance gardeners toward Nature was indeed one of hostility; their objective, that of domination. Far from being Nature's helpmeets or partners, they made themselves her taskmasters. "They presume to do in what manner they list with nature, as if they were her superiors", William Harrison wrote in 1577.[18] One such gardener was the clergyman John Lawrence (1668-1732), a martinet whose garden was a parade ground on which plants were "Improv'd by Discipline, like a martial band".[19] Another who presumed to do what he chose with Nature was Lord Fairfax, who figured in a series of poems by Andrew Marvell (1621-1678).[20] For Fairfax gardening was not a respite from but a continuation of the "warlike studies" he had pursued during a long military career. His garden was square and walled, laid out "in the just figure of a fort"; and within it he "stupif'd" and "enforced" Nature's creations:

> See how the Flow'rs as at Parade
> Under their Colours stand displaid;
> Each Regiment in order grows,
> That of the Tulip, Pinke and Rose.[21]

To Horace Walpole in the eighteenth century it was clear that the purpose of the formal gardens was not to celebrate Nature but actually to "oppose" her. Modern scholars too have commented on Renaissance horticulture's palpable hostility toward Nature. Nature was "overcome" in the gardens of the Belvedere, Comito wrote.[22] Hyams described the Villa d'Este's gardens (*fig.* 6.6) as "regular, symmetrical,

---

[18] Harrison's *Description of England* appeared as part of the second edition of Holinshed's *Chronicle*.

[19] Laurence, *Paradise Regain'd, or the art of gardening* (1728), p.16; quoted Prest 1981, p.101.

[20] It is worth remarking that according to Vita Sackville-West (1929, p.42) – who was herself an accomplished poet of the garden – Marvell's appreciation of uncultivated Nature, reflected in his bitter aspersions on Fairfax, "was not at all proper to the seventeenth century".

[21] "Upon Appleton House", xliii (Marvell 1927, v.1, p.69).

[22] Comito 1978, p.153.

ordered, *anti-natural*" (my italics).[23] Strong wrote of the same gardens that they were "a *coup d'oeil* aimed at establishing immediately in the mind man's total control over the forces of nature."[24] These remarks can be applied generally. The gardens of the Renaissance were intended to be, not the apotheosis of Nature but her nemesis.

The Renaissance garden thus asserted Man's dominion over Nature. The garden had become *his* domain and in it Nature was *his* creature, existing meekly within the tight restraints that he placed upon her. Curbed and enfeebled, she appeared as a gaunt caricature of herself; and her organic fabric was often impossible to discern in the spare, tidy and closely-cropped symmetries into which she had been forced.[25]

It would be mistaken to regard the radical innovations brought about by Renaissance horticulturists as a mere shift in taste. They should be seen, rather, as arising from a startling new view of Nature as a force of immense, lethal, malevolence.

This was not how Nature had been experienced previously. To be sure, the medieval mind, as Kenneth Clark has written, found Nature to be "disturbing, vast and fearful".[26] Yet the dangers inherent in Nature had been mitigated in the Middle Ages by an awareness of her benevolent, or at least harmless, aspects. Thus Dante, immediately after the opening lines of the *Divine Comedy* in which he recalled the terrors "almost as bitter as death" that he encountered in the tenebrous forest, went on to refer to "the good I discovered there" – *del ben ch'I vi trovai*. Later, as already noted above, he wrote appreciatively of the "dense and living forest" that he beheld. Petrarch too did not experience much amiss as he passed through the "inhospitable and wild forests" – *boschi inospiti e selvaggi* - of the Ardennes (#176). It was outlaws and not Nature that posed the greatest threat there, but not even they intimidated Petrarch, who writes that for him it was "sweet to be alone and unarmed there where Mars takes up arms without warning" - *Dolce m' è sol senz' arme esser stato ivi, dove armato fier Marte, et non acenna*, (#177). Clark himself, having written of the fearsome aspect of

---

[23] Hyams 1971, pp.132, 134.

[24] Strong 1998, p.20.

[25] John Evelyn thought the gardens of his day looked as if they were made of pasteboard and pine planks and that they smelled "more of paynt then of flowers and verdure" (in a letter to Sir Thomas Browne, quoted Strong 1998, p.221). At the very outset of the Renaissance the suggestion was already being made (Alberti 1966, IX:iv) that gardens should be given the "geometric shapes that are favored in the plans of buildings". Cf Thacker 1979, p.93.

[26] Clark 1949, p.8.

Nature, then went on to say that "in this wild country man may enclose a garden".²⁷ And it is clear that the medieval garden was not inspired by anything like the Renaissance determination to oppose and subdue Nature. Medieval gardens were, rather, a shelter from Nature's harshness, perhaps an evocation of the Garden of Eden, and the dangers from which they provided refuge were a perennial consequence of the Fall and not a suddenly-rising threat of unprecedented lethality that called into question the very survival of the human race.

The Renaissance garden has none of the sweet and gentle loveliness of its medieval predecessor. The latter, by the same token, is not a triumphalist proclamation of man's success in subjugating and transforming Nature and thereby eliminating the terrible dangers Nature posed. If the medieval garden is a loving, artistic, affirmation of Nature's charm, the Renaissance garden, as Cotton said of Chatsworth, was created "[de]spite Nature".

The new perception of Nature as a malevolent, lethal force is expressed in a number of early Renaissance paintings. Uccello's "The Hunt" (*fig.*6.9) shows twenty or more well-armed men, supported by twice as many hunting dogs, at the edge of a forest. Despite their numbers, the men seem fearfully hesitant (*fig.*6.9,a,b) about entering the dense, dark wood, as if sensing that Death waiting there could well seize them too, along with their prey.

The relation of Death and Nature is also apparent in Pollaiuolo's great print, "Combat" as it is sometimes called (*fig.*6.10), that depicts two groups of naked men engaged in what is evidently a struggle to the death. The impenetrably dense background of denuded trees and ripe crops against which the struggle takes place is mysterious, but one senses that it is somehow associated with the fatal outcome that is in the offing.²⁸

In Giovanni di Paolo's "Death on Horseback" (*fig.*6.11), the association of Nature with death is explicit. The indescribably sinister figure of Death rides out of the massive, dense forest that is his home to snare his next victim, who stands immobilized with fear.²⁹

In these works Death seems associated with, is almost identical to, Nature herself. Nature is not a source of loveliness, or a comfort.

---

[27] Clark 1949, p.8.

[28] Hall (2005, p.74) interprets that link as follows: "This affinity between leaves and muscles suggests that it is the autumn of all their lives. The grim reaper will cut down both crops and men indiscriminately". But the plants are not engaged in combat with each other, as the men are, and I tend to think that it is they – the plants – that somehow *are* the grim reaper (or perhaps he is hiding in them)!

[29] In the contemporary "Triumph of Death" in Palermo the figure of Death also appears to have emerged from the impenetrable gloom of the surrounding forest.

Instead, she hides within herself – or more correctly, she *is* - a mortal menace that will at any moment leap out of concealment and carry another helpless human to his or her doom.[30] This was a very different view of Nature from that which had prevailed earlier. It is not how Dante saw Nature, or Petrarch. Boccaccio, too, would not have recognized it.

What then caused the change? What brought about this drastic, disturbing new view of Nature?

I speculate that it was – the plague. The plague of 1348-1350, known as the Black Death, is by any measure one of the greatest calamities in recorded history. At least one-third (and by some estimates more than one-half) of western Europe's population succumbed to it, and it severely disrupted the social and economic fabric of European life.[31] One can scarcely exaggerate the sense of hopelessness that it instilled in those who had not, or had not yet, been infected. "There was such a fear", a Florentine chronicler wrote, "that no one knew what to do"; another chronicler feared that it would bring about "*la sterminio della generazzione umana*" - the extinction of the entire human race.[32] "On all sides is sorrow…", Petrarch wrote to his brother, who was the sole survivor of 35 monks in his monastery.[33] His letter continues: "Everywhere is fear. When has any such thing been even heard or seen; in what annals has it ever been read that houses were left vacant, cities deserted, the country neglected, the fields too small for the dead and a fearful and universal solitude over the whole earth?…[34]

---

[30] Clark (1949, pp.46, 177) writes of Leonardo's "consciousness of the infinite, unknown destructive powers of nature". His studies of rocks, water and landscapes, Clark remarks, show "the forces of nature rising in revolt against man with his absurd pretence to ignore them, or use them for his advantage", an interpretation (with its sense of Nature violated by human exploitation) that evokes the 20th century Romantic naturalist too strongly to be plausible. It seems likelier that those studies reflect an acute awareness of the lethal dangers that Nature posed to defenseless Man in the era of the plagues. Leonardo's awareness of those dangers is evident from the report of Kruft (1994, p.59) that Leonardo, "under the impact of the great plague of 1484/85" in which about one-third of the population of the Duchy of Milan died, conceived a radically new design for a plague-resistant town based on the principles of decentralization and hygiene.

[31] For example, "Because of the chaos of the present age the judges have deserted the courts [and] the laws of God and of man are in abeyance" – *Decameron* (conclusion of the sixth day.)

[32] Villani Bk. I, end of chap.1, quoted Meiss 1951, p.66

[33] Quoted Deaux 1967, p.92. It was the plague that brought about the greatest calamity of Petrarch's life, the death of his lover, Laura.

[34] Despite the magnitude of this catastrophe there are some historians who believe that the Black Death had little if any lasting impact on European society or culture. Huizinga for example, in his *Waning of the Middle Ages,* attributes to

The plague did not end with the Black Death (*figs.* 6.12, 6.13). For three centuries thereafter Europe continued to be assaulted by wave after wave of outbreaks. Although the severity of outbreaks gradually diminished they were still so lethal three hundred years after the Black Death that in 1630 about one-third of Venice's population perished; and about one-fifth of London's population died in the Great Plague of 1665-1666.

In the three and a half centuries during which these outbreaks recurred no valid understanding was reached about what caused the sickness or what could be done to cure those stricken by it. Familiar remedies such as penitential prayer or the massacre of Jews, no matter how zealously they were resorted to, proved unavailing. Nothing seemed to prevent the plague from coming back, and each – seemingly arbitrary - recurrence heightened people's feelings of helplessness. No one knew when the plague would strike again, no one knew what to do when it did, and no one understood why it kept on returning. As John Donne said in a sermon he preached while the calamitous outbreak of 1625 was still raging in Britain:

> God can call up ... a plague that shall not onely be uncureable, uncontrollable, unexorable, but undisputable,

---

causes other than the plague itself phenomena that common sense tells us must surely have been consequences of it. "At the closing of the Middle Ages" he declares, "a somber melancholy weighs on people's souls. Whether we read a chronicle, a poem, a sermon, a legal document, even, the same impression of immense sadness is produced by them all"(p.31). Huizinga does not connect this "immense sadness" to the experience of the plague, however, but describes it as an expression of the "asceticism of the blasé, born of disillusion and satiety" (p.37). Similarly, he attributes the terror-filled view of death that came to the fore in the late fourteenth century, not at all to the plague but to "a kind of spasmodic reaction against an excessive sensuality" (p.141). The morbid tone of French poets of the period, he also says, arose from "a sentimental need of enrobing their souls with the garb of woe", and evidently it too was not a consequence of the plague (p.34). Another historian, Millard Meiss, in his *Painting in Florence and Siena after the Black Death,* also minimizes – despite his book's title - the effects of the plague. He reports that in the second half of the fourteenth century artists turned away from the naturalism of Giotto and his circle, while Boccaccio and other humanists repudiated their enthusiasm for the literature of Classical paganism. Meiss argues that these reactions would "inevitably" have occurred anyway, though he concedes that they were made "far more acute" by the experience of the plague. G. G. Coulton's view of the Black Death's impact is also ambiguous. "This catastrophe did deeply affect the later course of European civilisation" he writes, on the one hand: while on the other declaring that by the time of the Renaissance "most men had forgotten even this notorious calamity"! (Coulton 1930, p.101.) Coulton overlooks the fact that people in the Renaissance were themselves subjected to recurring assaults of the plague.

unexaminable, unquestionable; a plague that shall not onely not admit a remedy, when it is come, but not give a reason how it did come.[35]

Thus, in the centuries after the Black Death the plague continued to haunt the lives and the imagination of people in western Europe. Had the Black Death been a discrete occurrence the memory of it may not have played a significant role for long. As it was, however, the experience of the Black Death itself was reworked and channeled into new forms of expression as each outbreak of the plague was followed by another. Florence, which holds our interest here as the birthplace of the concept of symmetry, suffered an outbreak of the plague an average of every 8 years between 1400 and 1490.[36] The plague was thus a familiar, recurring fact in the lives of the great 15th-century artistic and intellectual figures of Florence among whom the symmetry norm originated.[37] The accumulated experience of previous outbreaks, starting with the Black Death, was part of their inheritance at birth, and was further elaborated on an average of more than once a decade throughout the course of their lives: and it was in the gloom of this grim aura that they passed all their days.[38]

---

[35] Quoted Gilman 2009, p.203.

[36] Morrison et al, 1985.

[37] Pius II, who is credited as the first person known to have used the word "symmetry" in its modern sense, was stricken by the plague when he was in Basel in 1439. "The sickness raged so fiercely" he recalled in his memoirs (Pius 2003, vol.1, pp.40-41), "that more than three hundred people were buried in a single day".

[38] It must be acknowledged that literary references to the Black Death and subsequent outbreaks of the plague are few and (with the exception of Boccaccio's extraordinary eyewitness description of Florence during the plague) generally rather insubstantial. As Tuchman (1978, p.109) points out, Froissart (born *circa* 1337) and Chaucer (born *circa* 1343), say almost nothing about it.[38] But this should not be taken to mean that people who lived through the Black Death were not deeply affected by the experience. Avoidance or postponement of the memory of traumatic events is after all a well-documented response (see the paper by van der Holk and van der Hart in Caruth, 1995). Defoe, who was about five years old during the Great Plague of the 17th century, did not write his fictionalized *Journal of the Plague Year* until half a century later. We find a more recent parallel in survivors of the Nazi Holocaust, who generally avoided mention of it, and seldom wrote about it, until the catharsis of the Eichmann trial in 1961 gave them permission to do so (Stern, 2000). Sometimes moreover *conscious* memory of the traumatic experience may be set aside permanently. We see this perhaps with Pepys, who described the Great Plague in numerous vivid entries in his diary but never mentioned it again after it passed. An exception is Venice, which to this day celebrates the *Festa della Madonna della Salute* with a solemn procession of thanksgiving for deliverance from the plague; the church of the Salute ("health") was built as an offering for protection against the plague of 1630-31. Silence about a trau-

This then was the experience of Nature during the Black Death and the plagues that followed in its train. It is this experience that gave rise to the hostile attitudes toward Nature that came to the fore during the fifteenth century and to the determination to gain mastery over her.

And it is in the light of this experience, I believe, that we must understand the radical new aesthetic of the Renaissance. Most manifestly in the garden, it led to the creation of an environment in which a person could indulge in the illusion that Nature no longer held sway, but was subjugated by Man and deprived of some of her most fundamental (and to Man, most menacing) attributes.

The Renaissance's new aesthetic of simplicity and symmetry, we may say, was rooted in the ambition to neutralize Nature's deadliness. Nature lurked in the impenetrable *foresta spessa*, to emerge who knew when. Renaissance Man resolved to deprive her of that hiding place. The simplified – symmetric - forms into which he forced Nature in his gardens created a visual environment that Man could easily monitor; it was too sparse and orderly for concealment. Untrammeled Nature's preference for visual confusion – the habitat of impenetrable obscurity in which she hid, preparing her next deadly strike – was now transformed by Man's agency into an environment that was transparent, predictable, controllable: and answerable to Man.[39] In this

---

matic experience, accordingly – whether the silence is temporary or permanent - does not necessarily mean that all memory of the experience has been erased. It may be buried, rather, in the unconscious mind. There, it enters the storehouse of the affected person's experience and may help shape (though not always in ways that are apparent) his or her perceptions, expectations and behavior. If the traumatic experience was an historical event it is shared with others who have also experienced it, and becomes an element of the wider culture that is transmitted to ensuing generations. It is a tricky undertaking, to be sure, to argue *ex silentio:* yet we must ask how likely it is that people who lived through a calamity as great as the Black Death were not deeply scarred by it – or that they would not have implanted their trauma in the generations that followed them? For later generations, indeed, the inherited (if eventually, largely unconscious) memory of the Black Death itself must have been entrenched by the accumulated trauma of subsequent outbreaks, including any that they experienced in their own lifetimes.

[39] There is a curious echo of this in *News from Nowhere* (Morris 2004, p.65), where the character Hammond says (evidently with Morris' approval): "Like the medievals we like everything trim and clean, and orderly and bright; as people always do when they have any sense of architectural power; *because then they know that they can have what they want, and they won't stand any nonsense from Nature in their dealings with her"*. The aesthetic of "trim and clean, and orderly" is clearly that of the Renaissance and not of the Middle Ages; but it is remarkable to see that Hammond associated it with the desire for control over Nature and not to have to "stand any nonsense" from her.

garden Man was Nature's master, and here, at least, *she* conformed to *his* every requirement. His fearful uncertainty and helplessness in face of death-dealing Nature could now be replaced by a sense of his dominion over her. He knew and determined what took place in even the smallest corner of his domain.

The plagues, I have suggested, constituted the "menacing environment" in which the concept of symmetry originated. Symmetry, by simplifying the visual habitat and making it predictable to man, was a device for defending himself – symbolically, to be sure – against an environment that tragic experience had taught him to fear and mistrust. It enabled Man to enjoy the illusion that he had gained ascendancy over malevolent Nature: that he had vanquished her. Had he not, after all, imposed tidiness, predictability, transparency – *symmetry*! – on the face of the earth?

I should perhaps repeat now my statement at the outset of this discussion that no data explicitly link this cause – the plague – to this effect – the emergence of the symmetry norm. I offer it here as an hypothesis that may seem plausible but that is, of course, highly speculative. I urge readers to withhold their judgment of it until they have read Note Seven, in which I attempt to account for the *decline* of the formal garden of the Renaissance and the so-called "natural" garden's return to the complex and unpredictable textures of Nature herself.

One indication of how radical an innovation the concept of symmetry was in the middle of the fifteenth century can be found in the difficulty people had in settling on a name for it. Leon Battista Alberti, who died in 1472, is the earliest theoretician of the idea known to us, though we have no reason to suppose that the concept originated with him.[40] He used the term *collocatio* for it, but no one else is known to have followed his example.[41]

Instead, some of Alberti's contemporaries, and occasionally even Alberti himself, used a variety of ponderous circumlocutions such as "the mutual correspondence of parts" or "this side answering that", and these would continue to be used for the next three hundred years.[42] In addition the concept was sometimes referred to obliquely,

---

[40] Alberti 1966, VI:3; IX:7; comp. I:9, and I:12.

[41] Alberti borrowed the term *collocatio* from Cicero, who used it to denote the component of rhetorical structure that deals with organization or arrangement: cf. Kemp 1977, p.356 and Payne 1999, p.75. (Alberti's *collocatio* is not to be confused with Vitruvius' *conlocatio*, for which see Scranton 1974.) I discuss the substance and the history of Alberti's concept in the appendix to the present Note.

[42] e.g. Alberti, 1966, IX:7, "... *ut mutuo dextera sinistris*". The circumlocution of parts "answerable to each other" occurs in English as early as 1579 in a letter from Hatton to Burleigh: see Nicolas 1847, pp. 125-126. Temple ("Garden of Epicurus") in

not with a specific term or phrase but by alluding to the (purportedly mirrored) two-sidedness of the human body.⁴³

---

the 17th century and Burke ("Essay on the Sublime …") in the 18th also employed "answering" to indicate bilateral symmetry.

⁴³ e.g. Alberti, op.cit., I:9, "*ac veluti in animante membra membris ita in aedificio partes partibus respondeant condecet.*" In the second half of the 15th century the notion that the human body is bilaterally symmetric was however still open to question. Thus Filarete (1965, Bk.1, ff. iii' – iv), after referring to Vitruvius' claim that the navel is centered on a man's body, demurred "*Ma a me' nonpare' pero che sia totalmente' imezzo* – "but to me it does not seem that it is totally centered": his remark (Bk.1, f.2v, ff) that the proportions of buildings should be those of man could therefore take a different meaning from that generally attributed to it. Dürer's *Vier Buecher von menschilicher Proportion* (1528) contains some asymmetric figures but we do not know whether their asymmetry was intended by Dürer or resulted from inaccurate copying by the engraver. As we saw in Note One, Leonardo da Vinci - superb empirical observer that he was - knew that natural forms are *not* bilaterally symmetric. Not just the face of his "Vitruvian Man"(*fig.*1.1) but its entire body are asymmetric. Its arms, for example, as well as the portions subdivided by vertical lines, are unequal in length, and its navel is not equidistant from the two sides of the body but closer to the right side of the figure. It is not usually recognized, moreover, that the body's proportions are not consistent with those specified by Vitruvius, for the height of Leonardo's figure is greater than the span of its outstretched arms, so that the "square" containing the figure is an oblong, and the "circle" is an oval. Also seldom noted is that the distance from the chin to the top of the forehead is not one-tenth the body's length, as specified by Vitruvius, and that the length of the foot is not one-sixth that of the body. Leonardo's seemingly disregard of Vitruvius' criteria – along with his claim to be illustrating them (Leonardo 1958, v.1, pp.213-4) - suggests that "Vitruvian Man" may be another Da Vinci code waiting to be cracked! It should be noted here that, as Hon and Goldstein (2008, p.117) correctly observe, Vitruvius "thought of the body in terms of proportions. He did not even call attention to the correspondence between its limbs". Among those to have mistakenly believed that Vitruvius thought in terms of bilateral symmetry are Tavernor (1998, p.43), who remarked "By *symmetria* Vitruvius meant … the mirroring of form across an axis, the modern reading of 'symmetry'": similarly Lowic (1983) in his discussion of di Giorgio's use of Vitruvius.

The view of the human body as symmetric and its application to the doctrine that buildings, too, must be symmetric, was not established before the middle of the sixteenth century – the earliest evidence for it seems to be Michelangelo's letter of December 1550 to an unidentified cardinal in which he argues that "*i mezzi sempre sono liberi come vogliono, siccome il naso che è nel mezzo del viso non è obligato nè all'uno nè all'altro occhio, ma l'una mano è bene obligata a essere come l'altre, e l'uno ochio come l'altro per rispetto degli lati e de' riscontri. A però ècosa certa che le membra dell'architettura dipendono dalle membra dell'uomo*". (This statement, incidentally, is among the considerations that call into question the claim of Vasari [1996, II, p.709] that Michelangelo "never consented to be bound by any law, whether ancient of modern, in matters of architecture". Ramsden [Michelangelo 1963, v.2, p.290f] is mistaken in attributing Michelangelo's argument to Vitruvius' doctrine of symmetry, for the latter addresses the proportions of a structure and is

Another word used from the outset for the mirroring of the left and right halves of a form was "symmetry", which in the end would become the standard term for it. "Symmetry" was not a new word, however. As we saw in an earlier Note, it had been used by Classical writers for the altogether different concept of proportions that are pleasing or harmonious.[44] It would continue to be used in this sense during the Renaissance and even down into modern times.[45] Its adoption in the fifteenth century for the concept of a form whose left and

---

not about bilateral symmetry. Cf. the discussions of this letter in Ackerman 1986, p.37ff. and Summers 1981, pp.418-446.) Vasari regarded the human body as symmetric and stated that a façade must be *"compartita come la faccia dell'uomo"*. His anthropomorphism extends to the entire human body, and to its functions as well as its form. *"Bisogna poi"*, he writes, *"che rappresenti il corpor dell'uomo nel tutto e nelle parti sililmente"* including *"un centro che porti via tutte insieme le brutezze ed i puzzi"* – see the introductory section *dell'Architettura* cap.vii. Wilson (1977, p.51) quotes the opinion of Sir Roger Pratt (1620-1685) that rooms within a house should be arranged symmetrically "as we find it to be in our own bodies". For comparable expressions by Pascal, Hogarth, Diderot *et al.* see Hon and Goldstein (2008, pp.128ff). This view is implicit in Montesquieu's (1825, p.616) likening ("Essay on Taste", 1825, p.616) of an asymmetric building to a deformed body: *"Un batiment avec ... une aile plus courte qu'une autre est ... peu fini qu'un corps avec ... un bras trop court"*. In more recent times we find Wölfflin (1946 p.27) declaring that *"die Forderung des Symmetrie ist abgeleitet von der Anlage unseres Koerper. Weil wir symmetrisch aufgebaut sind..."* Similarly Wittkower (1978, p.128): "Bilateral symmetry is the symmetry of the human body and for that reason of towering importance to mankind." Comp. Hommel (1987, p.20): *"Frontal beobachtet scheint der menschlicher Koerper vollendet symmetrisch gebaut"*. Edmund Burke in the eighteenth century (see fn. 80, *below*) and the nineteenth-century French architectural theorist Durand (2000, p.113) are rare voices rejecting the human body as an analogy to architecture.

[44] Perry (2000) suggests that it referred specifically to *correct* proportion.

[45] Cristoforo Landino, a younger contemporary of Pius and Alberti, equated symmetry with *"vera proportione"* (quoted Panofsky 1972, p.27); cf. *"le loro simetrie"* of Manetti (1970, p.51, l.316) which is clearly about the proportions of buildings (though the 20th-century English translation renders it nonsensically as "symmetry"); and also Paolo Cortesi's references to *"germanica symmetria"* and *"prisca symmetria"* in his *De Cardinalatu* (c.1510) Bk II, cap.2; text in Weil-Garris 1980, p.76 and fn.28, p.102. Dürer's book on *"menschlicher Proportion"* (fn.43, above) was published in Italian in 1591 under the title *Della Simmetria dei corpi humani*, suggesting that for the Italians at least, *"simmetria"* is the equivalent of *"Proportion"*. I have not yet seen a copy of Wendel Dietterlin's rare pattern book, *Architectura von Austheilung Symetria und Proportion der fünf Seulen*, (Nuremberg 1598), that also appears to use the two terms as separate concepts; the Latin edition, also published in 1598, is entitled similarly, *Architectura: de constitutione, symmetria, ac proportione quinque columnarum*. Here and elsewhere we find instances in which *symmetria* and *proportione* are clearly not synonyms though both apparently allude to the proportions of an object. The distinction between the two terms however remains to be clarified.

right halves mirror each other was therefore by no means a foregone conclusion. It was moreover both a baffling and an inauspicious choice, for it meant that the lexicon of aesthetic theory now employed the same word for two altogether unrelated ideas. The inevitable result was a blurring of the distinction between the two concepts for which it was being used. The confusion was particularly acute in the realm of architecture, where issues of symmetry (in the new sense) and of proportion often had to be addressed more or less concurrently.

Possibly the earliest reference to the concept that we possess actually uses the term "symmetry" for it. On the exterior side walls of his new palace in Pienza, Pope Pius II (d.1464) wrote in his autobiographical *Commentarii*, a doorway is set off to one side of the central axis and it is matched by a fake (but visually identical) doorway at an equal distance on the other side of the center (*fig.* 6.14a).[46] This arrangement was required, Pius explained, "*ad servandam simmetrie gratiam*" – for the sake of symmetry – and it is clear that he intended the term to be understood in the modern sense.[47] We do not know how widespread this meaning of *simmetria* was at the time the pope wrote his memoirs, or who first used it in this way (there is no reason to suppose that it was Pius who did so); but we may perhaps infer from the fact that Pius did not explain what he meant by the term that in his day "symmetry" had already become a recognized meaning for the mirroring of the two lateral halves of a shape.

It is evident that with Pius we are very near the inception of the concept, in the period when old tastes and precepts had only just started to be discarded and the application of the new notion of symmetry was still far from rigorous. Thus Pius, for all his modern sensibilities, also loved the paintings of Giotto, the sculpture of Maitani and the medieval cathedrals of England.[48] The city that he rebuilt and named after himself, Pienza, also belongs to both eras, for on two sides of the piazza on which the papal palace stands there are buildings,

---

[46] I am reminded of the sardonic remark of Pascal (*Pensées* Sec.1:27): "*Ceux qui font les antithèses en forçant les mots sont comme ceux qui font de fausses fenêtres pour la symétrie: Leur règle n'est pas de parler juste, mais de faire des figures justes.*"

[47] Pius II, 1984, v.2, p.547: "*in orientali latere quod oppidi plateam respicit cum media porta tenere non posset ad servandam simmetrie gratiam due ianue addite sunt quarum altera muro obducta clause uestigium pre se ferret altera ad quotidianum usum mansit aperta. In occidentali latere idem fecere*". Pius does not explain why the doors could not have been centered, but cf. the suggestion of Mack (1987, pp.50-51). Mack states only that "there were two smaller doors symmetrically placed" (p.51) and evidently does not recognize that Pius' is the first known use of "symmetry" in the modern sense.

[48] Mack 1987, p.31; C. Smith 1992, p.48.

contemporary with the palace, whose idioms are unambiguously medieval; the piazza itself is very far from being symmetric (*fig. 6.14b*).[49] Indeed, the papal palace, which Mack declares "is emphatically symmetrical" is not that at all: for as Mack himself reports, the bays of its outer walls, for no apparent reason, vary irregularly in width by as much as 1.7 meters. These considerations do not negate the fact that ideas about symmetric design also played a role in the design of Pienza's new structures. They indicate, rather, that the imperative, *symmetrie gratiam*, was applied selectively - and perhaps understood imperfectly - by Pienza's builders and patron.[50]

Pius' *Commentarii* were not published until 1584, more than a century after his death. The first known appearance in print of "symmetry" with its new meaning is therefore to be credited instead to *Hypnerotomachia Poliphili*, the bizarre erotic novel by Francesco Colonna that Aldus published in Venice in 1499.[51] By my count, the word "symmetry" occurs twenty times in this book. In nine of those instances it is clearly to be understood in the modern sense of "bilateral

---

[49] The presence of many medieval stylistic elements in Pienza may lead one to question Mack's characterization of it as "a Renaissance City".

[50] Mack 1987, pp.51, 76. It may be useful to point out here that Wittkower's ideas about the dominant role of theories of proportion in Renaissance architecture find no confirmation in Pienza's structures. And this notwithstanding the letter Biondo Flavio wrote to Pius in September 1462 (Mack, 1961 p.228) praising the proportions and the harmonious relationship of the individual parts with one another that he discerned in Pienza's new papal palace. Pius himself did not refer in the *Commentarii* to the proportions of the buildings in Pienza except to state, in passing and without elaboration, that the plan of the papal palace is a square: "*Palatium quadratum fuit*" (Pius 1962, v.II, p.546). We do not know whether Pius' remark points back to the *ad quadratum* of medieval times or forward to the symmetry of the Renaissance. It could be either – though, as it turns out, the plan, with the porticoes on the southern end, is 36 meters wide but 39 meters long and thus far from square (Mack (1987, pp.44-45). Comp. Pius's description (1961, p.548), of the length and width of the gallery, that he clearly gives in order to suggest its great size, and not to call attention to its proportions (for which purpose he would have had to – but does not – also give the gallery's height). We therefore have no empirical evidence to support Biondo's letter, which is sycophantic in tone and incorrectly refers to the new cathedral as dedicated to "St Matthew". The architectural principles that guided the construction of Pienza's papal buildings are unclear – perhaps reflecting the eclecticism or tentativeness of the period of transition to Renaissance ideals – and I do not believe that Biondo's references to the proportions of the papal palace do anything to clarify them.

[51] The citations here are from the Methuen facsimile London, 1904 of the first edition by Aldus (Colonna, 1499). The acrostic by which Godwin (Colonna 1999, pp. xiii ff.) convincingly identified Francesco Colonna as the author was known at least as early as 1635 (Vershbow 2013, p.42). The attempt of Lefaivre (1997) to attribute authorship of this work to Leon Battista Alberti is to say the least unpersuasive.

symmetry.⁵² We read, for example, that the channels cut through a pyramid are "symmetrically... distributed" – *symmetriatamente ... distributi* – in the structure (b, ii'); that the wreaths on one wall of a courtyard are "arranged symmetrically" – *symmetriato congresso* - with those on the opposite wall (f, iv'); that box-trees in a garden are shaped as "symmetric moons" – *symmetriate lune* (u, iii'); and that palm trees are planted symmetrically – *symmetriatamente* - (m, iii') in a row along a hedge.⁵³

The "symmetry" in these and a number of other passages almost certainly refers to forms whose two lateral halves mirror each other – the new meaning of the term - and not to their proportions. In other passages, though, the term is clearly used in the Classical sense to refer to the proportions of a form. Thus, all the parts of the Pantheon are built *cum observabile Symmetria* – with "the same symmetry", that is, in accordance with a single system of proportion (c, v'); and the "entire symmetry" - *tuta la Symmetria* - of a portal is derived from the size of the squares on which the structure's columns rest (c, i'). In other passages the "symmetry" of a shape – we infer, its proportions – is explicitly identified as beautiful: as in Poliphilo's appreciation of the *exquisita Simmetria* of a pyramid (a, viii'), or of the *elegante & symmetriato* design of a building (y, iii'). It is safe to assume that Colonna is referring in these passages to the structures' proportions. There are however some other passages in which it is not possible to determine which of the two meanings of "symmetry" he intended. When he wrote that a palace is "symmetrical in its architecture" – *pallatio ... di symmetriatta architectura* - (e, viii'), for example, we do not know whether he was referring to the structure's proportions or to the mirroring of its two lateral halves. At no point did Colonna explain what he meant by "symmetry". Nor did he acknowledge that he used the term in two distinctly different senses.⁵⁴

---

⁵² Colonna did not use Alberti's *collocatio* for "symmetry", though he may have known *De re aedificatoria*, the first printed edition of which had appeared fourteen years before the publication of *Hypnerotomachia*.

⁵³ In his translation of *Hypnerotomachia Poliphili* (Colonna 1999) Godwin twice paraphrases with "symmetric" passages in which the term is not directly indicated in the original Italian: the "symmetrical" courtyard (p.96: *vide* f,iiii') was originally *aequabile*; while the "upright symmetry" of the obelisk (p.131: *vide* h,vi) was originally *aequalitate statario*. This is not to criticize the translator, however, for the context seems to indicate that *aequabile* and *aequalitate* could indeed do duty as synonyms for "symmetry" (in the modern sense), though I am not aware of other instances in which they are used in this way.

⁵⁴ Stewering (2000), who perceives Nature's forms as symmetric, misrepresents Colonna's use of "symmetry", and fails to recognize his frequent use of the term to mean "beautiful proportions".

Colonna's ambiguous use of "symmetry" indicates, as one might have expected, that the word became a source of confusion from the moment it acquired the additional meaning of shapes whose two lateral halves mirror each other. In a fanciful and rather obscure novel such as *Hypnerotomachia Poliphili* this confusion was perhaps not of much consequence. Sebastiano Serlio's treatises on architecture, on the other hand, were among the most widely read of the Renaissance. Their influence extended beyond Italy to France, Spain, England and the Low Countries, and by the end of the sixteenth century several had been translated into all of the principal west-European languages.[55]

In his *Fourth Book of Architecture* (1537) Serlio, discussing one of his designs for a city gate, Serlio stipulated that the postern on one side of the main portal must be matched by a false (*"finta"*) postern on the other side of it.[56] This, he explained, was required *"per servar la simmetria"* - "for the sake of symmetry"- and because his drawing of the structure shows that the false postern was identical to the real one both in appearance and in its distance from the center, we can be confident that in this passage Serlio intended *"simmetria"* to be understood in the modern sense.

The context and phrasing of Serlio's remarks are of course strikingly similar to Pius' description of the real and fake doorways in the walls of the papal palace in Pienza. We have no grounds for supposing that Serlio derived his ideas and terminology from Pius' *Commentarii* (which at the time existed only in a few manuscript copies). The resemblances between the two passages must therefore be explained either as a coincidence or, perhaps more plausibly, as an indication that both men drew from the same (though to us unknown) school of thought.

There is, though, a significant difference between the two accounts. Pius, as we noted, evidently did not believe it was necessary to explain what he meant by "symmetry". Serlio on the other hand, as part of his discussion of the fake postern, evidently *did* feel the need to do so, from which we may infer that the term was no longer as widely known as it had been in Pius' day, nearly a century earlier. Serlio therefore gave his readers a definition of the term, telling them that *"Simmetria"* means *"corrispondenzia proportionata"* or, "proportionate correspondence". With this definition he laid bare the problem inher-

---

[55] Serlio 1996, I, xxxi-xxxv; pp.470-471.

[56] Serlio 1996, v.1, p.260: "*Ma per servar la simmetria, che vuol dir corrispondenza proportionata, è necessario farre un' altra finta. La misura della porta cosi è da fare, che quanto serà la larghezza dell'apertura, sia la metà di esse aggiunta all'altezza*". It was of course a *non sequitur* to declare that the false postern was needed to make the design symmetric; a functioning postern would have had the same effect.

rent in the use of the one term for two different concepts: and in fact made the problem an acute one.

"*Corrispondenzia proportionata*" is an opaque phrase that is without precedent in the literature of aesthetic theory, and suggests that Serlio may not have been entirely clear in his own mind whether he intended to use "symmetry" for the *correspondence* of a structure's two lateral halves (the modern meaning) or for its *proportions* (the Classical meaning).[57]

Later, to be sure, in his *Seventh Book*, which was published posthumously in 1575, Serlio used "symmetry" in a way that leaves us in no doubt that he understood the word in its modern sense. But this was of little consequence for the history of the word because the *Seventh Book* was not translated into other European languages until the twentieth century, and its unambiguous use of "symmetry" in the modern sense is not present in Serlio's earlier book. There, indeed, immediately after defining symmetry as "proportionate correspondence", Serlio went on to describe the optimal *proportions* of the gateway he was writing about, thus giving the misleading impression that "symmetry", as he was using the term, was not about bilateral correspondence at all but about proportions. This confusion was heightened a few years later, but still during Serlio's lifetime, when Flemish and French translations of the *Fourth Book* were published in Antwerp by Pieter Coecke van Alst.[58] In these editions Coecke dropped mention of the false postern in Serlio's Italian text and merely declared that, "for the sake of symmetry", the gateway's *proportions* would have to be such-and-such.[59] For Coecke's readers, therefore, "symmetry" had nothing to do with the modern sense of the term but simply meant "well-proportioned".

Serlio's reference to the *need* for a second – if fake – postern, as well as Pius' statement that a fake doorway had been inserted "for the sake of symmetry", reminds us that from its inception the concept of

---

[57] Hon and Goldstein (2008, p.118), who recognize the problematic nature of the term, suggest that Serlio may have intended to merge the two concepts. "According to Serlio", they write, "symmetry involves both proportion ... and correspondence", but this is contradicted by Serlio's unambiguous use of "symmetry" in the *Seventh Book* to mean "bilateral symmetry". It should be noted, of course, that the addition of a second postern in Serlio's gateway, while it made the design symmetric, did not affect its proportions, which would have been the same whether or not each flank housed a postern.

[58] He was the father-in-law, as it happens, of the elder Brueghel.

[59] "*Toute porte de cité a besoin de poternes: mais pour garder la symétrie, c'est-à-dire, correspondance proportionnée, est besoin d'ensuivre par cette manière, qu'autant que sera la latitude ou largeur de l'ouverture de la porte soit ajutée la moitié d'icelle à sa hauteur*".

symmetry has had a prescriptive as well as descriptive aspect. That is, it not only defines what a symmetric shape *is* but requires that the things we make *should be* shaped symmetrically.

In its prescriptive aspect the concept of symmetry makes a rather startling appearance in Serlio's *Seventh Book*. There, in Chapter 62, we learn that in a certain Italian city whose citizens cared greatly about architecture a rich but miserly man lived in the house his grandfather had built back in the days when good architecture still lay buried – *ancora sepolta*. This house was flanked on either side by newer buildings whose fine design only made the miser's house seem all the uglier (*piu brutta*) by comparison. So offensive was this deformed (*difforme*) house, indeed, that the very sight of it induced feelings of nausea and queasiness (*nausea & fastidio*) in the prince who ruled the city. What caused the prince to react in this way is not a mystery. The façade of the house was very obviously asymmetric. The twenty principal windows on it comprised at least eight different shapes and sizes and were arranged asymmetrically. Moreover, the entrance to the building was not centered on the façade, something that (Serlio tells us) is very contrary to good architecture (*"cosa che e molto contraria alla buona Architettura"*).

The prince tried to persuade the miser to improve the building's appearance but he, caring (in Serlio's telling of it) more for his money than for the decorous appearance of the city, always replied that he would like to do as the prince asked but that for the time being he was short of funds. Eventually the prince's patience ran out and he warned the miser that he would confiscate and demolish the house unless it were rebuilt within one year in the style of its neighbors. The miser capitulated. He called in the city's best architect and ordered him, without regard to cost, to alter the house's appearance in a way the prince would find pleasing. The architect tore down the entire façade and built a new one in its place; the asymmetric plan of the interior of the house was modified only to the extent that a room was partitioned to create an entrance hall for the newly-centered doorway to lead into. The drawing (*fig. 6.1*) with which Serlio illustrates this account shows that the main objective of the renovation was to transform the house's façade from an asymmetric to a symmetric layout. This involved rebuilding the windows (whose appearance was modernized during the process) and moving the entrance to the center of the structure.[60]

---

[60] Also as part of the renovation, a heavy cornice was placed between the two principal floors. Serlio says that this episode took place during his lifetime, which means that a date even before the end of the 15th century (Serlio was born in 1475) is possible; and that it could have been Serlio himself who designed the new façade. It should be noted that Serlio does not mention the *proportions* of the build-

Albeit less colorfully, Serlio described two other projects in which older houses were given symmetric facades. In Chapter 66 he discussed a well-built house that suffered from a number of drawbacks, "the clearest error being that the door of this house is not in the centre, as it should be – and also the windows have a certain inequality" (*fig*.6.15). The owner of his house wanted "not to appear inferior to his neighbors" who "unerringly build with good arrangements". By this, Serlio explained, he meant that "as a bare minimum they adhere to *simmetria*". The façade was rebuilt in symmetric form.[61] In the second project, Chapter 67, Serlio described how the owner of two adjoining asymmetric houses wished to build a single façade onto the two structures, "putting the door in the center, as is necessary".[62] Where there were formerly two interestingly asymmetric facades there is now a single, rather bland, symmetric one instead.

Serlio's narrative, as we see, is set in a time when enthusiasm for the principles of "good" architecture was not only fervent but was matched by revulsion – strong enough to induce feelings of nausea! – at the taste of an earlier generation. The recent changes had at their core the unequivocal rejection of asymmetric design. Feelings on this point ran so high that the presence of even a single asymmetric building was thought to detract from a city's appearance, and social and political pressure could be brought to bear to compel its owner to spend substantial amounts of money on the merely cosmetic transformation of its façade from an asymmetric to a symmetric design. The intensity of the feelings aroused by asymmetric design is quite startling. It suggests that the desire for symmetry was not based on aesthetic considerations alone but may have had deeper and more complex and irrational origin – possibly, the one discussed in the first portion of this Note.[63]

---

ing – evidently they were not among the things that had made it seem *difforme* – and they were not altered as part of the renovation.

[61] We can infer that the new facade would have won less grudging approval from Serlio if its windows had been equidistant from each other, but they had been installed only recently and the owner, wanting "the least disruption and expense possible", did not wish to re-arrange them. Although not equidistant, their arrangement on either side of the central axis – the newly-built doorway – is now symmetric.

[62] Serlio 2001, Bk. VII, caps. LXII. LXIII

[63] But the rejection of asymmetric design may not have been quite as widespread as Serlio implied. In Bk.III (90v) Serlio wrote of the "disordered and discordant" effect created by the asymmetries of the Baths of Diocletian, which he compared unfavorably to the Baths of Antoninus, with their "correspondence in all parts" and the "harmony" that resulted from it. He went on however (94v) to apologize to "supporters and defenders of ancient things" if they were offended by his criti-

Pius II, Colonna and Serlio are evidently the only Renaissance writers who used "symmetry" in the sense of bilateral symmetry. As we have already noted, when other Italians used the word they invariably did so with its Classical meaning of harmonious proportion. And it was more often than not in this sense too that "symmetry" was used in England before the end of the nineteenth century. Thus for John Shute, whose architectural treatise was published in 1563, the dimensions of a Tuscan column were to be determined by "the order and rule of Symetria" that, as he explained, require a "parfaicte knowledge" of arithmetic.[64] Clearly, he was referring here to the mathematical calculations needed to determine the optimal proportions of a column.[65] In 1611, when Pike published his English translation of Serlio (it was based on Coecke's Flemish translation) he stated what the dimensions of a structure must be if it is to conform to "semetry, that is due measure" – in other words, if it is to have good proportions.[66] For Henry Wotton, too, a decade after Pike, symmetry had to do with good proportions: as he put it, "*Symmetria* is the convenience that runneth between the Parts and the Whole".[67] When he wished to refer to what we now call symmetry Wotton used the term "Uniformitie" instead. This, he claimed, is "the great Paterne of Nature" and is exemplified by our bodies "than which there can be no Structure more uniforme ... each side agreeing with the other, both in the number, in the qualitie and in the measure of the Parts".[68] Somewhat later in the seventeenth century we find the writer of an unsigned letter stating that

---

cism of Diocletian's structure. We see from this that there were contemporaries of Serlio who did not share his disdain for asymmetry. Tantalizingly spare though this reference is, it is the only source that tells us of the existence of a school of thought in the sixteenth century that appreciated asymmetric design.

[64] Shute 1563, p.iiii. He added, borrowing from Vitruvius, that the rule of "Symetria" is based upon "the Simetrie of a strong man".

[65] Half a century after Shute Dallington (1605), p.13 described the limbs, feet and arms of the giant statue in the Pratolino garden as being "symmetricall to his head". It is an obscure statement, and the fact that it refers to paired members of the body *may* mean that Dallington was using the term in the modern sense (with the head representing the central axis of the body) and not to suggest that those members were well-proportioned in relation to the head. There is no way of being sure, however.

[66] Serlio 1982, Bk IV, cap.1, fol.5v.

[67] Wotton 1968, p.119. Comp. *ibid*, p.54: "in some windowes and doores the symmetry of two to three, in their breadth and length".

[68] *ibid*, p.21. We saw earlier that Wotton, following Vasari, advanced the case for symmetric design without using any term for it by arguing that buildings must resemble the well-shaped male body with the principal entrance, like the mouth, in the center and windows, "like our eyes, be set in equall number and distance on both sides".

in Roger Pratt's work at Raynham Hall "there was somewhat in it divine in the symmetry of proportions of length, height and breadth which was harmonious to the rational soul".[69] Clearly here too "symmetry" refers to the apt proportions of a design.[70] In much the same way Addison, in 1712, equated "symmetry" with "the beauty of an object".[71] The "fearful symmetry" of Blake's tiger (1794) establishes that the term's meaning as proportion was still current at the end of the 18th century.

The word "symmetry" in its modern sense made its first, albeit ambiguous, appearance in French in 1623, when Pierre Le Muet published his influential *Manière de bâtir pour toutes sortes de personnes*. Like Serlio almost a century earlier, Le Muet seems to have been uncertain about which of the word's two meanings he really had in mind. Under the heading, "*La belle ordonnance consiste en la simmetrie*" – beautiful arrangement consists of symmetry – he first defined symmetry as that which requires "the parts equally distant from the middle to be equal to one another".[72] Yet on the very next line (and still under the same heading) he went on to declare that the parts of a building that are equally distant from the middle must be correctly proportioned – "*proportionnées*" - in relation to each other and to the overall structure.[73]

In the English version of *Manière de bâtir*, published in 1670, the ambiguity of the French original was abandoned in favor of the origi-

---

[69] Text in Gunther (1928, p.133), who dates the letter *circa* 1663.

[70] In his modestly-titled *True Intellectual System of the Universe* (1678) the Cambridge neo-Platonist Ralph Cudworth listed "symmetry and asymmetry" among "the basic essences". I have not seen this rather rare work, however, and do not know in which senses Cudworth used those terms. See the article, "Ralph Cudworth", in Richards (n.d.). The first unambiguous use of "symmetry" in the modern sense by an English author occurs seven years after Cudworth's work was published, in Temple's *Garden of Epicurus* (1685), and is discussed further on in this Note.

[71] *Spectator* No.411, June 21, 1712.

[72] Le Muet 1623, p.4.

[73] "*Selon la largeur, elle consiste à faire que les parties esgalement esloingnees du miliere soient esgalees entre elles. Que les parties soient proportionnées au total & entre elles. Selon la hauteur elle consiste à faire que les parties esquelles mesmes symétrie aura esté observee pour le regard de la largeur, soient aussi de mesme niveau en leur hauteur. Car il peut arriver qu'une partie symétrique en largeur ne le sera point en hauteur. Pour exemple, les demies croisees, lesquelles vous pouvez asseoir en pareille distance du milieu de l'edifice, neantmoins les frontons qui leur feront imposés n'arriveront pas à la hauteur de ceux des croisees entieres; ainsi ce qui fera symétrie en largeur, ne le sera pas en hautcur ; partant tels ouvrages sont à eviter.*"

nal definition of symmetry as harmonious proportion. "Fair ordering and comeliness", it reads, "consisteth in the *symmetry or equal proportions*" [my italics] of the parts of a building.[74] Another consideration indeed leads one to question the extent to which Le Muet ever really *did* understand "symmetry" in its modern meaning. A number of engravings that appear in both the French and English editions of *Manière de bâtir* show designs of buildings whose main entrances as well as certain other features are in a manifestly asymmetric relation to the overall façade *(fig.6.16)*. "Symmetry" in these buildings, because it cannot mean *bilateral* symmetry, is therefore likely to refer to their *proportions*.

Another influential architect and theorist, Claude Perrault (1613-1688), attempted to resolve the confusion between symmetry as "proportion" and symmetry as "correspondence" by declaring that there are "two kinds of proportion". One of these, that he says is "very difficult to discern", consists of "the proportional relation of the parts". The other, that is "very apparent", is "called symmetry", and is "a balanced and fitting correspondence of parts that maintain the same arrangement and position".[75] It is not clear why Perrault regarded symmetry as a "kind of proportion", too – what did he gain by doing so? – but the confusion engendered, ultimately, by Serlio's *corrispondenzia proportionata* may be the explanation.

In the early eighteenth century the same confused double meaning of "symmetry" appeared in Sebastien Le Clerc's *Traité d'architecture* (1714), an English translation of which, by Ephraim Chambers, the encyclopedist, was published in 1732.[76] Le Clerc required that there be pilasters on both sides of a window "to make a symmetry", which implies that he understood the word in the modern sense; yet he also used the word "symmetry" to refer to the proportions of certain arrangements of columns.

In England the earliest occurrence of "symmetry" with the meaning of "bilateral symmetry" in an original text – i.e., one not translated from a foreign tongue - was in Temple's "Garden of Epicurus" (1685). In this essay Temple introduced the concept of *sharawaggi*, which he claimed was a Chinese method for designing buildings and landscapes that intentionally dispelled with "any order or disposition of parts that shall be commonly or easily observ'd".[77] Temple con-

---

[74] Le Muet 1670, p.3. "Equal proportion" is not to be understood in the modern sense of "all of the same size" but as a consistent system of proportion throughout a structure.

[75] Perrault 1993, pp.53, 50.

[76] I have seen only the English translation.

[77] Temple 1731, v.I, p.186. Honour (1962, p.144) suggests that Temple may have learned about the design of Chinese gardens from far-east travelers he met during

trasted this type of design (which of course was necessarily asymmetric) with English designs whose "beauty... is placed chiefly in some certain proportions, symmetries or uniformities". That these three latter terms are not merely synonyms and that Temple here means "symmetry" in the sense we understand it today can be inferred from the context, which contrasts the English manner (by which trees are "ranged so, as to answer one another") with the irregular, *sharawaggi*, way of doing things.[78]

The new meaning of "symmetry" started to be used with some frequency in English literary circles around the middle of the eighteenth century. We find Walpole, for example, telling his friend Horace Mann in 1750 that he was "almost as fond of the ... want of symmetry in buildings as in grounds of gardens".[79] Burke's role in the adoption of this new use was especially important. In his "Essay on the Sublime and Beautiful", which first appeared in 1756, Burke denounced the fashion of "disciplining" Nature and "teaching her to know her business" by reducing her forms to "squares, triangles and other mathematical figures with exactness and symmetry" – the latter term clearly referring to symmetry in the modern sense. [80]

---

his embassy in The Hague. Lang and Pevsner (1949) on the other hand declare that according to Sinologists "*sharawaggi*" is not a Chinese word. Similarly OED on "Sharawaggi". Honour, (*op.cit.*, p.145), though without citing authorities, finds Chinese and Japanese origins for it. Similarly, Clark 1944. Lewis (1960, p.102, n.) suggests that the word was probably invented as a hoax by Temple. Murray, 1998, gives the concept a Japanese rather than Chinese origin and claims to have "resolved" the whole problem. For the "insistent asymmetry" of Japanese architecture see Ramberg (1960).

[78] According to Temple the Chinese "scorned" roads laid out in straight lines and flanked by symmetrically-planted trees. It is curious to note that, almost 150 years after Temple, William Chambers (1772, p.52) reported that roads in China are laid out with "exact order and symmetry". See Lovejoy 1955a, pp.122-135, for a good account of the reservations Chambers had about his contemporaries' understanding of Chinese design.

[79] Quoted Tunnard 1978, p.83. Some years later Walpole (1891, v.IX, p.70) wrote a catty description of the Duke of Modena having "a mound of vermilion on the left side of his forehead to symmetrise with a wen on the right". (A wen is a benign cyst of the skin.) In his book on gardening Walpole (1995, pp. 25-6; 29) deplored the "fantastic admirers of symmetry" who "corrected" the shapes of trees, and he dismissed "symmetrical" gardens as "unnatural". Comp. Hogarth's (2007, pp.21-28), equation of "symmetry" with "uniformity".

[80] "Essay on the Sublime and Beautiful", Part III, Section 4: "And certainly nothing could be more unaccountably whimsical, than for an architect to model his performance by the human figure, since no two things can have less resemblance or analogy, than a man and a house, or temple: do we need to observe, that their purposes are entirely different? What I am apt to suspect is this: that these analo-

Nevertheless, the earlier meaning of "symmetry" also continued to be current in England and we find Burke himself reverting to it when he wrote of someone who had "symmetrized every disproportion".[81] The lexicographers stayed with the older meaning, alone. Dr Johnson, notably, defined symmetry as the "adaptation of parts to each other; proportion; harmony; agreement of one part to another". (The last of these is too ambiguous to allow us any confidence that what the great Doctor had in mind was intended in the modern sense. Do the parts "agree" because they mirror each other or because the appearance of the one is in some sense compatible with that of the other?) The *Encyclopedia Britannica*, in its initial appearance in 1771, also stuck to the traditional usage, defining symmetry as "the just proportion of the several parts of any thing, so as to compose a beautiful whole". In the middle of the nineteenth century Ruskin, in *The Stones of Venice*, used the term in this sense with his reference to the "exquisite symmetry and richness" of the canopy over a tomb.[82] The older meaning of symmetry, indeed, has survived into our own day and age, as we see from P. D. James' description, in one of her fine detective novels, of the "attractive symmetry in the ... proportion between the strong walls and roof" of a house.[83]

In England "symmetry" would retain its Classical meaning until well into the nineteenth century, and it was not generally unders-

---

gues were devised to give credit to the work of art, by showing a conformity between them and the noblest works in nature; not that the latter served at all to supply hints for the perfection of the former. And I am the more fully convinced, that the patrons of proportion have transferred their artificial ideas to nature, and not borrowed from thence the proportions they use in works of art; because in any discussion of this subject they always quit as soon as possible the open field of natural beauties, the animal and vegetable kingdoms, and fortify themselves within the artificial lines and angles of architecture. For there is in mankind an unfortunate propensity to make themselves, their views, and their works, the measure of excellence in everything whatsoever. Therefore, having observed that their dwellings were most commodious and firm when they were thrown into regular figures, with parts answerable to each other; they transferred these ideas to their gardens; they turned their trees into pillars, pyramids and obelisks; they formed their hedges into so many green walls, and fashioned their walks into squares, triangles and other mathematical figures, with exactness and symmetry; and they thought, if they were not imitating, they were at least improving nature, and teaching her to know her business. But nature has at last escaped from their discipline and their fetters; and our gardens, if nothing else, declare we begin to feel that mathematical ideas are not the true measure of beauty."

[81] Burke 1796, #55.

[82] Ruskin 1903-13, v.XI, p.84. Ruskin also used "symmetry" in the modern sense.

[83] James 2005, Kindle version at 5763.

tood in the modern sense until the twentieth century.[84] Moreover, the use of "corresponding parts" for bilateral symmetry continued in England until at least the first decade of the nineteenth century.[85] In France, by contrast, the modern meaning of symmetry appears to have been securely established by the third quarter of the eighteenth century, when Montesquieu discussed the concept at some length in the section "Des Plaisirs de la Symétrie" of his *Essai sur le Gout*.[86] The English translation of this essay (published in 1777) reflects the continuing confusion in England between the two meanings, sometimes rendering "symétrie" as "symmetry" and at others times, nonsensically, as "proportion". It is perhaps indicative of the difference between the two countries with respect to this word that, although the French crystallographer Haüy reported in 1800 that snow crystals quite often have *"un charactière particulier de symétrie"*, the English explorer Scoresby was still describing them as "regular" in 1820: and it was not until 1880 that the term "hexagonal symmetry" was first used for them, in a paraphrase by Huxley of Scoresby's description.[87]

The muddle between the two meanings of the word "symmetry" has continued into modern times. In a chapter entitled "The Aesthetics of Proportion" Umberto Eco wrote that "mainly due to the influence of Vitruvius ... the concept of symmetry was very common" in medieval plastic art: but on the following page – this is a chapter about proportion! – he referred to double-headed eagles and two-tailed mermaids as examples of medieval symmetric design.[88] We may be confident that whatever inspired the creators of those designs it was not "symmetry" in the Classical sense used by Vitruvius when he set forth his ideas about proportions.[89] Nor is Eco the only modern scholar to mistake Vitruvius' concept of symmetry for bilateral symmetry. In

---

[84] Among the more curious explanations of "symmetry" in the Classical sense is that of J. B. Ker (1840, pp.104-5) who defined it as "complete order, proportion" and claimed that it implied "a state devised by the Supreme Being". He derived the word from the Dutch "*sij'm met rije*", which he translated as "we come into a duly regulated state of things". For a less idiosyncratic use of the older meaning of symmetry see, for example, Charlotte Bronte's description in *Villette* (1853, p. 279) of her heroine's "pale small features, her fairy symmetry, her varying expression".

[85] Gandy 1805, p.vii: "architectural design in general should be uniform, that is, having corresponding parts on each side of a centre".

[86] Montesquieu 1825, pp.616-7.

[87] Huxley 1887, pp.60, 62.

[88] Eco 1986, pp.39-40.

[89] Eco's supposition that Vitruvius enjoyed great influence in the Middle Ages is a rather idiosyncratic one.

their fine edition of Serlio's *Books* Hart and Hicks cite Vitruvius, I,ii,3-4 on symmetry to explain Serlio's "proportional correspondence".[90] Vitruvius of course used the term to indicate proportions, not the mirroring of a form's two lateral halves; and as we have seen it is clear from the context that it was in the latter sense that Serlio used "symmetry" when he referred to the necessity of balancing the postern on one side with a postern on the other. The concept of bilateral symmetry to which - in a perhaps rather muddled way Serlio was referring - is not a Vitruvian concept.

Another relatively recent instance of the confusion between the two concepts of symmetry is Wittkower's characterization of bilateral symmetry as "a primary aspect of proportion".[91] His definition of bilateral symmetry as "the balance of parts between themselves and the whole", is *sui generis* and not one that I think anyone else would recognize. If anything, it could be understood as a definition of harmonious or pleasing proportions.

Aside from the confusion engendered by the two meanings of the term, "symmetry" in the sense of the mirroring of the right and left halves of a form remained an elusive concept well into the 19th century. A drawing that the architect Downing presented to readers of his *Cottage Residences* clearly shows an asymmetric structure (*fig*.6.17). Downing however, although he acknowledged that his design was not symmetric "in shape", nevertheless insisted that it was symmetric "in bulk and in the mass of composition". Fortunately, "symmetrically irregular", the term he devised for such structures, never caught on. In any case, as we see from the illustration, the distribution of the building's bulk is *not* equal, the wing on the right being both taller and broader than the one on the left. Downing predicted that this design would bring its owners "more intense and enduring pleasure" than a "regular" house.[92]

It took the better part of five hundred years for the meaning that Pope Pius II attached to the word "symmetry" to become generally accepted. Ironically, by the time this happened scholars had come to realize that there are in fact numerous distinct types of symmetry, to which they have given such names as "translational symmetry", "rotational symmetry", "helical symmetry", etc.[93] Thus "symmetry" in the sense introduced in the fifteenth century is now only one of several types of symmetry, and to be literally correct one should refer to it

---

[90] Serlio 1996 vol.I, p.449 fn.72.

[91] Wittkower 1978, p.123.

[92] Downing 1844, p.3.

[93] Weyl 1952, pp.41*ff*.

specifically as *"bilateral* symmetry". Most people nowadays, however, mean "bilateral symmetry" when they say "symmetry", and I have followed popular usage here.

Before concluding this Note we should briefly consider the word "asymmetry" which, as we saw earlier, literally refers to a shape that is "without symmetry". An insidious aspect of these terms is their implication, not only that asymmetry lacks that which symmetry possesses (rather than, perhaps, the other way around) but also that symmetry is somehow the appropriate standard, the norm, while asymmetry is an aberrant – somehow defective or erroneous - version of it: a deviation from the norm.[94] (Perhaps it is this that explains why we sometimes hear that a shape is "almost symmetric" but never that it is "almost asymmetric".) In view of what we have seen in previous Notes to be the overwhelming predominance of asymmetric forms both in Nature and in human artifacts, it is surely the presence of symmetry and not its absence that ought to seem remarkable and set us in search of an explanation. In the real world it is asymmetric shapes, not symmetric ones, that constitute the norm!

The negative connotation of the word asymmetry is apparent in the earliest known use of the term in English, when "symmetry" was still used to refer to good proportions. It was with this sense that John Evelyn used it when he associated "asymmetrie" with the "want of decorum and proportion" exemplified by Gothic buildings, that he

---

[94] According to Wittkower (1978, p.123) an asymmetric human body (as if there are human bodies that are *not* asymmetric!) "evokes reactions such as pity, irritation, or repulsion". Arnheim (1977, p.36) is among those who have expressed the opinion that symmetry is the norm from which asymmetry deviates. His bold pronouncement has it that "matter is grouped symmetrically around the vertical axis unless intervening forces modify this simple equilibrium... We may say that what requires explanation about any particular shape is not its symmetry but its asymmetry". Other statements of the *normative* nature of symmetry include the one in *Roget's Thesaurus* that equates symmetry with "shapeliness, finish, beauty"; and another in the *Encyclopedia Britannica* on-line edition that declares that "symmetry in nature underlies one of the most fundamental concepts of beauty". Presumably, these definitions mean that asymmetric forms are not beautiful and that nature's forms *are* symmetric. Weyl (1952, p.16) associated symmetry with normative values in another way, suggesting that symbols of justice and everlasting truth are "naturally" presented in symmetric, frontal view. This, he says, is the reason why "public buildings and houses of worship, whether they are Greek temples or Christian basilicas, are bilaterally symmetric". But he is factually incorrect. Some of the most notable "public buildings", such as the Palazzo della Signoria and the Bargello in Florence, the Palazzo Publico in Siena, or the Doge's Palace in Venice, have asymmetric facades. So among many others have the Parthenon, the Pantheon, the basilica of St Mark in Venice and the cathedral of Notre Dame in Paris.

thought of as "fantastical and licentious" and lacking "any just proportion".[95] A few years later Boyle, in his essay "Discourse of things above reason"(1681) contrasted "harmonious" truths with others that are "not symmetrical", and went on to refer to the latter as "asymmetrical or unsociable" – obscure terms in this context, to be sure, but clearly not intended as laudatory.[96] This use of asymmetry to denote that which is inharmoniously proportioned and irrational continued into the nineteenth century.[97]

It was not until late in the nineteenth century that "asymmetry" started to be used without reference to proportion but as the antonym of "symmetry" in the sense of "bilateral symmetry". But just as the positive connotation of the older meaning of symmetry was absorbed into the new meaning of the term, so too did the negative connotation of asymmetry as the antithesis of symmetry-as-proportion become absorbed in some measure into the new meaning of asymmetry.

Appendix: Alberti's Collocatio

Leon Battista Alberti's *collocatio* is noteworthy as the earliest extant formulation of the concept of symmetry, and also because Alberti regarded it as one of the three essential components of good design.[98] Art historians however have either ignored *collocatio* altogether,[99] or minimized its scope,[100] or explained it in terms that bear absolutely no resemblance to anything Alberti ever wrote.[101]

---

[95] Freart, 1664, in Evelyn's unpaginated introduction to his translation of Freart's architectural treatise. Friedman (1998, 153ff), incorrectly assumes that Evelyn used "symmetry" and by implication, its opposite, in the modern sense.

[96] "Discourse of Things Above Reason" in Boyle 1979, p.235.

[97] For example: "There was asymmetry and disproportion", Erasmus Middleton, *Biographia Evangelica*, 1810, vol.III, p.90.

[98] Alberti 1966a, Bk.IX, cap.5 – "*praecipua esse tria haec in quibus omnis quam quaerimus ratio consumetur numerus, et quam nos finitionem nuncupabimus et collocatio*". The requirements of *collocatio* must be attended to at the very outset of work on a new project: "*quare in primis observabimus ... ita ut muto dextra sinistris... aequatissime conveniant*" (ibid., Bk.IX, cap.7.) Alberti concluded his discussion by declaring that he had now shown what beauty is and what it consists of: "*itaque et quidnam sit pulchritudo et quibus constet partibus...*".

[99] e.g. Wittkower 1949, etc; Borsi 1986; Burckhardt, 1985. Heydenreich (1996, p.44), refers to "the fundamental laws of architecture contained in ... *collocatio*"

No doubt part of the blame for this rests with Alberti himself. His presentation of the concept is often turgid and inept, and is scattered haphazardly (and without always being identified by name) in different sections of *De re aedificatoria*. He began his discussion of it with the oracular pronouncement that it pertains to *"situm et sedem"* ("siting and seating"), whatever that may mean; and then added that it is easier to see when it is done poorly (*"ubi male habita est"*) than to indicate rules for doing it well (*"quam intelligatur per se qui decenter ponenda sit"*). It is doubtful, he went on to say, whether rules can help a person meet the requirements of *collocatio* if he lacks innate good judgment (*"ad iudicium insitum natura animis hominum"*).[102]

These remarks might lead one to suppose that that *collocatio* is a subtle concept that can be grasped only by people with superior minds. Yet it is nothing of the sort. Indeed, in Alberti's own telling of it *collocatio* is a very simple notion that can be understood at once by just about anyone. It consists of two elements. One is descriptive: it is the

---

and then says nothing further about it. It is curious to note Wittkower's skittishness about discussing, not just Alberti's *collocatio*, but symmetry in general: "Renaissance architects", he wrote, (*ibid*, p.70), "always regarded symmetry as a theoretical requirement, and rigidly symmetrical plans are already found in Filarete, Francesco di Giorgio and Giuliano da Sangallo". Wittkower did not mention Alberti, or *collocatio*, in this context, or explain what the theory in that "theoretical requirement" may have been. He added, though without explanation, that "in practice this theory was rarely applied". That symmetric design is "rarely" found in Renaissance architecture will come as a surprise to most people.

[100] Kruft (1994, pp. 46-7), mistakenly limits *collocatio* to architectural design. Poeschke (2008, p.186) described *collocatio* as *"die Symmetrie eines Gebaeudes als spiegelbildiche Anordnung seiner Teile"* adding that it *"erhaelt sonnst quasi den Rang eines Naturgesetzes"*, an accurate definition as far as it goes though also mistakenly limiting *collocatio* to architecture. Gadol too (1969, pp. 109-110), with her definition of *collocatio* as "architectural symmetry in the modern sense", limits *collocatio* to architecture. Perhaps echoing Wittkower, and also without explanation, she adds that that Alberti "did not intend his remarks [on *collocatio*] to be carried out". Oechslin (1985) is one of the few who declared, without reservation, that "Alberti set forth the rules of mirror-reflection [i.e. bilateral symmetry]."

[101] Hersey (1977) characterizes *collocatio* as "a question of choice and distribution". Rykwert's two shots at defining the term both fall short. In Alberti 1965 (p.252) he translated *collocatio* as "relation", while in Alberti 1988 (p.422) he rendered it, no less vacuously, as "decisions that determine the arrangements of a building". Tavernor (1998, p.46), solemnly intones that *collocatio* is "what would be called planning today", but with the proviso that its results be "such that man, society and cosmos are in complete harmony". This stipulation is Tavernor's nonsensical embellishment, and if adopted would lead to the permanent cessation of all construction work everywhere! See also Pelt and Westfall 1993, p.275; Mateer, 2000, p.48; Pennick 2012, p.67; and Luecke 1994, p.82.

[102] Bk.IX, cap.7.

notion of bilateral symmetry – the precise mirroring of the appearance of the left and right halves of a form. The other is prescriptive: it is the axiom that if we want the things we make to be beautiful we must make them symmetric.

Alberti had little to say about the first – the descriptive - element of his concept other than to emphasize that with *collocatio* the mirroring of the left and right halves of a shape is exact, so that every feature of one of the halves is accurately mirrored by the other.

He discussed the prescriptive element at greater length. The ancient Greeks, he claimed, learned what beauty is by studying Nature's forms; and because those forms are invariably symmetric ("*dextra sinistris ... convenirent*") Greek architects always took great pains to ensure that, in whatever they made, even the smallest details ("*in minutissimis*") on one side were matched precisely ("*exactissime*") by those on the other. The imperative of imitating Nature's symmetry was also obeyed by artists, who understood that in their statues, pictures and ornaments all details must appear as twins ("*gemella videantur*").[103]

We are invited to believe, therefore, that *collocatio* is the restatement of a long-forgotten principle of Classical art. Alberti claimed that he discovered it by carefully examining "every building of the ancients, wherever it might be, that has attracted praise".[104] This is an implausible claim on the face of it, and is not made less so by the fact that Alberti did not publish any details of his research, or even name the buildings he examined; no drawings or notes he may have made in connection with those studies are known.[105] There is indeed no evidence that Alberti ever inspected an ancient Greek building, not even the temples at Paestum which are only 50 miles or so south of Naples.[106] The only independent knowledge we have of Alberti's familiarity with Classical ruins is a remark by Pius II, who referred to him as "a scholar and a very clever archaeologist" and quoted a report

---

[103] This confirms my point that *collocatio* is not limited, as Krufft and others have stated, to architecture alone.

[104] Alberti, 1966, VI:1, 3, 6. Notwithstanding its title, Alberti's *Descriptio Urbis Romae* is a guide to the mapping or surveying of the city, and does not describe any of the structures within it.

[105] The only ancient structure he described in *De re aedificatoria* (IV: 3) were the ruined walls of Antium Anzio, his description of which is limited to the banal statements that the walls followed the winding line of the coast and that they must have been very long.

[106] Kunst (n.d.) properly rejects the notion that the ruins of Paestum were only discovered in the middle of the 18th century.

from Alberti about raising an old Roman ship from the bed of a lake near Albano.[107]

But even if we suppose for the sake of argument that Alberti *had* examined all the buildings he claimed to have examined, his view that symmetry is a principle of Classical art and architecture would not be tenable. For despite what Alberti - and so many after him - supposed, the concept of symmetry (as we saw in Note Three) was known in the ancient world, if it was known at all, only rather briefly and as an esoteric doctrine shared by a small number of people: even Euclid appears to have been ignorant of it. The extreme rarity (if not complete absence) of symmetric design in the surviving physical relics of the ancient world bears this out. Alberti also claimed to have seen perfectly "twinned" statues. This too is a baffling report, for Alberti did not identify any of these statues, and none like them appear in the standard work on Classical sculptures known in the Renaissance.[108]

Alberti's claim that the Ancients regarded Nature's forms as symmetric can also be dismissed. There is no literary evidence to support this claim, and natural forms are not shown as symmetric in surviving works of art from the Classical era; in reality, of course, Nature's creations are *not* symmetric. Indeed, it seems as if Alberti himself inadvertently acknowledged as much. In a curious passage, he remarked that the resemblance between the right and left halves of some statues he had seen was greater than one can expect to find in Nature's own creations, in which "we hardly ever see one feature so exactly like the other" (*"in cuis operibus ne nesum quidem naso similem*

---

[107] Pius II, 1962, p.316 (=Dec. 1462-June 1463). See also Biondo 2005, pp.188-192.

[108] Bober and Rubenstein (2010). (The Warburg Institute's *Census of Antique Works of Art and Architecture known in the Renaissance* is now available in a searchable database at www.census.de.) The reliefs on Trajan's Column and the Arch of Titus, as well as on some lesser relics, would have been known to Alberti, but they too do not uphold his claims about the symmetry of Classical sculpture. Alberti's younger contemporary, Mantegna (1431-1506), who is described by Clark (1981, p.122) as "striving for archeological accuracy" in the backgrounds of his paintings set in the Roman era, clearly did not think that Roman architecture was symmetric. In his *Saint James addressing the Demons* (Tietze-Conrat, 1955, pl.9) the saint is standing under an arch whose interior is decorated with irregularly-shaped and spaced coffers. The triumphal arch in *Saint James before Herod Agrippa* (*ibid*, pl.11) is almost astonishingly asymmetric (the right-hand side of the architecture has *not* been cut off. Note the much narrower – yet more broadly-fluted – column on the right). In *The Martyrdom of Saint Christopher* (*ibid*, pl.14) the large brick house has markedly asymmetric fenestration and its eaves are of different lengths (the one on the right is shorter). The funerary monument in pl.14 is set lower than the one in pl.15 in which we see the other half of the house's façade. Obviously, then, Alberti and Mantegna had a very different view of Classical architecture, at least in regard to its asymmetry.

intueamur.) The requirement of *collocatio*, it will be remembered, is that the two lateral halves of a form must mirror each other precisely – and it is this standard evidently that according to Alberti himself Nature falls short of. Thus, if the Ancients were diligent in their imitation of Nature, they would have created forms – and indeed *did* create forms - that, like those of Nature herself, are not symmetric.[109] To be sure, this is not an implication that Alberti acknowledged.

Separately, Alberti also argued that any combination of two disparate shapes is inherently offensive. We would be repelled, he wrote, by the sight of a dog that had one ear like that of a donkey, or of a man who had one hand or foot that was much larger than the other: or again, by the sight of a horse that had one gray and one black eye. Whether asymmetric arrangements are usefully characterized by such images may be doubted. Moreover, as he presented it, Alberti's point is to deplore the asymmetry of the two ears, not the inappropriateness of one of them. Does this mean that we would not be repelled by the sight of a dog whose two ears were – identically – shaped like those of a donkey?

In explaining why we should make our artifacts symmetric, then, Alberti can do no better than to say that that's how Nature and the Classical world make things, which is untrue; and that asymmetric forms are repellent, which is not only a matter of uninformed opinion but one that is contradicted by the undoubted pleasure we get from looking at many asymmetric forms, whether natural or man-made, whose loveliness, indeed, is often enhanced by their asymmetry.

Alberti's rationale for the symmetry norm thus rests on the the most inept of arguments. Yet it is also the case that the advocacy of symmetric design has not climbed to a higher intellectual level since his day – I am thinking, for example, of Montesquieu's argument that we enjoy symmetric designs because it is easier for us to comprehend them.

Although Alberti probably completed his architectural treatise some years before Pius built his palace in Pienza, we have no reason to believe that it was from Alberti that the pope acquired his knowledge of the concept of symmetry. Indeed, we may infer from the fact that Pius used *simmetria* and not *collocatio* for the concept, (as well as from the likelihood that the reason Pius did not explain the term *simmetria* was because he believed his readers would be familiar with it) that another version of the concept of symmetry, in addition to Alberti's, was current in the middle of the fifteenth century. It is more probable that Francesco Colonna, author of *Hypnerotomachia Poliphili* derived *his*

---

[109] Sir Henry Wotton (1958, p.94), ever the lover of paradox, cited Quintilian to justify his remark that sometimes the imitation of nature can lead to results that are "too naturall".

knowledge of the concept from that source than from either Alberti or the pope. What that source may have been it is impossible for us to determine. We are unable to trace the origins of the concept any further back than the mid-fifteenth century writings of these three men.

And just as we cannot attribute the origin of the idea of symmetry to Alberti so too are we unable to attribute its subsequent history to his influence. If anyone played an influential role in propagating the idea of symmetry that person was probably Sebastiano Serlio (1475-1554) whose books, popular in France and the Low Countries, may well have been the medium by which the concept of symmetry first reached beyond the Alps.

In the past several decades art historians have made much of Alberti's importance.[110] However, there is no evidence at all of the influence of *collocatio* either during Alberti's lifetime (he died in 1472) or later. Not a single writer before the twentieth century is known to have referred to Alberti's views on bilateral symmetry; and no one else ever adopted his term for it.[111] Perhaps nothing illustrates more vividly Al-

---

[110] However, the scholarly "Societe International Leon Battista Alberti" seems now to be defunct; its journal *Albertiana* has not appeared since about 2008 (see www.silba.msh-paris.fr). Dissenting from the academic consensus is Krufft (1994, p.49), who remarks that Alberti "never attained the widespread impact that Vitruvius, Serlio and Vignola enjoyed for centuries".

[111] One may question, indeed, Alberti's influence in general. Writers in the first century or so of the Italian Renaissance are restrained in their references to him. Manetti (1970, p.55, l.384) mentions him merely as someone who "gave precepts" about the Classical manner of building. Biondo (2005, v.I, p.191) characterized Alberti as "*geometra nostro tempore egregius*" and as the author of "*elegantissimos … libros*" on architecture, i.e., the *De re aedificatoria* - far from fulsome words, but perhaps more so than those of Vasari who, while acknowledging Alberti's reputation criticized much of his architectural work and commented that writers receive more attention than architects, even though the latter may know more about the subject than the former! Palladio (1997, p.5) listed Alberti among "other excellent writers who came after Vitruvius" but cited him only on a few relatively minor matters, such as the design of roads. Only Serlio pulls out the stops. Alberti, he writes, was "expert in both theory and practice" and he was "greatly praised as an architect". (His admiration for Alberti did not lead him, however, to adopt *collocatio* as his term for symmetry. He chose instead to refer to it as *simmetria*.) These few references do not add up to much; they surely do not confirm the view of Alberti's towering influence and achievement that has been current for the past century or so, during which Alberti has been the subject of a seemingly endless outpouring of adulatory treatises. Indications of the reluctance of modern scholars to acknowledge Alberti's relatively minor stature and influence are not hard to come by. Saalman, for example (Manetti 1970, pp.28-29) writes of the "profound" influence of Alberti's work on Manetti's *Life of Brunelleschi* but soon acknowledges that Manetti is "in as profound a contrast with Albertian principles and practice of architecture as was Brunelleschi himself". Similarly, Panofsky (1972, p.27) in

berti's lack of influence over the subsequent history of the concept of symmetry than the fact that although Wotton owned an exceptional copy of *De re aedificatoria* it was not Alberti but Vasari whom he cited as the source of his ideas on the subject.[112]

The historical significance, if any, of Alberti's *collocatio* does not lie in its influence, accordingly, but in the fact that it is the earliest surviving (albeit very flawed) attempt to formulate a rationale for symmetric design.

---

his great essay on the concept of the Renaissance, declares but without giving evidence for it that Leonardo da Vinci and Dürer were among "Alberti's followers" and then seemingly contradicts himself by acknowledging that Alberti's "method of determining and recording human proportions was, and even remained for some time, unique" (we are not told when the period of uniqueness ended, or under whose aegis this occurred). Rykwert and his colleagues, in their edition of *De re aedificatoria*, declare that "Alberti's contemporaries accepted *De re aedificatoria* as a model of learned Latin writing immediately", but offer no evidence to support their claim, whether we understand it to refer to Alberti's command of Latin prose or to the substance of his book. Equally, Weil-Garris and Damico (1980), writing of the influence of Alberti as well as of Vitruvius on Cortesi, cope with the fact that the evidence for that influence is not really there by allowing themselves to say: "In the traditional way Cortesi uses sources without identifying them. It is instructive that the names of Vitruvius and Alberti are never mentioned"! Boase, (1979, p.53), also without documentation, claims that "Vasari seems to have absorbed Alberti's theories" but acknowledges that there is "little direct trace" of them in Vasari's works. Clark (1983, pp.100-105) claims that Uccello, Piero della Francesca and Leonardo da Vinci were greatly influenced by Alberti's *della Pittura* but acknowledges that the evidence for this too is slim. Consistent with my opinion that Alberti's influence is a modern contrivance, it is perhaps worth noting that the statue to him in the church of Santa Croce was erected no more recently than at the beginning of the 20th century, and with funds contributed by a member of the Alberti family.

[112] Wotton 1968, p.117. Wotton, who became provost of Eton, gave his copy of *De re aedificatoria* to the Eton College library, where it is still to be found.

6.2 Late-medieval garden

6.3 Agugliaro: Villa Saraceno

6.4 Rome: Palazzo Farnese

6.5 Windsor Castle gardens, c. 1725.

6.6 The Villa d'Este

6.7 Villa di Castel Pulci [113]

---

[113] Zocchi 1757, pl.8

THE SYMMETRY NORM AND THE ASYMMETRIC UNIVERSE 203

6.8   Botticelli's "dense and living forest"

6.9   "The Hunt" by Paolo Uccello (1397-1475)

6.9a "The Hunt" (*detail*)

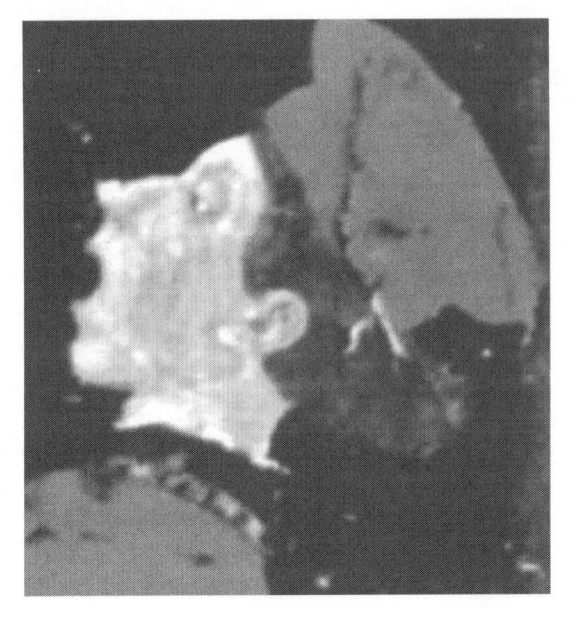

6.9b Detail of 6.9a

6.10 "Combat" by Antonio Pollaiuolo (1433-1498)

6.11 "Death on Horseback" by Giovanni di Paolo (1395-1482)

6.12 Giovanni del Biondo (active 1356-1399):
Florence during the 1374 plague

6.13 Baccio del Bianco (1604-57): The Plague in Florence in 1630 (*detail*)

6.14 Pienza, the cathedral and (*right*) the papal palace, the "*simmetrie*" of which Pius II wrote has been disturbed by the bricking-up of the inner area of the false doorway.

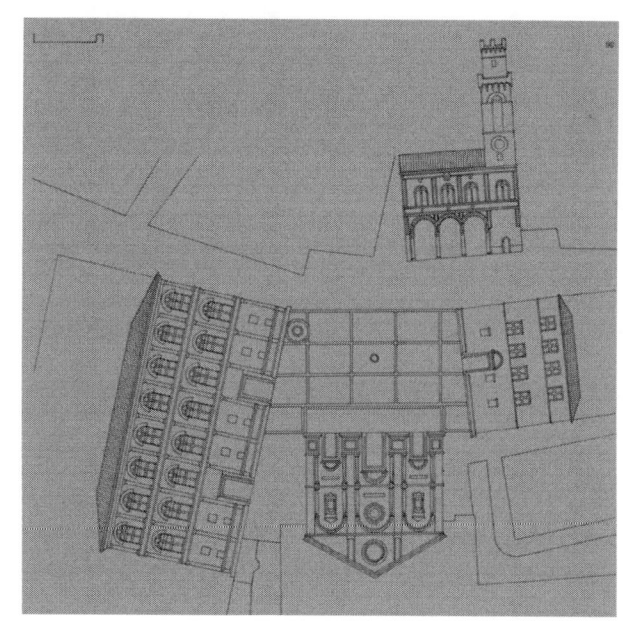

6.14b Pienza, plan showing (clockwise) town hall (top), episcopal palace, cathedral and papal palace.

6.15 Serlio: Asymmetric façades "corrected"

THE SYMMETRY NORM AND THE ASYMMETRIC UNIVERSE   211

6.16 Le Muet, "symmetric" house façade[114]

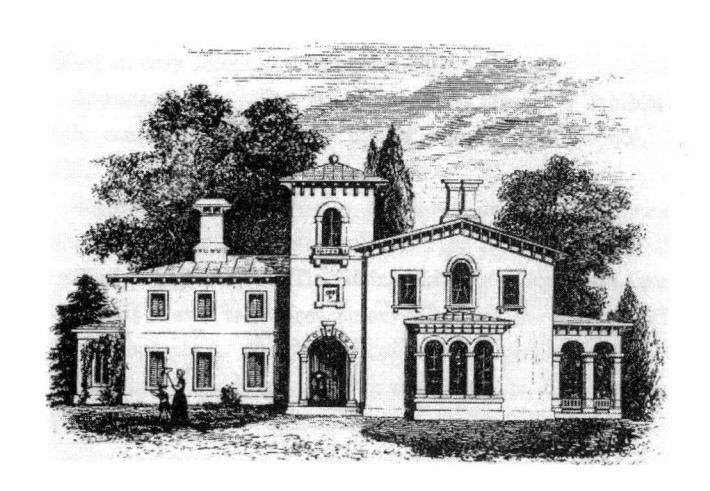

6.17 Downing's "symmetric irregularity"

---

[114] Le Muet 1623, p.29.

THE NATURAL GARDEN IN ENGLAND

7.1 High Wycomb (designed by Humphrey Repton)

Note Seven

> *"The shift to Nature in the form of landscape gardens sprang from an eagerness to break free from symmetry."*
> - Max Friedlaender (1969, p.29)

In England at the beginning of the eighteenth century the formal garden of the Renaissance gave way to what became known as the "natural" garden, sometimes also known as the "English" garden.[1] The change was by any standards revolutionary (*figs*. 6.5, 7.1, 7.2). For two centuries gardens had been characterized by stark geometric shapes, artificial contrivances and symmetric arrangements. Now informal, free-flowing design became the norm, along with an emphasis on variety of texture, color and form; intimate vistas; the discretely contrived interplay of light and shade; and unabashed visual complexity.[2]

The natural garden, for all that it was meticulously designed, gave the impression - *non murato ma veramente nato*[3] - that it stemmed from Nature's plan and not, like the Renaissance garden, from the will of Man. Here Man was Nature's patient and enthusiastic collaborator -

---

[1] "Natural garden" begs the question, to be sure, of how "natural" anything that is designed and cultivated by humans can be. In the Aristotelian view (*Physics*, 192:68; Hardie and Gaye trans.), that enjoyed much currency during the Renaissance and for long thereafter, "art partly completes what nature cannot bring to a finish, and partly imitates her". Shakespeare ("Winter's Tale", Act 4, Sc. 4) expressed the thought thus: "This is an art which does mend nature, change it rather, but the art itself is nature". In other words: Nature is fulfilled, not falsified, when she is improved by Art. Sir Joshua Reynolds (1997, Discourse XIII) however insisted that gardening "is a deviation from Nature".

[2] Comp. Pevsner 1964, p.174: "The English garden ... is asymmetrical, informal, varied, and made of such parts as the serpentine lake, the winding drive and winding path, the trees grouped in clumps and smooth lawn (mown or cropped by sheep) reaching right up to the French windows of the house".

[3] "Not built but born". This felicitous phrase is Vasari's. He coined it however for the Palazzo Farnese (*fig*.6.4), a structure in whose decidedly *murato* appearance it is impossible to discern even a hint of the *nato*.

perhaps merely her helper - and certainly not her conqueror. The spirit of Renaissance horticulture, that had regarded Nature as a threat and aimed at her subjugation, was nowhere evident.

We suggested in Note Six that the Renaissance gardener's belligerence toward Nature was a response to the deadly plagues that ravaged Europe for more than three centuries. Only an end to that terrible threat, we may speculate, could allow a more benign perception of Nature to take hold and to be manifested in horticulture. *And indeed, the emergence of the natural garden and the radically changed view of Nature that made it possible coincided with the end of the era of the plagues.*

The change from the one to the other can be observed in the works of two seventeenth-century contemporaries. We have already referred to Charles Cotton (Note Six). Cotton's dyspeptic remark in *Wonders of the Peake* that the beauty of Chatsworth's gardens was achieved, not *by* Nature but *despite* her, places him and those gardens in a familiar Renaissance context. What helped form Cotton's perception is suggested, I believe, by the chilling metaphors, drawn from the lexicon of disease, that he used to describe the valley of the river Derwent and, by extension, Nature herself.[4] They bring to mind the fact that Cotton wrote the poem a scant fifteen years after the Great Plague of 1665-1666 in which about one-fifth of London's population perished.

William Temple was born two years before Cotton; his essay, "Upon the Gardens of Epicurus" appeared four years after the publication of *Wonders of the Peake*. Nevertheless, the difference between the two works is fundamental: it is the difference between two eras' perception of Nature. Where Cotton regarded Beauty and Nature as antithetical, for Temple beauty was the happy outcome of Man's cooperation with her. (His essay, indeed, would play a role in the transition to the new style of gardening.) Cotton's poem seems haunted by the catastrophe of 1665, but nothing Temple wrote so much as hints at it. Neither Cotton nor Temple could know, of course, that with the Great Plague the era of plagues in England had at last come to a close.[5] But

---

[4] For Cotton the Derwent was a "blue scrofulous scum"; and the land through which it flowed was "so deform'd" that it resembled nothing so much as "impostumated boyles", "warts and wens" - and even "Nature's pudenda"! This is the same Derwent that, a little more than a century later, Wordsworth would celebrate as "the fairest of all rivers".

[5] Defoe reverted to the earlier epoch with his *Journal of the Plague Year* (a fictional account of the Great Plague), published in 1722. Mullett (1936) suggests that Defoe may have written this work in the expectation that the outbreak of the plague

that knowledge, completely absent from Cotton's verse, is implicit in the fearless embrace of Nature that we find in Temple's essay.[6]

If the end of the era of the plagues encouraged people to acquire a new view of Nature and, in consequence of it, to recognize the visual, intellectual and emotional barrenness of the Renaissance garden, it was the advent of a new aesthetic principle that brought them, specifically, to the vital, free-flowing forms of the natural garden. This was the principle of variety.[7]

Initially, this principle was discussed in the context of literary theory, but as early as the first half of the seventeenth century it was also being talked about in terms of garden design. It thus became a precursor of the natural garden of the eighteenth century.[8] "All the beauties of gardening", Spence records Pope saying, "might be comprehended in one word, variety".[9]

A distinction should be drawn between two applications of this principle. In one, the value of variety is seen primarily in instrumental terms. When "E.K.", in his dedicatory epistle to Spenser's *The Shepeardes Calendar* (published in 1579) remarked that we are often "singularly delighted with the shewe of naturall rudeness, and take great pleasure in ... disorderly order", it was not because he regarded variety – disorder – as an end in itself. Rather, it was because he believed that what he called "the daintie lineaments of beautye" could most pleasurably be experienced in conjunction with their opposites. As he explained: "So oftentimes a dischorde in Musick maketh a comely concordance: so great delight tooke the worthy Poete Alceus to behold a blemish in the joynt of a wel shaped body".[10] Rather similarly, Sir

---

that was then devastating Marseilles would soon spread to England. It turned out however that the Marseilles outbreak was the last that afflicted western Europe.

[6] As noted below, Temple actually *preferred* the formal garden, but only for the banal reason that it was easier to design and create.

[7] Ogden (1949) states that "aside from the principle of decorum there was probably no aesthetic principle ... regarded as more important" during the sixteenth and seventeenth centuries. The evidence of a preference for variety in the *sixteenth* century however is at best very slight.

[8] Humphreys (1937, pp.39-69) finds the precursors of the natural garden in a revolt against "the sheer boredom" of the formal garden, along with a number of other factors, of which delight in Nature's "infinite variety" is only one.

[9] Spence 1964, p.48.

[10] Comp. Spenser's own "dischord oft in Musick makes the sweeter lay" - *Faerie Queene* III.ii.15.

Henry Wotton (1568-1639) reported enthusiastically about the application of the principle of variety in the gardens of Ware Park, whose owner

> did so precisely examine the tinctures, and seasons of his flowres, that in their setting, the inwardest of those which were to come up at the same time, should be always a little darker than the outmost, and to serve them for a kinde of gentle shadow, like a piece not of Nature, but of Arte.[11]

Here too variety has an instrumental purpose, with the darker flowers used to heighten the colors of the others.

Another application of the principle of variety in the seventeenth century was the fashion of including an area of wilderness in an otherwise formal garden. The main part of the garden, Bacon declared in 1625, "is best to be square ... not too busy or full of work" – in other words, it was to be laid out in the formal fashion – but fully one-third of the garden's overall acreage was to be given over to what Bacon called a "heath". This was to be "framed, as much as may be, to a natural wildness", and with flowers strewn all over it, "here and there, not in any order".[12] The point of doing so, evidently, was to offer a contrast between the two, though it is unclear whether the contrast was valued for its own sake or to heighten the beauty of the formal garden. We should not make too much of Bacon's suggestion, however, for his "heath" conceded little to natural forms. As Dutton remarks, its wilderness was a "phantasy of meretricious artificiality" that would have evoked the withering scorn" of proponents of the natural garden.[13]

More than a century later the idea of antithetical arrangements within a single confine remained current, as we see from the epistolary novel, *Felicia to Charlotte* by Mary Collyer, that was published in 1749. Writing in breathless style to Charlotte, Felicia reports that one side of her garden in the country exemplifies "the beauty of art" - "The hedges, that are on each side of the principal walks, are formed of ev-

---

[11] Wotton 1968, pp.110-111. The final phrase of this sentence establishes Art in juxtaposition to Nature, and not as her servant or ally.

[12] The concept of an irregular portion within a regular garden can be traced to Pliny (1952, vol.1, p.390): "*et in opere urbanissimo subita velut illati ruris imitatio*".

[13] Dutton 1950, p.50. For a detailed description of one "wilderness", that bears out Dutton's remark, cf. Malins 1966, p.13.

er-greens, resembling walls, adorned, at proper distances, with pilasters which, with eternal verdure, branch into all the decorations of architecture *etc. etc.*" On the other side of the garden by contrast there stands "the triumph of nature"- "The uncultivated wildness, which pleases without method and without design, charming most where the easy confusion and agreable [*sic*] disorder render art superfluous and labour vain."[14] One gets the distinct impression that for Miss Collyer the difference between the two sections was not a device to call attention – by the device of contrast - to the fineness of the cultivated garden but was welcomed for its own sake.

In fact, from the outset we find instances in which variety was celebrated for its own sake, its complexity inherent in itself and not only in the contrast it created to its opposite. The earliest example of the appreciation of variety that Ogden cites is one such instance. It occurs in the statement by Coverdale, in 1541, that God made the grounds of the Garden of Eden "not like on every side, but in many places set up pleasantly". The suggestion here is evidently that it was the variations in the garden that made it pleasant. Ogden also cited a French work, the English translation of which was published in 1594, that celebrated the fact that the world is filled with "things of dislike and contrarie qualitie". According to the French author, "nature is so desirous of contraries, making of them all decency, and beautie; not of things which are of like nature". In somewhat the same vein, Ogden noted the remark by Henry Peacham in 1606 that he found a certain landscape painting "most pleasing, *because* [my emphasis] it feedeth the eye with varietie".[15]

The supreme expression of pleasure in the diversity of Nature's forms, colors and textures – and not altogether coincidentally, the first recorded attack on the formal garden – is the blind Milton's vision (1667) of the first garden, with its boundless glories "powr'd forth profuse":

---

[14] Collyer 1749, pp.38-9. The term "agreeable disorder" came originally from *The Villas of the Ancients* (Castell 1728, p.27), and appears to be part of a progression that led from "E.K.'s" "disorderly order" in 1579 to Wotton's "delightful confusion" in 1624, and to Pope's "harmoniously confused" (1713: Windsor Forest). The less felicitous "easy confusion" appears to have been of Collyer's own devising.

[15] There can only have been a moderate degree of "delightful confusion" in this garden. It evidently was composed of a number of zones, each with a distinct *formal* design. It was in other words a collection of small formal gardens joined to each other in a rectangular grid.

> ... from that Saphire Fount the crisped Brooks,
> Rowling on Orient Pearl and sands of Gold,
> With mazie error under pendant shades
> Ran Nectar, visiting each plant, and fed
> Flours worthy of Paradise, which not nice Art
> In Beds and curious Knots, but Nature boon
> Powrd forth profuse on Hill and Dale and Plaine
> Both where the morning Sun first warmly smote
> The op'n field, and where the unpierc't shade
> Imbround the noontime Bowers: Thus was this place,
> A happy rural seat of various view;
> Groves whose rich Trees wept odorous Gumms and Balme,
> Others whose fruit burnisht with Gold'n Rinde
> Hung amiable...[16]

Note how "Nature boon" in her profusion is unhindered here by the "nice Art in Beds and curious Knots" that characterized the Renaissance garden. Note too Milton's description of the "various view" – not to be captured with the first glimpse – that presented itself to the eye from this happy rural seat: and how the brooks (of nectar!) flowing through the grounds do not run in straight channels but in "mazie error", i.e., they wander about in maze-like fashion.[17] Virtually the entire program of the 18th century's natural garden is anticipated in Milton's description. How radical it was for its time can be seen from the fact that two of Milton's contemporaries thought that the trees in the Garden of Eden had been planted in straight rows (Evelyn) or in quincunx (Sir Thomas Browne).[18]

We have already mentioned Sir William Temple's essay, "Upon the Gardens of Epicurus". Lovejoy regarded it as "the probable beginning of the new ideas about [gardening] which were destined to

---

[16] *Paradise Lost*, Bk.IV, 237-249 (Milton 1958, p.79). Milton's vision of the Garden's free-flowing and lushly varied forms was anticipated in the first half of the 17th century by some Continental artists, among them the Brueghels, Rubens and Poussin.

[17] Sherbo 1972.

[18] Prest 1981, p.90.

have consequences of such unforeseen range".[19] It should be noted, however, that Temple was not at all one of those who,

> "Tir'd of the scene parterres and fountains yield,
> He finds at last he better likes a field."[20]

Indeed, his essay contains a lengthy passage celebrating the formal gardens of his time, one of which he described in detail and deemed was "the perfectest figure of a garden I ever saw."[21] Among the points Temple argued in favor of the formal garden was that "in regular Figures 'tis hard to make any real or remarkable Faults".[22] This is surely an extraordinary criterion, and helps one to sympathize with Walpole's acerbic remark about the "want of ideas, of imagination, of taste" shown by Temple "when he dictated on a subject that is capable of all the graces that a knowledge of beautiful nature can bestow".[23]

Nevertheless, Temple *did* acknowledge that under certain circumstances gardens laid out entirely on irregular lines can be beautiful, and it is his brief statement to this effect that gives his essay its historical significance.

"Forms wholly irregular", he wrote, could if done well combine "many disagreeing Parts into some Figure which shall yet, upon the whole, be very agreeable". Indeed, he conceded that such arrangements might "for ought I know have more Beauty" than the conventional gardens of his day. Temple claimed to have seen gardens designed along these lines (unfortunately, he does not tell us where they were) and then added that he had heard from people who had been in China about the way gardens, houses and decorative objects were designed there.

In England, he wrote, "the Beauty of Buildings and Plantings is placed chiefly in some certain Proportions, Symmetries, or Uniformities; our Walks and our Trees ranged so, as to answer one another, and at exact Distances". By contrast people in China "…scorn this Way of Planting, and say a Boy that can [count to] an Hundred may plant Walks of Trees in their strait Lines, and over against one another, and

---

[19] Lovejoy 1955a.

[20] Pope, "Moral Essays" Epist. IV, 87-88.

[21] Temple 1731, v.1, pp.170-190.

[22] *Ibid*, p.186.

[23] Walpole 1995, p.33.

to what Length and Extent he pleases... But their greatest Reach of Imagination is Employed in contriving Figures, where the Beauty shall be great, and strike the Eye, but without any Order or Disposition of Parts, that shall be commonly or easily observ'd. And though we have hardly any Notion of this Sort of Beauty, yet they have a particular Word to express it; and where they find it hit their eye at first Sight, they say the *Sharawadgi*[24] is fine or admirable, or any such Expression of Esteem.[25]

Temple advised his readers not to try the Chinese method in their own gardens. "I should hardly advise any of these Attempts in the Figure of Gardens among us; they are Adventures of too hard Achievement for any common Hands; and though there may be more Honour if they succeed well, yet there is more Dishonour if they fail, and 'tis Twenty to One they will". Thus, although Temple *can* be credited with introducing the concept of *Sharawaggi* to England he was not an advocate of its adoption for English landscapes or gardens.[26]

The real herald of the new movement was not Temple but the third Earl of Shaftesbury (1671-1713), who in 1710 announced his dislike of the formal garden and his yearning for Nature's untrammeled forms. "I shall no longer resist the Passion growing in me for Things of a *natural* kind" he wrote, "where neither *Art*, nor the *Conceit* or *Caprice* of Man has spoil'd their *genuine Order*, by breaking in upon that *primitive State*. Even the rude *Rocks*, the mossy *Caverns*, the irregular unwrought *Grotto's*, and broken *Falls* of Waters, with all the horrid Graces of the *Wilderness* itself, as representing Nature more, will be the

---

[24] On Sharawaggi see fn.77, p.186, *above*.

[25] Temple 1713, p.186. Temple added that the fabrics of "Indian Gowns or the Paintings upon their best Skreens or Purcellans" have a "Beauty ... of this kind without Order". Temple's criterion of beauty hitting the "eye at first sight" shows how deeply that requirement – which as we saw originated in the early Renaissance as a corollary to the requirement for symmetry - was rooted in the aesthetics of his time. The application of this requirement to *Sharawadgi* is implausible; the two are fundamentally in contradiction to each other.

[26] Walpole was in the end not convinced by Temple's description of Chinese design. In the Chinese garden, he wrote, (1995, pp. 38-9), "nature, it seems [is] as much avoided, as in the squares and oblongs and strait lines of our ancestors". Chinese landscapes he added, are a "gaudy scene ... the work of caprice and whim". Chambers (1772, p.157) went further and rejected the opinion that Chinese design is always irregular. The Chinese, he wrote, are "no enemies to straight lines because they are generally speaking productive of grandeur...nor have they any aversion to regular geometrical figures".

more engaging, and appear with a Magnificence beyond the formal Mockery of princely Gardens."[27]

These sentiments were echoed, if in somewhat more measured terms, by Joseph Addison (1672-1719). Addison's statement on the natural garden comes as something of a surprise because his ideas about architectural beauty have about them, on the contrary, the distinct tone of the Renaissance's aesthetic minimalism. In *The Spectator* No.415 of June 26, 1712, he expressed his appreciation of the interior of the Pantheon and his disapproval of the interiors of Gothic cathedrals. His reasons were essentially those of Filarete 250 years earlier. No figures have a greater "Air" to them, he declared, than the concave and the convex, for in them "we generally see more of the Body". The Gothic interior, by contrast, is one of "Confusion", for the sight of it is "split into several Angles [and therefore] does not take in one uniform Idea, but several Ideas..." Sentiments like these, when applied to horticulture, had led to the rigidity and artificiality of the formal garden.[28]

Just the previous day however, in the *Spectator* No.414 of June 25, 1712, Addison had written in an entirely different vein about the design, not of buildings but of gardens. He contrasted the natural free forms of the Chinese – no doubt he had learned about them from Temple's essay – to those of British gardeners:

> "Our British Gardeners, on the contrary, instead of humouring Nature, love to deviate from it as much as possible. Our Trees rise in Cones, Globes, and Pyramids. We see the Marks of the Scissars upon every

---

[27] "The Moralist" pt. III, sect. ii (Shaftesbury 1749 v.3, p.235). How far Shaftesbury's enthusiasm would have carried him is an open question. As Sir Joshua Reynolds pointed out (Discourse XIII) only a habitat that man has not shaped has a "genuine order" untouched by human art or caprice: and therefore it is not a garden. Paradoxically, Shaftesbury also favored *simplicity* of design, for which see Havens 1953.

[28] Addison had earlier (*Spectator* No. 62, May 11, 1711) expressed his scorn for the "Goths in poetry", as he called them "who, like those in Architecture, not being able to come up to the beautiful Simplicity of the old Greeks and Romans, have endeavoured to supply its Place with all the Extravagances of an irregular Fancy". However, ten years earlier, in his *Remarks on...Italy* ("From Rome to Naples"), Addison found a balance between the old and new aesthetics of simplicity and variety. Of the Rotunda, or Pantheon, he wrote, "I must confess the eye is better fill'd at first entering the Rotund, and takes in the whole Beauty and Magnificence of the Temple at one view", but he also praised the interior of St Peter's for its "greater Variety of Noble Prospects".

Plant and Bush. I do not know whether I am singular in my Opinion, but, for my own part, I would rather look upon a Tree in all its Luxuriancy and Diffusion of Boughs and Branches, than when it is thus cut and trimmed into a Mathematical Figure: and cannot but fancy that an Orchard in Flower looks infinitely more delightful, than all the little Labrynths of the most finished Parterres".

Addison had begun his essay by discussing the relationship between Art and Nature. Standing on its head the Renaissance view that the task of art is to improve nature by simplifying her forms, he declared that Art is "very defective" in comparison with Nature. It may attain the beautiful, the strange, the polite or the delicate, but it has nothing of the "Vastness and Immensity which afford so great an Entertainment to the Mind of the Beholder". Its designs moreover are incapable of reproducing the "August and Magnificent" qualities of Nature herself:

There is something more bold and masterly in the rough careless Strokes of Nature, than in the nice Touches and embellishments of Art. The Beauties of the most stately Garden or Palace lie in the narrow Compass, the Imagination runs them over and requires something else to gratifie her; but, in the wild Fields of Nature, the Sight wanders up and down without Confinement, and is fed with an infinite variety of Images, without any certain Stint or Number.

Addison recalled the "artificial Rudeness" of some French and Italian gardens he had seen and declared it to be "much more charming than the Neatness and Elegancy" of the formal garden.[29] He then went on to make the radical – and in the event highly influential - suggestion that an entire estate be "thrown into a kind of Garden" in such a way as to increase both the pleasure and the profit that its owner derives from it:

---

[29] We do not know which these gardens were. Addison's statement is valuable for the light it casts on the prevailing view – e.g. Hays (Benes and Harris 2001) - that "irregular" gardens did not appear in France until the end of the eighteenth or the beginning of the nineteenth centuries.

> A Marsh overgrown with Willows, or a Mountain shaded with Oaks, are not only more beautiful, but more beneficial, than when they lie bare and unadorned. Fields of Corn make a pleasant Prospect, and if the walks were a little taken care of that lie between them, if the natural Embroidery of the Meadows were helpt and improved by some small Additions of Art, and the several Rows of Hedges set off by Trees and Flowers, that the Soil was capable of receiving, a Man might make a pretty Landskip of his own Possessions.

In these few sentences Addison set down the program that, in the ensuing decades, would transform the appearance of the English landscape and its gardens.

Some of the most prominent writers in England added to its intellectual foundations. Pope's role is well known, though his enthusiasm for Nature's freely flowing forms and visual complexity was less wholehearted than is often recognized. As a very young man Pope found himself disliking both the ordered artificiality of the formal garden *and* the untamed aspects of Nature, whose creations he described as "chaos-like together crush'd and bruis'd". He placed himself between these two extremes in a manmade world that is –

> "… harmoniously confus'd:
> Where order in variety we see,
> And where, though all things differ, all agree. [30]

– a paradoxical formulation, this, that perhaps does not invite close analysis. Pope's reference on another occasion to "the amiable simplicity of unadorned nature" moreover casts doubt on whether the middle ground he sought really exists, for nature is neither simple nor unadorned and often (as Pope's contemporaries Addison and Burke, among others, recognized) is anything but "amiable".[31]

In the fourth of his "Moral Essays" (dedicated, one notes, to Lord Burlington, whose avid Palladianism was far from compatible

---

[30] "Windsor Forest", Pope 1831, v.1, p.51.

[31] Pope's "amiable simplicity" is perhaps to be understood as an echo of Renaissance ideas. Some 18th century aesthetic thinking resurrected those ideas with regard to every medium of design, including Nature's designs: see Havens, 1953.

with the ideals of the natural garden[32]) the mature Pope offered both a critique of the formal garden and a manifesto of the revolution against it. He invited his reader to spend a day with him at the villa of "Timon", which has been identified as Sir Robert Walpole's Houghton Hall:

> At Timon's villa let us pass a day;
> Where all cry out, "what sums are thrown away;"
> So proud, so grand; of that stupendous air,
> Soft and agreeable come never there,
> Greatness with Timon dwells in such a draught
> As brings all Brobdignag before your thought.
> To compass this, his building is a town,
> His pond an ocean, his parterre a down:
> Who but must laugh, the master when he sees,
> A puny insect shivering at a breeze!
> Lo, what huge heaps of littleness around !
> The whole a labour'd quarry above ground.
> Two Cupids squirt before: a lake behind
> Improves the keenness of the northern wind.
> His gardens next your admiration call;
> On every side you look, behold the wall!
> No pleasing intricacies intervene,
> No artful wildness to perplex the scene;
> Grove nods at grove, each alley has a brother,
> And half the platform just reflects the other.
> The suffering eye inverted Nature sees;
> Trees cut to statues, statues thick as trees;
> With here a fountain never to be play'd,
> And there a summerhouse that knows no shade;
> Here Amphitrite sails through myrtle bowers,
> There gladiator fight or die in flowers;
> Unwater'd, see the drooping seahorse mourn,
> And swallows roost in Nilus' dusty urn.

All this empty excess, Pope predicted, will be unavailing, and the land will one day return to pursue its authentic purposes:

---

[32] Dr. Johnson (1810, v.3, p.155) remarked that Pope "can derive little honour" from his penchant for associating his work with the names of aristocrats such as Burlington. See also the discussion of Burlington's Chiswick House and its garden on p.220*ff.* below.

> Another age shall see the golden ear
> Imbrown the slope, and nod on the parterre,
> Deep harvests bury all his pride has plann'd,
> And laughing Ceres reassume the land.

Pope to be sure did not reject the notion of refashioning Nature's works to create gardens. But there were limits to what might be done:

> Something there is more needful than expense,
> and something previous e'en to taste – 'tis sense.
> Good sense, which only is the gift of Heaven

To someone designing a garden he offered this advice:

> To build, to plant, whatever you intend,
> To rear the column, or the architecture to bend,
> To swell the terrace, or to sink the grot,
> In all, let Nature never be forgot;
> But treat the goddess like a modest fair,
> Nor overdress, nor leave her wholly bare;
> Let not each beauty every where be spied,
> Where half the skill is decently to hide.
> He gains all points who pleasingly confounds,
> Surprises, varies, and conceals the bounds.
> Consults the genius of the place in all
> Tells the waters or to rise or fall,
> Or helps th' ambitious hill the heaven to scale,
> Or scoops in circling theatres the vale:
> Joins willing woods, and varies shades from shades;
> Now breaks, or now directs, th'intending lines...[33]

... Good advice indeed. But Pope never decided how completely he wished to disown the principles of the formal garden or to affirm those

---

[33] In a slight variation – different perhaps because not constrained by the requirements of meter – Pope told Spence (1964, p.159) that "All the rules of gardening are reducible to three heads: - the contrasts, the management of surprises, and the concealment of bounds". Variety, he added in reply to Spence's question, "is included mostly in the contrasts". He then quoted the two lines of verse above and said they were inspired by Horace's *omne tulit punctum...* (which however refers to the pleasure of mixing the useful with the agreeable).

of the natural garden. His own garden, of which a plan survives (*fig.*7.3) reflects only dimly the principles that were manifested in the gracious tranquility of the natural garden. Although irregular and asymmetric in its layout, Pope's garden had too many straight rows of paths and trees to be more than an unhappy compromise between the conflicting values of the formal and natural garden.[34]

No one had a more telling critique of the formal garden or was a more effective spokesman for what he called "the modern taste in gardening" than Horace Walpole (1717-1797). Witty, eccentric, energetic, Walpole's accomplishments include the first Gothic novel (*The Castle of Otranto,* 1764) as well as the design of his house, Strawberry Hill, that helped to stimulate the Gothic Revival; the books that he published at his Strawberry Hill Press are still valued by collectors for their fine design. Walpole's abhorrence of the formal garden has a curious aspect to it, for he was the son of Sir Robert Walpole, whose gardens at Houghton Hall may have been the ones pilloried by Pope. In *The History of the Modern Taste in Gardening* (1780) the younger Walpole did not refer to the Houghton by name but one wonders whether he did not have it, too, in mind:

> When the custom of making square gardens inclosed with walls was ... established, to the exclusion of nature and prospect, pomp and solitude combined to call for something that might enrich and enliven the insipid and unanimated partition. Fountains, first invented for use ... received embellishments from costly marbles, and at last to contradict utility, tossed their waste of waters into air in spouting columns. Art, in the hands of rude man, had at first been made a succedaneum to nature; in the hands of ostentatious wealth, it become the means of opposing nature; and the more it traversed the march of the latter, the more nobility thought its power was demonstrated. Canals measured by the line were introduced in lieu of meandering streams, and terrasses were hoisted aloft in opposition to the facile slopes that imperceptibly unite the valley and the hill... Statues furnished the lifeless spots with

---

[34] Pope was not the only one to hesitate. Streatfield (1981, p.36) makes the point that even Kent used symmetric layouts, such as in the groupings of trees in Holkham and Euston and in his unexecuted hillside scheme for Chatsworth.

mimic representations of the excluded sons of men. Thus difficulty and expence were the constituent parts of those sumptuous and selfish solitudes; and every improvement that was made, was but a step farther from nature... To crown these impotent displays of false taste, the shears were applied to the lovely wildness of form with which nature has distinguished each various species of tree and shrub. The venerable oak, the romantic beech, the useful elm, even the aspiring circuit of the lime, the regular round of the chestnut, and the almost molded orange-tree, were corrected by such fantastic admirers of symmetry. The compass and square were of more use in plantations than the nurseryman. The measured walk, the quincunx, and the etoile imposed their unsatisfying sameness on every royal and noble garden ... and symmetry, even where the space was too large to permit it being remarked at one view, was ... essential.[35]

The "tiresome and returning uniformity" and "symmetrical and unnatural design" that Walpole castigated had characterized the gardens of the nobility and gentry everywhere in England.[36] It was literary men like Addison, Pope, Walpole and Burke who provided the ideas that led to the rejection of the formal garden and pointed the way back to designs incorporating natural forms. But it was a series of hugely talented and entrepreneurial garden designers who helped instill in moneyed landowners enthusiasm for the new ideas, and drafted plans for putting them into effect. The singular achievement of Charles Bridgeman (1680-1738) and William Kent (1685-1748) was to reverse the previous order of things. Instead of extending the formal garden into the countryside they brought the countryside into what now became the natural garden. It was by them, Walpole wrote, that the garden was "set free from its prim regularity, that it might consort with the wilder country without". Bridgeman, Walpole wrote, "ba-

---

[35] Walpole 1995, pp.25-27. Walpole (*ibid*, p.43) claimed that his father's garden at Houghton was planted in a "simple though still formal style", but Pope's testimony that contradicts this – if indeed Pope was referring to Houghton – seems more reliable.

[36] *ibid*, p.29.

nish'd verdant sculpture, and did not even revert to the square precision of the previous age. He ... disdained to make every division tally to its opposite, and although he still adhered much to strait walks with high clipped hedges, they were the only great lines; the rest he diversified by wilderness". Walpole's highest admiration was for Kent who, as he declared, "leaped the fence and saw that all nature was a garden":

> He felt the delicious contrast of hill and valley changing imperceptibly into each other, tasted the beauty of the gentle swell, or concave scoop, and remarked how loose groves crowned an easy eminence with happy ornament, and while they called in the distant view between their graceful stems, removed and extended the perspective by delusive comparison.
>
> Thus the pencil of his imagination bestowed all the arts of landscape on the scenes he handled. The great principles on which he worked were perspective, and light and shade. Groupes of trees broke too uniform or too extensive a lawn; evergreens and woods were opposed to the glare of the champain, and where the view was less fortunate, or so much exposed as to be beheld at once, he blotted out some parts by thick shades, to divide it into variety, or to make the richest scene more enchanting by reserving it to a farther advance of the spectator's step...
>
> But of all the beauties he added to the face of this beautiful country, none surpassed his management of water. Adieu to canals, circular basons, and cascades tumbling down marble steps, that last absurd magnificence of Italian and French villas. The forced elevation of cataracts was no more. The gentle stream was taught to serpentize seemingly at its pleasure ... The living landscape was chastened or polished, not transformed. Freedom was given to the forms of trees...[37]

The revolution in taste that celebrated Nature and embraced her freely-flowing forms, her pervasive asymmetry, her seemingly boundless visual variety of colors, shapes and textures, changed the appearance of English gardens and parks. Beyond that, though, its

---

[37] *ibid*, pp.43-45.

scope proved to be surprisingly limited. For, while it eradicated the hostility toward Nature that prevailed earlier during the era of plagues, it did not eradicate the *fear* of Nature that had been the cause of that hostility. Rather, and most paradoxically, it joined it to the new enthusiasm for Nature, creating an ingenious blend that combined acknowledgement of the objective fact of Nature's menacing potential with pleasure in the loveliness of Nature's forms. Thus, while Nature remained "dark, uncertain, confused",[38] her danger was now experienced as something – pleasurable! It became, as Addison said, an "agreeable kind of horror"[39]. Burke called it the Sublime and described it as "delightful horror". Its ruling principle, he wrote, arises "in all cases" from the "ideas of pain and danger" that Nature's creations can arouse in us. These, he insisted, give us more intense pleasure than we can get from looking at Nature's conventionally beautiful forms.[40]

Lovejoy claimed that in the eighteenth century "the primacy of irregularity was no longer limited to the theory of landscape-design" but was extended to architecture, too.[41] But that claim greatly overstates the matter. By and large, the advent of the natural garden was not accompanied by a similar revolution in the design of English buildings. The nobility and gentry, which must give Nature free rein in their gardens, continued as before – or perhaps with all those Palladian designs, went on *even more* resolutely than before – to build their houses in rigidly formal, symmetric style.[42] Thus in 1726, when the

---

[38] Burke 1939, Part 2, Sect.ii. During the Renaissance people sometimes referred approvingly to the foreboding that the gloom of a church's interior could instill in a person. Alberti, for example, wrote approvingly of the "*horror qui ex umbra excitatur*" – quoted, with other examples, Germann 1973, pp.56-57. It is possible that these sentiments anticipate the eighteenth century's enthusiasm for Nature's terrors. In our banal age of mass culture we can hear a debased variant of this paradoxical pleasure in the shrieks that emanate from people as they thrill to the terror of riding on roller-coasters.

[39] Addison, *Remarks on Italy* ("Geneva and the Lake").

[40] Burke 1939, Part 1, Sect. viii.

[41] Lovejoy 1955b.

[42] The dissonance or contrast between house and garden upheld, whether intentionally or not, the new values of variety and contrast. It was only in the Renaissance that the dreary insistence on consistency prevailed, so that the house and its grounds were shaped by the same aesthetic themes. (I am reminded of men who, if they are wearing a blue shirt, believe it necessary for that color to be "picked up" by a similar blue in their necktie!) Wotton was perhaps the first in England to call this rule into question, with his dictum that that although gardens should be (in his very limited sense) irregular in appearance, the houses that

innovative principles of natural gardening were already widely accepted, Lord Burlington began building Chiswick House (fig.7.4), which inaugurated the Palladian revival in England and gave renewed vigor to the earlier fashion for symmetric architecture. Yet the *gardens* of Chiswick house were largely designed by William Kent, the selfsame gardener whom Horace Walpole greatly admired as one of the foremost practitioners of the natural garden movement!

This is not to say that there were not voices advocating asymmetric architecture. In one of his lectures Joshua Reynolds commented on the design of additions to existing buildings:

> ... As such buildings depart from regularity, they now and then acquire something of scenery by this accident, which I think might not unsuccessfully be adopted by an architect, in an original plan, if it does not too much interfere with convenience. Variety and intricacy is a beauty and excellence in every other of the arts which address the imagination; and why not in architecture."[43]

A few asymmetric houses were indeed built. Vanbrugh, despite the relentless symmetry of his most notable buildings (above all, Blenheim Palace) gave asymmetric form to the house he designed for himself, the grandiloquently-named Vanbrugh Castle.[44] But these are exceptions. Almost invariably, the buildings set in the graciously freeflowing, asymmetric landscapes and gardens of the eighteenth century were symmetric.

The fundamental difference between the antecedents of Renaissance horticulture and Renaissance architecture may help account for this circumstance. The Renaissance architect had access to an almost inexhaustible supply of Classical artifacts and ruins that could provide him with authentic models on which to base, or on which he could *claim* to be basing, his designs. The designer of a Renaissance garden or landscape however had no such guides available to him. At best, he could hope to infer the principles of Classical garden design from a

---

stood in them should not be. Comp. the point of Wilson (1977, p.17) that in the Elizabethan era it became increasingly common for a preference for symmetric house fronts to be matched by a preference for asymmetric interiors.

[43] Reynolds 1997, p.243.

[44] Somewhat later, in the Regency era John Nash designed a number of asymmetric structures, most notably Cronkhill in Shropshire (Pevsner 2010, pp.141-2).

few ambiguous literary passages, such as Pliny's descriptions of his villas and the grounds in which they stood, or the skeletal remains of one or two ruined gardens such as those of Hadrian's villa in Tivoli. The Renaissance garden, in consequence, strident though its assertions of principle were, could never rival the Renaissance building in its Classical authenticity.

It suffered from a further disadvantage. Compounding its questionable Classical paternity was the fact that it was only by the suspension of belief, and by accepting manifestly fanciful claims regarding the ideal forms of Nature's creations, that anyone could overlook its contrived and artificial appearance and believe that there was anything natural about it. It was easy to accept that a Renaissance building looked "classical", but the fiction that the Renaissance garden looked "natural" was a very tenuous one, indeed.

The Renaissance garden then was neither manifestly Classical nor manifestly natural. It had served the important function of providing Man with a symbolic victory over Nature during those long, long years when Nature was identified with the unspeakable terrors of the plague. But when the time came that that function was no longer needed, the aesthetic itself – inauthentic and ungratifying as it was – could be discarded with few if any misgivings. That time came, of course, with the end of the era of plagues, which removed the psychological (and perhaps the principal) need for this aesthetic. The formal garden was now rapidly dismantled, as though it had never really been more than the stage set that John Evelyn thought it resembled.

There are a number of reasons why, on the other hand, and with only brief intervals, buildings continued to be designed symmetrically. I hope to discuss this matter in a later publication. For now, I will limit myself to a very brief statement of what I think may be the heart of the matter.

Symmetry, as we have seen, is the aesthetic of domination. It came into being to demonstrate Man's domination over Nature. When the plagues finally came to an end, symmetry was readily adapted as an instrument of another form of domination: that of Man over Man.[45]

---

[45] The end of the era of the plagues coincided with the Glorious Revolution of 1688 and the rise of the Whig aristocracy. This period witnessed the final but most ambitious manifestation of Renaissance horticultural principles, exemplified by the creation of immense estates laid out in geometrical shapes, including arrow-straight roads that stretched out from the main house in every direction. The ele-

This function had been anticipated very early on in the relentless symmetry of the two first – immense – buildings of governmental bureaucracy - the Procuratorial buildings of Venice's Piazza San Marco, and the Medicis' Uffizi. Their design conveys nothing of their function; they have all the opacity of a bank of filing cabinets. They offer the eye nothing to explore and thereby ensure that all will see what everyone else sees and, of course, *only* that which those in power wish o show. Symmetry is the domineering aesthetic of authoritarianism (*figs.* 7.5, 7.6). It is veiled, indifferent, unpliable, joyless; it is impressive and uninviting, intimidating and not enlivening. And as the world becomes increasingly subjugated by the centralized power of state and corporation, symmetry will continue to be an effective weapon in the arsenal of control.

---

ment of domination in the aesthetics of these grounds is finely described by John Prest (1981, pp.94-5): "we feel ourselves to be in the presence of autocracy, for if anything is out of place in an avenue or formal garden, the autocrat can spot it at once, and so to can the functionary whom he employs, and of the restless search for domination which Hobbes attributed to mankind".

THE SYMMETRY NORM AND THE ASYMMETRIC UNIVERSE 233

7.2 Stourhead (note the asymmetric bridge)

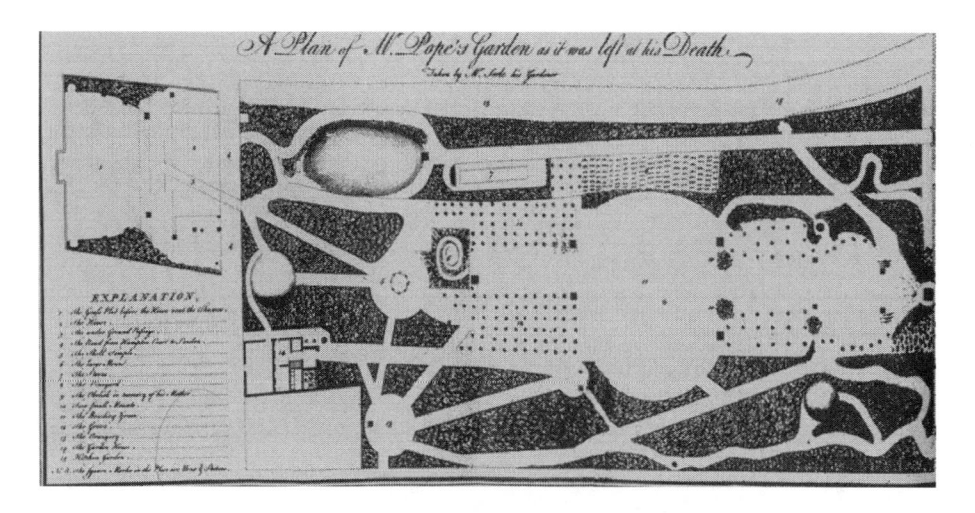

7.3 Plan of Pope's Garden in Twickenham.

7.4 London, Chiswick House

7.5 Paris, Rue Castiglione. Bombastic, opaque, joyless: ordered.
(The column is surmounted by a statue of Napoleon.)

7.6 London, MI6 intelligence agency headquarters

WITTKOWER AND THE SANTA MARIA NOVELLA FAÇADE

8.1 In this image Wittkower's line drawing of Santa Maria Novella is laid over a photograph of the façade, with the scale of the drawing adjusted so that the widths of the upper storey in both are identical. The combined image shows that the upper level does not fit into a square based on the structure's width, as Wittkower claimed, for both the sides and the top of the pediment extend beyond it. (Wittkower never explained why he did not include the horizontal strip between the upper square and the lower two in his construct. Nor did he account for the fact that the middle of the 15 "squares" in the attic is not centered on the structure.) On the lower level the actual sides of the façade extend well beyond Wittkower's drawing, thus establishing that the overall façade fits into a rectangle and not, as Wittkower claimed, a square. This image therefore refutes Wittkower's entire hypothesis.

Note Eight

According to Rudolf Wittkower the concept of symmetry was ignored by most Renaissance architects, among them Leon Battista Alberti. The few who took any notice of it at all treated it as a merely "theoretical" idea and "rarely applied" it in their designs.[1] Consistent with this opinion, Wittkower did not refer to issues of symmetry in his celebrated analysis of the façade – attributed to Alberti[2] – of the church of Santa Maria Novella in Florence. That façade, Wittkower wrote, was "the most important" of the Renaissance, and it "set the example" that would be followed by architects for centuries to come. What made the façade so significant, Wittkower said, and established Alberti as a preeminent Renaissance theorist, was that the design of the façade was based on Classical theories of proportion that Alberti himself had revived.

Wittkower's thesis was that the Santa Maria Novella façade is "exactly circumscribed by [an imaginary] square"; that "the place and size of every single part and detail" of the entire design is "fixed and defined" by a system of proportion based on the progressive halving

---

[1] Wittkower 1949, p.70. Gadol, (1969, pp.109-110), a follower of Wittkower, departs from him by very sensibly defining *collocatio* as "architectural symmetry in the modern sense", but she then returns to the orthodox fold by claiming, on the basis of no authority at all, that Alberti "did not intend his remarks [on *collocatio*] to be carried out" As I point out at the end of this appendix, the three church facades that are known to have been Alberti's work are all symmetric.

[2] Although the attribution of the Santa Maria Novella façade to Alberti is generally accepted the evidence for it is far from conclusive. It rests primarily on a letter to the humanist poet Landino, a contemporary of Alberti, (quoted by Mancini 1882, p.461), which establishes a connection between Alberti and the Santa Maria Novella façade but leaves the nature of that connection unclear. In his first, 1550, edition of the *Lives*, Vasari stated only that Alberti designed "the door on the façade of Santa Maria Novella"; in the 1568 edition he added that Rucellai, patron of the project, received from Alberti, his friend, "not only advice but the actual model" for the new façade. That statement is an ambiguous one and its accuracy a century or more after the event, is open to question. No model of the new façade is known to exist and no contemporary source mentions it. Millon's (1994, p.24) suggestion that for Alberti models were "not a vehicle to present an idea to a client but a means to study and realize an idea" casts some further doubt on Vasari's report. The attribution of the Palazzo Rucellai to Alberti is called into question by Mack (1974).

of that square; that this system of proportion is "the Leitmotif of the whole façade"; that Alberti's *concinnitas* is its intellectual foundation; that the "chief characteristic" of *concinnitas* is *eurhythmia*, which Wittkower described as "the Classical idea of maintaining a uniform system of proportion throughout all parts of a building"; that this idea had been an "axiom of all Classical architecture"; and that Alberti's "strict" application of this system of proportion established the Santa Maria Novella façade as "the first great Renaissance example of *eurhythmia*".[3]

These propositions became - and remain - the standard account, not only of the façade of Santa Maria Novella itself but of some of the basic principles that are said to underlie Renaissance architecture; and they established Wittkower as one of the most influential art historians of modern times.[4]

Yet Wittkower's thesis, for all its elegance and the acclaim it has enjoyed, was deeply flawed at the outset and remained deeply flawed even after the four revisions of it that he published over the

---

[3] Wittkower *op.cit.*, pp. 45-7; 33; p.33,fn.5; and Wittkower, 1940-1941, p.1, fn.4 and p.8, fn.2. Wittkower never indicated how he determined what the dimensions of the Santa Maria Novella façade are, and it is remarkable that he was never challenged to do so. Although Wittkower did not acknowledge his debt to Heinrich Wölfflin's (1889) analysis of the façade's proportions, the line drawing that Wölfflin published with that paper (fig.5, p.48) is uncannily similar to the well-known one of the façade that Wittkower published 60 years later. Wölfflin in turn acknowledged that his analysis was based in part on the statement of Thiersch (1902, IV, I, p.39) that "Harmony results from the repetition of the [proportions of the] main figure of the work in its subdivisions" – "*das Harmonische entsteht durch Wiederholung des Hauptfigur des Werkes in seinen Unterabteilungen*" - a concept that bears more than just a passing, even if unacknowledged, resemblance to the one Wittkower presented as *eurhythmia*.

[4] For general surveys of the influence of Wittkower's work see Millon (1972), and Payne (1994). Among those endorsing Wittkower's analysis of the Santa Maria Novella facade are Gadol (1969, pp.112-114); Borsi (1989, pp.61ff); Evans (1995, p.248); and Tavernor (1998, pp.99-106). More recently Hatfield (2004), has referred to "…the remarkable system of proportions that is best described in a memorable discussion by Rudolf Wittkower". For dissenting views cf. Lorch (1999, pp.45-46) and Ostwald (2000). In the preface to the third edition Wittkower himself attested to the wide influence of his book, though one might question his statement there that Scholfield (1958) was among those who "took [his] cue" from it: and perhaps even more so his modified statement, in the fourth edition (Appendix III), that Scholfield's book was "partly derived from" *Architectural Principles in the Age of Humanism.* Scholfield (*op.cit.*, pp.35, 39, and comp. pp.51-2) argued that Wittkower's stress on the importance of neo-Platonism in Renaissance theory of architecture "has little to recommend it" and that Wittkower's musical theory "does not…explain all the facts of proportion as it was practiced in the Renaissance". Scholfield, (*ibid.*, p.55 fn.3), did however accept Wittkower's analysis of the Santa Maria Novella façade.

course of thirty years.⁵ We can start by noting some problems with his attempts to link Alberti's ideas to Classical architectural theory.

Wittkower's claim that *eurhythmia* was an "axiom of all Classical architecture" ignores the fact that our knowledge of ancient Greek and Roman architectural theories is too limited to sustain plausible generalizations about *any* of their axioms. In particular, Wittkower's claim ignores the uncertainty of scholars today about the meaning of *eurhythmia*. Schofield, indeed, declares that *eurhythmia* as it has come down to us has "no recognized meaning at all".⁶ Uncertainty about what *eurhythmia* means applies *a fortiori* to Vitruvius, Wittkower's sole source for the meaning of the term.⁷ Although one would not know this from reading Wittkower, it is widely agreed that Vitruvius' used *eurhythmia* "so sketchily that his entire concept of it is not clear".⁸ What *does* seem clear however is that *eurhythmia* is not the same thing as "proportion", a concept that is served in Latin by the word *proportio*.⁹ And for Vitruvius at least *proportio* is definitely not the Latin

---

⁵ The first appearance of the study was as part of Wittkower 1940-1941; this essay is referred to here as "the initial version". Successive revised versions appeared in the first edition of *Architectural Principles in the Age of Humanism* (Wittkower 1949, pp.36-41); second edition (Wittkower 1952, pp.36-41); third edition (Wittkower 1962, pp.36-41); and fourth edition (Wittkower 1971 pp.41-47). My remarks here are based primarily on, and cites the pagination of, the fourth and final edition, which was published shortly before Wittkower's death in 1971, and which differs from the third edition only in minor stylistic alterations and in having a new introduction. I identify differences between the fourth and earlier versions when they illustrate significant changes in Wittkower's analysis. Wittkower noted in the original version that it was written in wartime London without access to a copy of the Latin text of Alberti's *De re aedificatoria*, and that he relied instead on "the still unsurpassed" (though in fact at that time the only) English translation of 1755 by Leoni, and on the Italian translation of 1750 by Bartoli. A short train ride however would have brought Wittkower to the library at Eton, where Wotton's copy of *De re aedificatoria* – see M.R. James, *A descriptive catalogue of the manuscripts in the library of Eton College*, 1895 - remained on the shelves until at least August, 1941, when Eton's rare books were sent for safety to the vaults of the Bodleian in Oxford (email communication from an Eton College librarian, Dec.20, 2011).

⁶ Scholfield 1958, p.18; he adds that, although "not obviously nonsense", translations of the term "unfortunately... convey very little sense"- a point illustrated by such renderings of *eurhythmia* as a "nameless grace", Foat (1915); as "abstract beauty, but not necessarily visual beauty, a sense of fine crafting", Wilson Jones (2003, p. 43); and as "shapeliness ... simple, inherent proportions of each element", Taylor (2003, p.25).

⁷ Vitruvius I,ii,3.

⁸ Scranton 1974.

⁹ It is far from clear what role ideas about proportion played in Classical architecture. Coulton (1982, p.66) calls into question whether any modular system was used by Greek architects, at least before the Hellenistic period. Addison (1705, at

equivalent of the Greek *eurhythmia* – as Wittkower would have us believe – but of *analogia*.[10]

Wittkower's attempt to link Alberti's ideas to the concept of *eurhythmia* was also not helped by the fact that Alberti himself never used the term. At first, Wittkower addressed this difficulty by declaring (though without explanation) that "Alberti's definitions coincide to a larger degree with those of Vitruvius than is generally admitted".[11] Sensibly, Wittkower deleted this claim from the later versions of his work.

He did however retain his initial assertion that Vitruvius' *eurhythmia* "is covered by" Alberti's *concinnitas*. "Covered" is an ambiguous term, to be sure, but Wittkower's failure to identify anything else that *concinnitas* also "covers" obliges the reader to conclude that Wittkower regarded *eurhythmia* and *concinnitas* as synonyms.

That however was clearly not Alberti's position. For as Wittkower acknowledged in the initial version, Alberti's *concinnitas* comprises the three distinct standards of *numerus*, *finitio* and *collocatio* and

---

2158-9) calls into doubt the adherence of the ancient Romans to the rules, if any, of proportion: some say, he wrote, that "the Ancients, knowing Architecture was chiefly design'd to please the Eye, only took care to avoid such Disproportions as were gross enough to be observ'd by the Sight, without minding whether or no they approach'd to a Mathematical Exactness: Others ... say the Ancients always consider'd the Situation of a Building, whether it were high or low, in an open Square or in a narrow Street, and more or less deviated from their Rules of Art, to comply with the several Distances and Elevations from which their Works were to be regarded." Addison, in the same discussion, quotes Desgodets, with regard to old Roman pillars, "that the Ancients have not kept to the nicety of Proportion, and the Rules of Art, so much as the Moderns in this Particular" and he cited opinions that blame the allegedly defective proportions of those pillars on the workmen of Egypt and other nations that sent their pillars, already shaped, to Rome.

[10] "... *a proportione quae graece* analogia *dicitur*" - Vitruvius III.i.1 – establishes this altogether unambiguously. Wittkower's erroneous equation of *eurhythmia* with "proportion" is taken directly (though without acknowledgment) from Granger's flawed translation in the Loeb Classical Library edition of Vitruvius. Granger, in turn, evidently derived it from Lewis and Short (1879, *ad loc*) who, venturing into Greek etymology, declared that *eurhythmia* means "beautiful arrangement, proportion, harmony of the parts" - for which their sole citation is the Latin text of Vitruvius I,ii,3, the passage in which Granger translated *eurhythmia* as proportion! Wittkower's use of Granger's translation, it must be said, raises a question about his command of Classical Latin. I would add that one may perhaps infer from Vitruvius III.i.1 ("*ex qua ratio efficitur symmetriarum*") and I.iii.3 ("*et ad summam omnia respondent suae symmetriae*") that the objective of *proportio* is not to achieve *eurhythmia* but *symmetria* (another confusing term in Vitruvius' use of it).

[11] First version, p.8, fn.2. Who those were who were wise enough not to "generally admit" this point is unknown.

is achieved only when all three are met.[12] Of these three however only *finitio* refers to a structure's proportions ("*aut maiorem minoremque redegeris*").[13] Clearly, if *concinnitas* encompasses *numerus, finitio* and *collocatio* it could not be a synonym for the alleged system of proportion that Wittkower wanted his readers to recognize as *eurhythmia*![14]

In the later versions Wittkower dealt with this difficulty *tout court* by deleting his earlier acknowledgement of the threefold nature of *concinnitas*. In its place he now substituted the statement that *concinnitas* is "a correlation of qualitatively different parts – Alberti's *finitio*".[15] Why Alberti would have employed two different terms for what (according to Wittkower) was the same thing remains an open question. Wittkower's "correlation of qualitatively different parts" is an opaque phrase, to be sure, and one without precedent, but it presumably refers to Wittkower's *idée fixe* about the requirement for a uniform system of proportion throughout a building.

More to the point though is that with this sleight of hand Wittkower redefined *concinnitas*, disencumbering it of *numerus* and *collocatio* and making of it merely a synonym for *finitio* (and thus by implication of *eurhythmia* as well)! Quite obviously this definition of *concinnitas* is different from Alberti's. Alberti nowhere declared that *concinnitas* refers to architectural proportion, or that it is attained (let alone that it can only be attained) by the application of a single system of proportions throughout a structure.[16]

---

[12] First version p.1, fn.4; p.8, fns. 1 and 2.

[13] *De re aedificatoria*, Bk. IX, cap.5.

[14] Alberti (1956, p.90f., quoted Panofsky 1972, p.26) offered a somewhat different concept of *concinnitas* in his *Della Pittura*, which was written about 1435, perhaps two decades before *De re aedificatoria*. He emphasized the notion of *concinnitas* as all parts of a work "agreeing with each other", which they will do so if "in quantity, in function, in kind, in color, and in all other respects they harmonize (*corresponderanno*) into one beauty". Without any apparent thought of *numerus, finitio* or *collocatio* this version of *concinnitas* is quite different, or less specific, than the one that appears in *De re aedificatoria* and Wittkower may mistakenly have relied on it instead.

[15] Fourth ed., p.42.

[16] We may mention here that Wittkower's discussion of Alberti's precepts for calculating architectural proportions is also flawed. Alberti stated that these proportions may be derived not only from harmonic chords but from arithmetic and geometric means, even though the ratios of the latter, such as 4:6:9 or 9:12:16 represent dissonances. In the initial version of his study Wittkower declared that Alberti required proportions to be based only on the ratios of harmonic chords: "Proportions recommended by Alberti are the simple relations ... which are the elements of musical harmony". Wittkower retained this misleading remark in all the postwar versions, but added to them the statement that for Alberti "The ratios

Wittkower's attempt to link Alberti's concepts to Classical architectural theory has a further flaw. As anyone familiar with Alberti's work should know, Alberti doubted the value of using literary sources to study Classical architecture. The best way to deduce the theories of the Ancients, he wrote, was to examine the ruins of their buildings.[17] And he dismissed Vitruvius in particular as a source for understanding Classical architecture on the grounds that Vitruvius was often simply unintelligible:

> [Vitruvius'] speech was such that the Latins might think that he wanted to appear a Greek, while the Greeks would think that he babbled Latin. However, his very text is evidence that he wrote neither Latin nor Greek, so that as far as we are concerned he might just as well not have written at all, rather than write something that we cannot understand.[18]

We have seen enough now to conclude that in attempting to derive Alberti's architectural theories from Classical sources Wittkower undertook a task that was bound to fail, no matter how questionable some of the procedures in which he indulged may have been. Unfortunately, Wittkower' tendency to circumvent the evidence would also manifest itself in the empirical portions of his analysis.

It is well known that the friars of Santa Maria Novella had required their architect – presumed by many to have been Alberti - to incorporate extensive portions of the existing medieval façade into his

---

of the musical intervals are only the raw materials for the combination of spatial ratios". He also acknowledged that Alberti was "well aware … that not every proportion using the mean method of calculation results in a musical consonance". These remarks of course do not really correct Wittkower's depiction of Alberti's methods for deriving proportions. Here as elsewhere we see Wittkower's disconcerting propensity to *appear* to correct an earlier statement – sometimes in a way that only adds another layer of error – but without acknowledging the effect of the correction on his overall thesis. It should also be pointed out that, contrary to Wittkower's position, musical proportions were used in architecture long before the Renaissance, Cluny being perhaps the best-known example (Prak, 1966).

[17] *De re aedificatoria* Bk.VI, i - "*Restabant vetera rerum exempla templis theatrisque mandata ex quibus tanguam ex optimis professoribus multa discerentur*".

[18] ibid, "... *sic enim loquebatur, ut Latini Graecum videri voluisse, Greci locutum Latine vaticinentur; res autem ipsa in sese porrigenda neque Latinum neque Graecum fuisse testetur, ut par sit non scripsisse hunc nobis, qui ita scripserit ut non intelligamus*". Krautheimer (1969: "Alberti and Vitruvius") declared that to Alberti Vitruvius was "only a starting point". He also declared, however that "Where Alberti really parts ways with Vitruvius is in his definition of the architect and of architecture", a statement that leaves one wondering what, in fact, the "starting point" could have consisted of once "architect" and "architecture" have been removed from it!

new design.[19] In the initial version Wittkower declared that there is "unambiguous" evidence that Alberti "believed himself to be faithfully continuing the existing portion of the façade."[20] For this claim to be consistent with Wittkower's thesis the retained portions of the earlier façade would have had to conform to a single system of proportion, based on progressively-halved squares, which Alberti then extended to the parts that he added to the structure. Although this possibility cannot be ruled out *a priori*, it requires one to believe that the medieval builders of the earlier façade had themselves worked in obedience to the requirements of what Wittkower represented as *eurhythmia*. But to believe that, of course, would be to deprive Alberti's façade of its distinction as the "Renaissance landmark of Classical *eurhythmia*" that Wittkower had bestowed upon it!

It transpires, though, that even by Wittkower's own reckoning not all parts of the Santa Maria Novella façade were derived from the 2:1 system of proportion that he alleged was used throughout the structure. In the same paragraph in which he characterized that system as "the Leitmotif of the whole façade", Wittkower acknowledged that the ratio of the height to width of the entrance bay is 3:2, and that the square incrustations of the attic are one-third of the attic's height. These ratios, of course, contradict Wittkower's fundamental thesis. Moreover, in the initial version Wittkower had also claimed, consistent with his "Leitmotif", that the volutes on the upper storey could each be fitted into an imaginary square one-half the size of the principal interior squares. In the postwar editions he moved the discussion of those squares from the body of his text to a footnote, where he now declared – *more suo* without addressing its impact on his proportional thesis - that those squares "are related to the height of the attic as 5:3, or to the height of the upper tier as 5:6". This too of course contradicts his thesis regarding the use of the 1:2 proportion throughout the structure.

---

[19] Borsi 1986, p.64; Kiesow 1962.

[20] The evidence is *not* unambiguous. Wittkower's argument rests in part in part on mistaken assumptions about which the earlier portions of the façade were, a matter on which he changed his original opinion. It also rests on Alberti's perhaps too-frequently quoted letter to de' Pasti about embellishing what has been built rather than spoiling what remains to be built. Ambiguous and possibly platitudinous as this statement is, Alberti did not write it about Santa Maria Novella but about his work on San Francesco in Rimini. In the 3rd and 4th eds. Wittkower changed his claim that Alberti wished his façade to be "a faithful continuation in idea and form" of the older parts of the structure and substituted for it the bland truism of "Alberti's patent wish to harmonize [Wittkower presumably used this term in a non-technical sense] his own work with the parts already *in situ*".

Another modification introduced with the 1949 edition was that the square incrustations, as Wittkower called them, of the attic were "related to the diameter of the [central portal's] columns as 2:1".[21] The full significance of this new datum first became apparent only in the third edition, in which Wittkower explained that "it is precisely the derivation of the system from the diameter of the column (Vitruvius' module) that differentiates Alberti's approach from that of the Middle Ages".[22] This modification shifted the entire derivation of the façade from the square in which Wittkower had first claimed that the façade was enclosed to the diameter of the columns flanking the main doorway. But since (according to Wittkower) the attic squares were not identifiably in a 2:1 relation to anything but the diameter of those columns (he said that they were in a 1:3 relation to the attic height) what was now left of Wittkower's entire thesis that "the place and size of every single part and detail" of the entire façade was "fixed and defined" by the progressive halving of the overall façade square – or indeed by any other consistent system?

Wittkower's *volte face* is buried in a mere footnote, his preferred *locus* for announcing fundamental alterations of his thesis. In the text above that footnote however he retained the principal statement of the thesis – the one in which he declared that every detail of the design derives from the imaginary square in which the entire façade is contained. It, along with the footnote that introduced the entirely different derivation from the columnar diameter, thus appear on the same page, seemingly as part of the same thesis: whereas in fact the one is a repudiation of the other.[23]

---

[21] 1st ed., p.49; and in all later editions. This ratio, it should be clear, is not connected with the halving of sizes that Wittkower referred to elsewhere, for it is one-half of something which is one-third of something else, i.e., the height of the attic.

[22] 3rd. ed, p.47, fn.1; also in 4th ed. The reference is to Vitruvius I.2.4, where the diameter *at the base* of the column is given as one of three possible modules for "sacred buildings" (*in aedibus sacris*).

[23] Wittkower's revised version of the analysis, based on the columnar module, is perhaps to be understood in the context of the criticism by Ackerman (1951) who, in a review of the first edition, rejected Wittkower's claim that Alberti's design for the Santa Maria Novella façade had been derived from the Classical model because, as Ackerman pointed out, it "lacks the module which connects plan to elevation". The design, according to Ackerman, was not Classical at all but "the rationalized offspring of the Gothic elevation *ad quadratum* which establishes interrelated modular squares within an embracing square". However, the module that Wittkower now purported to have found did not meet Ackerman's demand for a module that links elevation and plan. As we will see, Ackermann erred in accepting Wittkower's claim that the façade's design is based on the successive halving of squares.

Wittkower's revised thesis however is questionable for another reason, too. Examples of the columnar diameter being used as a module are to be found in pre-Renaissance buildings where not even a reckless scholar is likely to discern the influence of Vitruvius. Santa Maria Novella is often compared to the beautiful church of San Miniato al Monte (circa 1100) that looks down on Florence from across the Arno. The diameter of the un-tapered columns on San Miniato's façade is, by my calculations (based on measurements of my own photographs of the façade) employed as a module on many parts of the structure. It is multiplied by eight to create the diameter of the arches of the blind arcade that runs across the lower storey of the façade; the white marble panels below it are three-tenths the diameter of those arches, which is the same as the width of the recessed panels on the door of the central portal; the two sets of hatch-marks which so brilliantly link the two storeys, are also on this module.[24]

---

[24] Panofsky (1957) implicitly challenged Wittkower's view that the application of a single system of proportion throughout a structure is a Renaissance innovation. The entire system of a High Gothic cathedral, according to him, can be derived from as seemingly inconsequential a detail as "the cross section of one pier". Yet as Ackerman (1991, p.225) notes, in the late 14th century design of Milan's cathedral two different geometrical systems were employed, so that "the chief purpose of the triangle – to provide a unified correlation of the parts and the whole – is ignored". If we are to credit Heydenreich (1996, pp.16-7, 20), at the threshold of the Renaissance the design for San Lorenzo by Alberti's rather older contemporary Brunelleschi (1377-1446) evolved from the square of the crossing and is "governed by a single scale of proportions"; and his Santo Spirito is also based on the crossing square, from which the structure's parts have evolved "in strictly observed proportions" that are "still more exact in their proportional integration" than in S. Lorenzo. Heydenreich unfortunately did not disclose the procedures used to arrive at the measurements on which these statements are based, but one should perhaps not assume that they are necessarily more reliable than those employed by Wittkower. Battisti (1981, fig 197, p. 188) implicitly called into question the role of proportion in Brunelleschi's work by showing that the arches on the right-hand side of the nave of San Lorenzo vary inconsistently in height; as do all the nave arches of San Spirito (*ibid*, fig.216, p.213; p.197), where, moreover, the diagonals of the vaulting in a corner bay are unequal (*ibid*, pl.214). Battisti (*ibid*, p. 114) also discovered that the sides of the drum on which the great dome of Santa Maria del Fiore rests differ in length from one another. These differences have now been measured with pinpoint accuracy by Dalla Nagra (2004, text vol. p.36) whose photogrammetic survey shows that the drum is irregularly asymmetric, with a difference of 57cm. (22-1/2") between the shortest and longest side. Brunelleschi, who is known to have supervised work on the dome very closely, would have known this, of course; and so we may suppose that he accepted the fact that his greatest architectural feat would not have a base of "strictly observed proportions" to rest on. With regard to the prominence with which issues of proportion were considered by Renaissance builders I would add that Vasari – in condemning or praising the design of a building, and in his lengthy excoriation of

The objections raised up to this point would be less consequential if the actual dimensions of the Santa Maria Novella façade were consistent with Wittkower's analysis. Unfortunately Wittkower never disclosed what, in standard measuring units, the façade's dimensions are or how he determined what they are – a curious shortcoming, surely. Uncertainty about those dimensions was put to rest – albeit not completely – when the façade was measured by professional surveyors working under the aegis of the Institute for the Restoration of Monuments of the Faculty of Architecture of the University of Florence; the results were published in 1970.[25]

The survey's measurements, obtained with the use of photogrammetric techniques, are certainly very accurate. They are however incomplete, for the surveyors measured only the left-hand side of the façade. They did so on the grounds that what they mistakenly believed was "the perfect [bilateral] symmetry of the façade" – *la perfetta simmetria della facciata stessa* – made it unnecessary to incur the expense of measuring the other half.

The division of the two halves was set at a line drawn through the middle of the main door into the church. My own photographic analysis however establishes that this door is not accurately centered on the façade and so, because the surveyors left us with no indication of the width of the "half" that they did not measure, we do not know what the width of the entire façade is. We know the façade's height from the survey but that of course is not enough to tell us whether the façade *is* or is not a square.[26] In *fig*.8.1 I have proved that in fact the

---

Gothic architecture – refers only occasionally and in passing to issues of proportion. In his comments one does not even dimly hear references to the criteria stated by Wittkower. And see the excellent discussion by Anthony Blunt (1940, p.91). Blunt's important analysis, which invites reconsideration of the role of rationalistic schemes of proportion during the Renaissance, is seldom referred to by other scholars, for reasons which possibly have more to do with Wittkower's commanding influence than with Blunt's perfidious character and conduct: (among those he acknowledges in the preface to *Artistic Theory* is one "Mr. Guy Burgess").

[25] Bardeschi (1970: plates 1-4 and the section on criteria and methods used in the study on p.23 of the text volume). By a curious omission Bardeschi does not relate these findings – or even refer – to Wittkower's proportional scheme.

[26] The survey shows that the façade is 35.225 meters tall; the "half" that was measured is 17.825 wide. Assuming that this really was one-half of the façade's width would mean that the width of the structure is 35.650 meters, in which case the façade would be 0.425 meters (16-3/4") too wide to form a square. The main door is probably off-center by less than that amount but not, I suspect, by so much less that, given a reasonable margin of error, a square could be said to contain the entire façade. The final resolution of this matter will have to await another survey.

façade is *not* square and that Wittkower's famous diagram of it is inaccurate.

Nevertheless, other measurements obtained by the survey do provide a basis for empirically evaluating Wittkower's thesis. They fail to support Wittkower's claim that the height of the entrance bay is one-and-a-half times its width.[27] They also show that the two storeys of the structure are not the same height, as Wittkower claimed they were. The lower storey is 18.000m. tall, while the upper storey is 17.225m. If, as there is no reason to doubt, Alberti was free to determine the height of the upper storey, the fact that he did not make it the same as the height of the lower storey suggests that he was not interested in making the square of the upper storey equivalent – as it is in Wittkower's scheme – to each of the two squares that comprise the lower storey.

The survey's measurements also establish that on the left half of the attic the figures which Wittkower identified as "squares" are in fact oblong rectangles whose widths vary irregularly (the largest and smallest differ by about 6%), as do the spaces between them (by up to 62%).[28] Although the survey did not measure the *heights* of these rectangles they seem to be much more consistent with each other than their breadths, *but in no instance is the height of the rectangles one-third the height of the attic,* as Wittkower had claimed. Nor is the width of any of these rectangles twice that of the diameter of the columns, as Wittkower had stated in the later versions. Their average width is 5.79% greater than the columnar diameter. There is therefore no fixed relation between these "squares" and the base diameter of the columns on

---

[27] 4th ed., p.46. Comp. Bardeschi, pl. 2, showing that the entrance bay is 8.212m wide and 11.418m tall measured from the outer edge of the two columns at their base, and from the base of the columns to the top of the cornice. The actual height of the bay is therefore 90cm (35-1/2"), or 7.4%, less than the 12.318m (i.e., 3/2 of 8.212) called for by Wittkower. It should be noted, moreover, that the 2:3 ratio given by Wittkower for the proportions of a doorway is not found in *De re aedificatoria*. There, in I.12, Alberti states that the proportions should be either 1:2 or 1:1.414 (i.e., x√2, where x is a square the width of the entrance bay), to accord with which the Santa Maria Novella portal should have a height of either 16.414m or 9.373m. That its dimensions do not conform to Alberti's precepts give us reason to doubt Vasari's report (fn.2, *supra*) that the portal was designed by Alberti.

[28] Bardeschi, *op.cit.*, pl.2. From the left to the middle (the right-hand side of the attic was not measured) the widths of the rectangles, in meters, are as follows: 1.582; 1.564; 1.507; 1.506; 1.503; 1.520; 1.509; 1.492; and of the spaces between them: 0.944; 0.634; 0.624; 0.622; 0.598; 0.585; 0.585; 0.584. The variations in these measures do not bear out Wittkower's notion (4th ed, p.158) that "commensurability of measure [is] the nodal point of Renaissance aesthetics".

the lower story (or between the dimensions of these "squares" and the height of the attic).[29]

But even if Wittkower's description of the attic's "squares" and their relation to the column diameter and to the attic's height had been accurate they would not have sufficed to validate his thesis. What would have been needed is evidence of a consistent ratio linking the columnar diameter to *all* the other details of the façade – "the place and size of every single part and detail" of the structure, as Wittkower had claimed. Wittkower does not offer this evidence. Indeed, most of the details of the facade's design are ignored by him, leaving one to wonder what it was about the misnomered attic "squares" that led him to single *them* out. It should be noted that no later scholar has attempted to relate the columnar diameter to the details of the rest of the structure. My own efforts to do so – I have spent hours on that task – have yielded no such correlation. The empirical evidence for Wittkower's (revised) thesis therefore rests solely on factually incorrect and unexplained assertions about the dimensions of the attic "squares" in relation to the base of the column and the height of the attic.[30]

In 1971, a year after the Florence University survey was published, Wittkower issued the final edition of his *Architectural Principles in the Age of Humanism*. He did not modify his analysis of the façade to reflect the survey's findings, however. Indeed, he did not mention the survey.

Two seemingly empirical studies of the Santa Maria Novella façade have appeared since the publication of the Florence University survey. Franco Borsi, himself a professor of architectural history at the University of Florence, published his book-length study of Alberti in 1973, or two years after the publication of his own department's surveyed measurements of the façade of Santa Maria Novella.[31] In his book Borsi quoted, sympathetically and at length, Wittkower's analysis of the façade's proportions, and accompanied his text with an image in which his own line drawing is superimposed on the surveyed drawing of the façade made by his colleagues at the university. Curiously, Borsi did not refer to this image in his text, but it would seem

---

[29] Bardeschi, pl.2, shows that the diameters of the two columns on the left (those on the right were not measured) vary slightly, within a reasonable margin of error.

[30] Ostwald (2000) speculated that Wittkower's analysis "is traced on inaccurate drawings of the façade", as was the earlier analysis by Wölfflin. The "gross liberties" which Ostwald found in their analyses were not however detected by Evans (1995, p.248) who, on the contrary, described them both as "equally convincing". Ostwald's charge that the two analyses each transposed elements that are well behind the façade onto their elevations is left unexplained, but seems unfounded.

[31] Borsi, 1986, p.68. For the discussion of Santa Maria Novella see *ibid.*, pp.61-75.

to have been intended as confirmation of Wittkower's thesis. The result however is a fiasco. The upper-storey square in Borsi's drawing (which in fact turns out not to be a square) seems to be repeated on the lower storey (in fact, it is a shorter rectangle), where however it reaches down only to a point that is well above the threshold of the church; the "squares" enclosing the upper-storey volutes also prove to be rectangles, each of a different size, while a seeming semi-circle drawn from the right flank to demonstrate the relation between the upper storey and the volutes proves to be an arc of about 160 degrees.[32] Borsi's drawing too has a "no-man's land" between the "squares" of the two storeys, similar to that of Wittkower, and he too neither explained nor referred to it in his text; he also failed to mention the revised version of Wittkower's analysis relating the structure's proportions to the columnar diameter. Borsi did not relate the measurements taken by his own department's surveyors to Wittkower's analysis of the façade proportions, let alone acknowledge that the former refuted the latter.

A British architectural historian, Robert Tavernor, in a study of Alberti's work, included a line drawing of the Santa Maria Novella façade "overlaid with geometry and proportions derived from an encompassing square".[33] This drawing was based, Tavernor wrote, on a photogrammetric image of the façade that had been made in connection with an international exhibition about Alberti sponsored by the

---

[32] Naredi-Rainer (1997, p.179, n.9 and accompanying text), noted that the "square" in Borsi's line drawing of the façade of San Francesco, Rimini, is in fact an oblong. He charged Borsi with "manipulating" the evidence to conform to "the proportions he wanted" to find - "*Wunschproportionen*". Naredi-Rainer was just as unenthusiastic about Wittkower's work on the Santa Maria Novella façade. He rejected Wittkower's thesis regarding the progressively halved squares and noted that "Wittkower's proportions were inexactly drawn". I have not been able to obtain a copy of Naredi-Rainer's work, and know it only from references to it by Lorch (1999, pp. 45-46). Lorch congratulates herself on being the first to notice that Wittkower's system of squares cannot be related to the squares of the great volutes on the upper storey, yet seems unaware that the volutes can only be circumscribed by oblongs and that those oblongs are of different sizes because the two volutes differ from each other in both height and width.

[33] Tavernor 1998, pp.99-106. An indication of Tavernor's *modus operandi* is his acknowledgment (1998, p.103) that although "the façade lacks a precise symmetry... there can be little doubt that Alberti intended the composition of number and geometry to be regarded as perfect". How Tavernor came upon his knowledge of Alberti's undocumented intentions is unclear, as is the question of why Tavernor bothered to measure the structure in the first place if he already knew how Alberti intended it to look! Although Tavernor included Naredi-Rainer (1977) in his bibliography he did not mention the latter's reservations about Wittkower's analysis or his view that the measurements on which Wittkower based his analysis of the façade of Santa Maria Novella are incorrect.

Olivetti corporation and directed by Tavernor and Joseph Rykwert.[34] Photogrammetry uses sophisticated software to measure an object or parts of it with great precision – it is a very reliable procedure. Tavernor's image however is highly inaccurate. For example, although the "squares" in the attic and the spaces between them were shown by the University of Florence survey to be irregularly variable in width and in spacing, in Tavernor's image every rectangle has become a square of the same size except for the penultimate ones on the left and right, which however have the same dimensions as each other; the spaces between all of them are identical. Other irregularities in the structure have also been corrected in this image – for example all the horizontal lines of the frames enclosing the white panels on the lower storey are shown by Tavernor as being on the same plane whereas in reality some of the ones on the left slant upward toward the center. Also, the black-and-white stripes on the pilasters, which do not all match each other in reality, do so in Tavernor's image; and the great volutes on the upper story are the same size as each other. These anomalies cannot be reconciled with Tavernor's claim to be presenting a *bona fide* photogrammetric image. Tavernor's image is a concoction: a fraud. Like Borsi, Tavernor did not address Wittkower's revised version, which has the façade's proportions derive from the diameter of the column. Nor did he attempt to account for – indeed, he did not mention – the discrepancy between the measurements of his photogrammetric image and those made by the surveyors of the University of Florence.

We are obliged to conclude, then, that the evidence – for all that it is incomplete – clearly establishes that no rational system of proportion was used in the design of the façade of Santa Maria Novella.[35] Alberti did not use his standard of *finitio* on the façade, and nothing is gained by trying – as some do – to explain this fact away.[36]

---

[34] Tavernor 1998, p. xi. Precise measurements of any part of photogrammetric images can be made by using shareware programs such as Autodesk Design Review. Tavernor's image had been posted on www.bath/ac/uk/ace/uploads/alberti/smn-e-l.dwf but was removed, without explanation, shortly after I sent a message to Tavernor asking about the discrepancies between his image and the results of the Florence University survey. I have taken the liberty of posting Tavernor's image at www.keepahead.org/SMNis notsymmetric.dwf

[35] Saalman 1959 (p.94 and fns.11, 13), referring specifically to Alberti's contemporaries Brunelleschi and Filarete, suggests that the elevation may be inherent, as it were, in the plan, but this suggestive idea clearly does not apply to Santa Maria Novella, the relation of whose plan to elevation is altogether irrational.

[36] For example: "*a dimostrare che le misure necessariamente offerte dall' Alberti per realizionare le varie pari della composizione all'insieme di facciata non sottostanno rigidamente alle prescrizione del de re aedificatoria, ma si adattano con sufficiente elasticita a rendere communque un'immagine estremamente bilanciata e matura degli*

It must also be said that Alberti's criterion of *collocatio* too did not help shape the design of the Santa Maria Novella façade. The façade is *not* bilaterally symmetric, though its strong and (more or less) central axis somewhat obscures that fact; and in view of the Dominicans' requirement that the architect retain many portions of the medieval façade, which was asymmetric, it would have been impossible to make it symmetric.[37] In this respect, at least, Wittkower was some-

---

elementi architettonici utilizzati, constituendo un insieme basta sulla forma quadrata e sulle sue aggregazioni" - Nocentinni, 1992,p.43.

[37] Ironically, it is implicit in Wittkower's thesis of progressively-halved squares that the façade is bilaterally symmetric: and indeed, Wittkower's line drawings show a structure whose two halves mirror each other in every detail that he recorded on them. A simple test of whether or not the façade is symmetric – one readily available to Wittkower – is to trace the outline and other details of a photograph of the façade on tracing paper and then to reverse the sheet and determine whether the drawing still conforms to the details of the photograph. Today, this can be done even more accurately (as I have done) with any simple computer graphics program. The result of such procedures shows that the façade is not symmetric. Using this procedure, we also find that a square derived from the width of the upper storey extends from the peak of the pediment only to a point well above the attic, where it intersects the bottom of the circular window; that a somewhat wider square which contains the lateral tips of the pediment extends half way into the attic; and that a square derived from half the width of the lower storey is altogether too large for the upper. The irregularity of the attic "squares" is immediately apparent from this procedure. So are the differences between the two great volutes on the upper storey. These, it transpires, are of different widths, reflecting the fact that the upper storey is not centered on the lower; the volutes also differ from each other in height. Imaginary frames encompassing the volutes would therefore be of different sizes, and both would be oblongs, not squares. The procedure also shows that asymmetric arrangements abound on the façade. Specifically, we see that neither the main door nor the portal which contains it – both generally thought to be by Alberti - are centered on the façade or for that matter on each other; that the three smaller arches of the arcade on the right not only differ in width from each other but are significantly narrower than those on the left, which also differ in width from each other; that the arch over the right-hand portal, though wider than the others on its side, is not as wide as the arch over the left-hand portal; that the vertical white panels are all of different widths and that the horizontal lines of the upper row of them on the right-hand side of the façade are higher than those on the left, but that the bases of the four blind arches on the left-hand side are higher than those on the right; and that the black-and-white bands on the pointed arches of the *avelli* on the right side do not meet the horizontal bands on the walls at all the same points as their opposites on the left. (Kiesow 1962, p.3 gives the measurements of the *avelli*, starting with the one on the extreme left, as 2.34, 2.325, 2.34, 2.34, 2.33 and 2.33 meters, but I find that no two have the same width and that the difference between the widest and narrowest is 4.1% The Florence survey does not measure the widths of the *avelli* and its drawings represent them as being identical. These irregularities are not found on the long wall of tombs around the corner in the arcade which runs parallel to the

what justified in not mentioning *collocatio* in his analysis of the Santa Maria Novella façade.

A careful reading of Alberti's architectural treatise moreover raises doubts about whether Alberti intended *finitio* to be a standard that applies to the facades of churches or indeed of any other buildings. In chapters 5 and 6 of the Ninth Book of *De re aedificatoria* Alberti stated that *finitio* can be used for "squares and open areas" and for "platforms". These of course differ from facades by being horizontal and not vertical, and by not being integral parts of (three-dimensional) buildings. Alberti also stated that *finitio* can be applied to three-dimensional structures. However, he specified its use only for determining the proportions of various kinds of rooms. He did not state or imply that *finitio* could also be used for computing the proportions of a building's exterior.[38] *In fact, as far as we know Alberti never addressed the question of what the proportions of a church façade should be.* He did, to be sure, declare (VII.14), that façades of basilicas should be one and a half times as high as they are wide but it is clear that he did not intend this formula to apply to the dimensions of a church façade, for his discussion explicitly contrasts the design of basilicas (as palaces or halls of justice) to that of "temples", or churches.[39] In any case, even if we do

---

nave.) We have already pointed to the asymmetry of the arrangement of the attic's row of encrusted "squares", but the asymmetry of the ribbon of sail-like figures – a Rucellai device – which stretches across the width of the façade remains to be mentioned. (It is not of much matter however, being an asymmetry only because it is a continuous strip and not divided in the middle with the figures on one half reversing the direction of those on the other.) The specific distributions of asymmetric features in the lower portions of the structure do not appear to be guided by any aesthetic or philosophical program. Such, seemingly unprogrammatic, asymmetries are a commonplace in medieval churches. In Florence alone we can point to the earlier facades of Santa Croce and Santa Maria del Fiore and the surviving facades of Santa Maria Maggiore, San Miniato al Monte, and San Lorenzo, among others, as examples of medieval asymmetric facades. It scarcely needs saying that the irregular, asymmetric features of the Santa Maria Novella façade – so different from its representation in the line drawings of Wittkower, Borsi, Tavernor and others - preclude the possibility that a consistent system of proportion was applied to its design.

[38] In *De re aedificatoria* (IX.6) Alberti stated that harmonic chords can determine the ratios of "all the three lines of any body whatsoever" but he specified only the dimensions of "public halls, council chambers and the like" (IX.5), while ratios "not derived from harmony" are used for "the three relations of an apartment"(IX.6).

[39] Rykwert, Leach and Tavernor (Alberti 1988, p.396) write: "One of the problems of reading this passage is that no ancient basilica façade survives, and the passage must therefore be read in reference to Alberti's church facades". This is surely (1) a *non sequitur* and (2) mistaken on two grounds, the first being that Alberti was very clear that his discussion of basilicas did *not* apply to churches and the second being that none of Alberti's church facades is anywhere nearly one and a half

not yet know the overall dimensions of the Santa Maria Novella façade if is obvious that its height is very much less than one-and-a-half times its width.

It is baffling that Alberti never did prescribe the proportions of a church's façade.[40] Failing that, however, one might have expected to find a rational relationship between the height of the Santa Maria Novella façade and the plan of the church, yet no such relationship seems to exist. We are thus left to assume that the proportions of the façade were determined by contingent factors that are unknown to us today but are likely to have included the requirement imposed on the architect to preserve certain portions of the original structure. The fact that the façade does not reflect any of Alberti's ideas regarding *concinnitas* could suggest that the question of his contribution to the façade's design ought to be revisited. [41]

We conclude then that Wittkower's attempt to establish that the standard by which Alberti designed the façade of Santa Maria Novella was the criterion of proportion – *finitio* - has nothing to commend it. Moreover, his attempt to exclude *collocatio* from Alberti's *concinnitas* also has nothing to commend it and calls for no revision of our position that, for Alberti, symmetry was a requirement of the utmost importance. In fact, as we look at the three church facades – those of San Sebastiano and San Andrea in Mantua, and the unfinished facade of San Francesco at Rimini - that we know are by Alberti we find, ironically, that while they conform to the standard of *collocatio* (which is to say that they are symmetric) they do not conform to the proportions Wittkower defined as "*eurhythmic*".[42]

---

times as tall as it is wide. (There is some dispute as to whether Alberti's *latitudo spatii* in this passage refers to the internal measurements of the nave rather than to the width of the whole façade; but Leoni, from Bartoli, gives it as the façade's width, and Orlandi accepts this.) Of course, if Rykwert, Leach and Tavernor were correct that Alberti required church facades to be 3:2 Wittkower's entire hypothesis would be disproved and we would also have good reason to conclude that the Santa Maria Novella façade was not the work of Alberti!

[40] Lang (1965) proposed that the "all-embracing key to the whole building" in Alberti's theory is the ground plan. Ackerman (1954) made a similar point, though about 16th century architects, not 15th century ones as Lang mistakenly wrote. Yet the fact remains that Alberti said nothing on this subject.

[41] See Lorch (1999) for differing views of Alberti's contribution to the overall design.

[42] Wittkower 1971, pp.55, 58. Wittkower's drawing of the hypothetical complete façade of S. Francesco (*ibid*, p.46) renders its proportions as approximately 1:1.10 – not an "eurhythmic" ratio!

Works Cited or Consulted

Ackerman, James (1951): review of Wittkower's *Architectural Principles...* *Art Bulletin*, v. 33.

-- (1954): "Architectural Practice in the Italian Renaissance", *J. Society of Architectural Historians* v.13.

-- (1986): *The Architecture of Michelangelo.*

-- (1991): *Distance Points. Essays in theory and Renaissance art and architecture.*

-- (2002): *Origins, Imitation, Conventions.*

Adam, Leonhard (1936): "North-West American Indian Art and its Early Chinese Parallels", *Man* v. 36.

Addison, Joseph (1705): *Remarks on Several Parts of Italy etc., in the years 1701, 1702, 1703.* (Kindle ed.)

-- (1712): *The Spectator* No. 411, June 21, 1712.

Adler, Borrmann, Doerpfeld and others (1966): *Baudenkmaeler von Olympia* (repr. ed.)

Alberti, Leon Battista (1965): *The Ten Books on Architecture.* Leoni translation, ed. Rykwert.

-- (1966a): eds. Orlando and Portoghesi, *Leon Battista Alberti l'Architettura [De re aedificatoria].*

-- (1966b): *On Painting (della Pittura)* (rev. ed., trans. Spencer).

-- (1988): ed. and trans. Rykwert, Leach and Tavernor, *Leon Battista Alberti on the Art of Building in Ten Books.*

Albertini, Francesco (1863): *Memoriale di molte pitture e statue sono nella inclyta cipta di Florentia.*

Alexander, Christopher, Hansjoachim Neis and Maggie Moore Alexander (2013): *The Battle for the Life and Beauty of the Earth.*

Allen, Grant (1879): "The Origin of the Sense of Symmetry", *Mind*, v.4.

Alsop, Joseph (1982): *The Rare Art Traditions.*

Arnheim, Rudolf (1966): *Toward a Psychology of Art.*

-- (1977): *The Dynamics of Architectural Form.*

Bacon, Francis (1909): "Of Gardens" in *Essays, Civil and Moral* (Harvard Classics)

Bailey, Anthony (2011): *Velazquez and the Surrender of Breda.*

Bailey, Gauvin Alexander et al eds., (2005): *Hope and Healing. Painting in Italy in a ime of Plague, 1500-1800.*

Balanos, Nicolas (1938): *Les monuments de l'Acropole. Relevement et conservation.*

Bardeschi, Marco Dezzi (1970): *La Facciata di Santa Maria Novella*.

Bassin, Joan (1979): "The English Landscape Garden in the Eighteenth Century", *Albion*, v.11.

Battisti, Eugenio (1981): *Filippo Brunelleschi the complete work*.

Beazley, J.D. and Bernard Ashmole (1966): *Greek Sculpture and Paintings*. (repr.ed).

Bell, Corydon (1957): *The Wonder of Snow*.

Bell, Malcolm (1980): "The stylobate and roof in the Olympeion at Akagras", *American J. of Archaeology*, v.48.

Benes and Harris, eds. (2001): *Villas and Gardens in Early Modern Italy and France*.

Bentley and Humphreys (1961): *Snow Crystals* (Dover ed.)

Berenson, Bernard (1953): *Aesthetics and History*.

-- (1960): *The Passionate Sightseer*.

Bergman, David J. and Jacob S. Ishay (2007): "Do bees and hornets use acoustic resonance to monitor and coordinate comb construction?", *Bulletin of Mathematical Biology*, v.69.

Bernal, J. D. (1937): "Art and the scientist" in eds. Martin, Nicholson and Gabo, *Circle: International Survey of constructive art*.

-- (1955): review of Weyl's "Symmetry", *The British J. for the Philosophy of Science*, v.5.

Betts, Richard J. (1993): "Structural Innovation and Structural Design in Renaissance Architecture", *J. Society of Architectural Historians*, v.52.

Bialostocki, Jan (1963): "Renaissance Concept of Nature and Antiquity", *Acts of the Twentieth International Congress of Art History*.

Biondo, Flavio (2005): *Italy Illuminated*, ed. White.

Blomfield, Reginald (1892): *The Formal Garden in England* (repr. ed.)

Blunt, Anthony (1940): *Artistic Theory in Italy 1450-1600*.

Boardman, John (1968): *Archaic Greek Gems. Schools and artists in 6th and early 5th centuries*.

Boas, Franz (1907): "Notes on the blanket designs" in George T. Emmons, "The Chilkat Blanket", *American Museum of Natural History Memoirs* v.3, as reprinted in Jonaitis (1995).

-- (1927): *Primitive Art* (Dover repr. 1955).

Boase, T. S. R. (1979): *Giorgio Vasari. The man and the book*.

Bober and Rubinstein (2010): *Renaissance Artists and Antique Sculpture: a handbook of sources* (2nd.ed.)

Boccaccio, Giovanni (1972): *The Decameron* (trans. McWilliam).

Bonsanti, Giorgio (1997): *The Basilica of St. Francis of Assisi Glory and Destruction*.

Borsi, Franco: (1986): *Leon Battista Alberti The Complete Works*.

Boucher, Bruce (2000): "Nature and the Antique in the works of Andrea Palladio", *J. Society of Architectural Historians* v.59.

Boyle, Robert (1979): *Selected Philosophical Papers of Robert Boyle* (ed. Stewart).

Brink, Joel (1978): "Carpentry and Symmetry in Cimabue's Santa Croce Crucifix", *Burlington Magazine*, v. 120.

Brown, Beverly Louise and Diana E.E. Kleiner (1983): "Giuliano da Sangallo's drawings after Ciriaco d'Ancona: Transformation of Greek and Roman antiquities in Athens", *J. Society of Architectural Historians* v.42.

Buddenseig, T. (1971): "Criticism and Praise of the Pantheon", in ed. R. R. Bolgar, *Classical Influences on European Culture A.D. 500-1500*.

Bunzel, Ruth L. (1972): *The Pueblo Potter a study of creative imagination in primitive art*.

Burckhardt, Jakob (1985): *The Architecture of the Italian Renaissance* (ed. Murray).

Burke, Edmund (1796): "Letter to a Noble Peer".

-- (1939): *On the Sublime and Beautiful* (Harvard Classics)

Burke, John G. (1966): *Origins of the Science of Crystals*.

Burns, H. (1971): "Quattrocento Architecture" in ed. R.R. Bolgar, *Classical Influences on European Culture AD 500-1500*.

Businani, Alberto and Raffaello Bencini (1993): *Le Chiese di Firenze Quartiere di San Giovanni*.

Caglioti, Giuseppe, (1992): *The Dynamics of Ambiguity*.

Cantor, Norman (2001): *In the Wake of the Plague*.

Cardini, Franco and Massimo Miglio (2002): *Nostalgia del Paradiso: Il giardino medievale*.

Carmichael, Ann G. (1986): *Plague and the Poor in Renaissance Florence*.

Caroti, G. and A. de Falco (2002): "Geometric Survey for the Structural Assessment of the Architectural Heritage: the Case of the Cupola of the Baptistery of S. Giovanni e Reparata in Lucca", *International Archive of the Photogrammetry ... Sciences*, v.34.

Caruth, Cathy, ed. (1995): *Trauma: Explorations in Memory*.

Castell, Robert (1728): *The Villas of the Ancients*.

Chambers William (1772): *Dissertation on Oriental Gardening*.

Chiarini, Marco and Alessandro Marabottini, eds.(1994): *Firenze e la sua immagine. Cinque secoli di vedutismo*.

Choisy, Auguste (1865): "Note sur la courbure dissymétrique des degrés qui limitent au couchant la plate-forme du Parthenon", *Academie des Inscriptions et Belles-Lettres*, NS v.I

Choisy, Auguste (1996): *Histoire de l'Architecture* (repr.ed.)

Clark, H.F. (1944): "Lord Burlington's Bijou, or Sharawaggi at Chiswick", *Architectural Review*, v.110.

Clark, Kenneth (1949): *Landscape into Art*.

-- (1981): *The Art of Humanism*.

Cohn, Samuel K. (2002): *The Black Death Transformed: disease and culture in early Renaissance Europe.*

Cole, Bruce (1973): "Old and New in the Early Trecento", *Mitteilungen des Kunsthistorischen Institutes in Florenz*, v.XVII.

-- (1976): *Giotto and Florentine Painting1280-1375.*

Collyer, Mary (1749): *Felicia to Charlotte: being letters from a young lady in the country...*

Colonna, Francesco (1499): *Hypnerotomachi Poliphili ubi humana omnia non nisi somnium esse ostendit at que obiter plurima scitu sanequam digna commemorat* (London, 1904 facsimile ed.)

-- (1999): *Hypnerotomachia Poliphili*, trans. Godwin.

Comito, Terry (1957): *The Idea of the Garden in the Renaissance.*

Cook, R.M. (1972): *Greek Art. Its development, character and influence.*

Cooper, Frederick A. (1996): *The Temple of Apollo Bassitas*. v. 1.

Cotton, Charles (1683): *Wonders of the Peake* (2nd. ed.)

Coulton, G.G. (1930): *The Black Death.*

Coulton, J. J. (1982): *Ancient Greek Architects at Work. Problems of structure and design*, (2nd ed.)

Crawford, Virginia (1978): "Northwest Coast Indian Art". *Bulletin of the Cleveland Museum of Art*, v. 65.

Cresti, G. et al. (1987): *L'Avventura della Facciata.*

Crisp, Frank (1924): *Medieval Gardens.*

Crosby, Sumner McKnight (1987): *The Royal Abbey of Saint-Denis from its beginnings to the death of Suger,475-1151.*

Dallington, Robert (1605): *A Survey of the Great Dukes State of Tuscany.*

Darwin, Charles (1998): *Origin of Species*, (4th ed; Modern Library ed.)

Davis, Michael (2002): "On the Drawing Board: Plans of the Clermont Cathedral Terrace" in Wu, 2002.

Deaux, George (1960): *The Black Death 1347.*

Defoe, Daniel (1927): *Tour through the Whole Island of Great Britain*, (Everyman ed.)

Delougaz, P. (1960): "Architectural Representations on Steatite Vases", *Iraq* v.22.

Descartes, Renee (1824): *Oeuvres de Descartes Les Météores.*

Dillingham, Rick (1992): *Acoma & Laguna Pottery.*

Dinsmoor, W. B. (1950): *The Architecture of Ancient Greece*, (3rd ed.)

Doerpfeld, Wilhelm (1892): *Olympia.*

Doumas, Christos (1983): *Cycladic Art. Ancient Sculpture and Pottery from the N. P. Goulandris Collection.*

Downing, A.J. (1844): *Cottage Residences; or a series of designs ...* (2nd. ed.)

Dresser, William W. and Michael C. Robbins (1975): "Art Styles, Social Stratification and Cognition: an analysis of Greek vase painting", *American Ethnologist* v.2.

Duddy, Michael C. (2008): "Roaming Point Perspective: a dynamic interpretation of the visual refinements of the Greek Doric temple", *Nexus Network Journal* v.10.

Due Granduchi (1987): *Due Granducchi Tre Re e Una Facciata.*

Dupree, A. Hunter (1951): "Some letters from Charles Darwin to Jeffries Wyman" *Isis*, v.42.

Durand, J-N-L: (2000): *Precis of the lectures on architecture,* (trans. Pritt).

Dutton, Ralph (1950): *The English Garden* (2nd.ed.)

Eco, Umberto (1986): *Art and Beauty in the Middle Ages.*

Eisenman, Russel and H. K. Gellens (1968): "Preferences for Complexity-Simplicity and Symmetry-Asymmetry", *Perceptual and Motor Skills* v.26.

Emmons, George T. 1907): "The Chilkat Blanket", *American Museum of Natural History Memoirs* v.3, pt.4.

Etlin, Richard A. (1987): "Le Corbusier, Choisy, and French Hellenism: The Search for a New Architecture", *Art Bulletin*, v.69.

Evans, Robert (1995): *The Projective Cast. Architecture and its Three Geometries.*

Evelyn, John (1906): *The Diary of John Evelyn* (ed. Dobson).

Ferguson, Kitty (2008): *The Music of Pythagoras.*

Fergusson James, (1849): *An Historical Inquiry into the true principles of beauty in art.*

Festinger, Leon (1956): *When Prophecy Fails.*

Fewkes, Jesse Walter (1895-6):"Designs on Prehistoric Hopi Pottery" in *Seventeenth Annual Report of the Bureau of American Ethnology to the Secretary of the Smithsonian Institution.*

Filarete (1965): *Filarete's Treatise on Architecture* (ed. Spencer).

Fischer, J.L. (1961): "Art styles as cultural cognitive maps", *American Anthropologist* v. 63.

Fisher, Sally (1995): *The Square Halo and other mysteries of western art.*

Foat, F. W. G. (1915): "Anthropometry of Greek Statues", *J. of Hellenic Studies* v.35.

Foster, Philip (1981): "Lorenzo de' Medici and the Florence Cathedral façade", *Art Bulletin*, v. 63.

Frank, F.C. (1974): "Descartes' Observations on the Amsterdam Snowfalls of 4, 5, 6 and 9 February, 1634", *J. of Glaciology*, v.13.

Frankfort, Henry (1969): *The Art and Architecture of the Ancient Orient.* (4th ed.)

Freart. Roland (1664): *A Parallel of the Ancient Architecture with the Modern,* (trans. John Evelyn).

Friedlaender, Max J. (1969): *Reminiscences and Reflections* (trans. Magurn).

Friedman, Alice T. (1998): "John Evelyn and English Architecture" in eds. Therese O'Malley and Joachim Wolschke-Bulmahn, *John Evelyn's "Elysium Britannicum and European Gardening*.

Frisch, Karl von (1975): *Animal Architecture* (trans. Gombrich).

Frommel and Adams (2000): *The Architectural Drawings of Antonio da Sangallo the Younger and his Circle*.

Furukawa, Yoshimoro (1997): "Faszination der Schneekristalle - wie ihre bezaubernden Formen..." *Chemie in unsererZeit*, v.31.

-- and Wettlaufer, John S. (2007): "Snow and ice Crystals", *Physics Today*.

Gadol, Joan (1969): *Leon Battista Alberti Universal Man of the Renaissance*.

Gandy, Joseph (1805): *Designs for Cottages, Cottage Farms, and other Rural buildings, including gates and lodges*.

Gardner, Helen (2005): *Gardner's Art through the Ages*.

Germann, Georg (1973): *Gothic Revival in Europe and Britain*.

Gillerman. David M. (1999): "Cosmopolitanism and *Campanilisimo*: Gothic and Romanesque in the Siena Duomo Façade", *College Art Bulletin* v. 81.

Gilman, Ernest B. (2009): *Plague Writing in Early Modern England*.

Giorgio, Francesco di Martini (1967), *Tratatti di Architettura* (ed. Maltese).

Girouard (1978): *Life in the English Country House*.

Goethe, J. W. von (1963): "Kunst und Altertum" in *Aus einer Reise am Rhein, Main und Neckar*.

-- (1982): *Italian Journey* (trans Auden and Mayer).

Goldthwaite, Richard A. (1993): *Wealth and the Demand for Art in Italy 1300-1600*.

Gombrich, E.H. (1966): *Norm and Form*.

-- (1979): *The Sense of Order. A study in the psychology of decorative art*.

-- (2002): *The Preference for the Primitive. Episodes in the history of western taste and art*.

Goodyear, W.H. (1905): *Illustrated Catalogue of Photographs and Surveys of Architectural Refinements in Medieval Buildings*.

-- (1912): *Greek Refinements. Studies in temperamental architecture*.

Grew, Nehemiah (1673): "On the Nature of Snow", *Philosophical Transactions of the Royal Society*, v.8.

Gunther, R. W. T (1928): *The Architecture of Sir Roger Pratt*.

Hall, James (2005): *Michelangelo and the Reinvention of the Human Body*.

Hargittai, Istvan and Magdolna (1986): *Symmetry through the eyes of a chemist*.

-- (1994): *Symmetry a unifying concept*.

Haselberger, Lothar (1999): *Appearance and Essence, Refinements of Classical Architecture: Curvature*.

Hatfield, Rab (2004): "The funding of the façade of Santa Maria Novella", *J. of the Warburg and Courtauld Institutes*, v.67.

Hattenhauer, Darryl (1984): "The Rhetoric of Architecture: A Semiotic Approach", *Communication Quarterly*, v.32.

Hauser, Arnold (1965): *Mannerism. The Crisis of the Renaissance & the Origin of Modern Art*.

Havens, Raymond (1953): "Simplicity, a changing concept", *J. of the History of Ideas*, v.14.

Hawthorne, Nathaniel (1874): *Passages from the French and Italian Notebooks*.

Hays, David L. (2001): "'This is not a Jardin Anglais'. Carmontelle, the Jardin de Monceau, and Irregular Garden Design in Late-Eighteenth Century France", in eds. Benes and Harris, *Villas and Gardens in early modern Italy and France*".

Hemelrijk, Jaap M. (1984): *Caeretan Hydriai, Forschungen zur antiken Keramik* (2nd series, Kerameus v.5).

Hemelrijk, Jaap M. (2000): "Three Caeretan Hydriai in Malibu and New York" *Greek Vases in the J. Paul Getty Museum*, v.6.

Hersam, C., Nathan Guisinger, and Joseph Lyding (n.d.):"Silicon-Based Molecular nanotechnology", foresight.org/conference/MNT7/Papers/Hersa

Herlihy, David (1997): *The Black Death and the Transformation of the West.*

Hersey, David (1977): review of Heydenreich (1996): *JSHA*, v.36.

Heydenreich, L.H. (1937): "Pius II als Bauherr von Pienza", *Z. für Kunstgeschichte*, v.6.

-- (1996): *Architecture in Italy 1400-1500* (rev. ed.)

Hiscock, Nigel (2000): *The Wise Master Builder: Platonic Geometry in Plans of Medieval Abbeys and Cathedrals.*

Hiscock, Nigel (2002): "A Schematic Plan for Norwich Cathedral" in Wu, 2002.

Hogarth, William (2007): *The Analysis of Beauty* (ed. Paulson).

Holm, Bill (1965): *Northwest Coast Indian Art. An analysis of form.*

Holanda, Francisco de (2006): *Dialogues with Michelangelo* (ed. Hemsoll).

- (1963): Portuguese text (first two dialogs only): *Historia e antalogia da Literatura Portuguesa* v.16.

Hommel, Hildebrandt (1987): *Symmetrie in Spiegel der Antike.*

Hon, Giora and Bernard Goldstein (2008): *From Summetria to Symmetry, the making of a revolutionary scientific concept.*

Honour, Hugh (1961): *Chinoiserie. The vision of Cathay.*

Hooke, Robert (1665): *Micrographia.*

Hopkins, Clark (1979): *The Discovery of Duro-Europos.*

Horn and Born (1979): *The Plan of St Gall. A study of the architecture and economy of, and life in a paradigmatic Carolingian monastery.*

Hubbs, Carl and Laura (1944): "Bilateral asymmetry and bilateral variation in fishes", *Papers of the Michigan Academy of Science, Arts, and Letters*, v.30.

Huizinga, J. (1954): *The Waning of the Middle Ages* (Anchor ed.)

Humphreys, A. R. (1937): *William Shenstone. An eighteenth-century portrait.*

Hurston, Zora Neale (1983): "Characteristics of Negro Expression" (1934) repr. in *Zora Neale Hurston, The Sanctified Church.*

Hurwit, Jeffrey (1997): "Image and Frame in Greek Art", *American J. of Archaeology*, v.81.

-- (2002): "Reading the Chigi Vase", *Hesperia* v.71.

Hussey, Christopher (1967): *English Gardens and Landscapes 1700-1750.*

Huxley, T. H. (1888): *Physiography, an introduction to the study of nature.*

Hyams, Edward (1971): *A History of Gardens and Gardening.*

Iacopi, Irene (2008): *The House of Augustus Wall Paintings.*

Jablan, Slavik A. (1955): *Theory of Symmetry and Ornament.*

Jacobsthal, Paul (1925): "The Ornamentation of Greek Vases", *Burlington Magazine*, v.47.

Jaeger, F.M. (1917): *Lectures on the principle of symmetry and its application in all natural sciences.*

James, John (1982): *Chartres, the masons who built a legend.*

James, M.R. (1895): *A descriptive catalogue of the manuscripts in the library of Eton College.*

James, P.D. (2005): *The Lighthouse.*

Johnson, Samuel (1810): *The Lives of the Most Eminent English Poets with critical observations on their works* (new ed.)

Jonaitis, Aldona ed., (1995): *A Wealth of Thought. Franz Boas on Native American Art.*

Jourdain, Margaret (1948): *The Work of William Kent.*

Kahn, Charles H. (1960): *Anaximander and the Origins of Greek Cosmology* (repr. ed.)

Kallenberg, Mary Hunt and Anthony Berland, (1972): *The Navajo Blanket.*

Kellogg, Rhoda (1970): *Analyzing Children's Art.*

Kemp, Martin (1977): "From 'Mimesis' to 'Fantasie', the Quattrocento Vocabulary of Creation, Inspiration and Genius in the Visual Arts", *Viator*, v.8.

Kepler, Johannes (2010): *The Six-Cornered Snowflake.*

Ker, J.B. (1840): *Essay on the Archaeology of our popular phrases.*

Kiesow, Gottfried (1962): "Die gotische Suedfassade von S. Maria Novella in Florenz", *Zeitschrift für Kunstgeschichte*, v.25.

Kirk, G.S., J.E. Raven and M. Schofield (1983):*The Pre-Socratic Philosophers* (2nd. ed.)

Klarreich, Erica (2000):"Foams and Honeycombs", *American Scientist*, v.88.

Kliger, S. (1952): *The Goths in England.*

Koch, H (1955): Studien zum Theseustempel. *Abhandlung des Saechsischen Akademie der Wissenschafft*, v.47.

Korres M. (1999): *"Refinements of Refinements"* in Haselberger 1999.

Krautheimer, Richard (1969): *Studies in early Christian, Medieval and Renaissance art.*

Kruft, H-w (1994): *A History of Architectural Theory.*

Kunst, Christiane (n.d.): "Paestum Imagery in European Architecture", dialnet. unirioja.es/servlet/articulo? Codigo =2663376

LaChapelle, Edward (1960): *Field Guide to Snow Crystals.*

Ladis, Andrew (2008): *Giotto's O: Narrative, Figuration and Pictorial Ingenuity in the Arena Chapel.*

Landauro, Inti (2013): "A Greek Goddess Gets A Makeover", *Wall Street Journal* Aug. 28, 2013, sect. D1.

Lang, S. (1965): "L. B. Alberti's Use of a Technical Term", *J. of the Warburg and Courtauld Institutes*, v.28.

-- and N. Pevsner (1949):"Sir William Temple and Sharawaggi", *Architectural Review*, v.106.

Lawrence, A.W. (1967): *Greek Architecture.*

Le Clerc, Sebastien (1732): *A Treatise of Architecture.*

Lederman, Leon M. and Christopher T. Hill (2008): *Symmetry and the Beautiful Universe.*

Lefaivre, Liane (1997): *Leon Battista Alberti's Hypnerotomachia Poliphili.*

Leisinger, Hermann (1957): *Romanesque Bronzes. Church Portals in Medieval Europe.*

Lewis and Short (1879): *A Latin Dictionary.*

Lewis, W. S. (1960): *Horace Walpole.*

Libbrecht, Ken (2005): "The physics of snow crystals", *Rep. Prog. Phys.* v.68.

-- (2006): Ken Libbrecht's Field Guide to Snowflakes.

Licht, Kjeld de Fine (1966?): *The Rotonda in Rome. A Study of Hadrian's Pantheon.*

Livio, Mario (2006): *The equation that couldn't be solved. How mathematical genius discovered the language of symmetry.*

Lloyd, Joan E. Barclay (1986): "The Building History of the Medieval Church of S. Clemente in Rome", *J. Society of Architectural Historians*, v.45.

Lloyd, Seton (1980): *Foundations in the Dust*, (rev.ed.)

Lorand, Ruth (2003-4): "The Role of Symmetry in Art", *Symmetry: Culture and Science*, vols. 14-15.

Lorch, Ingomar (1999): *Die Kirchenfassade in Italien von 1450 bis 1527: Die Grundlagen durch Leon Battista Alberti und die Weiterentwicklung des Basilikalen Fassadenspiegels.*

Lorenzoni, Mario, editor (2007.): *La Facciata del Duomo di Siena. Iconografia, Stile, Indagini Storiche e Scientifiche.*

Lorris, Guillaume de and Jean de Meun (1995): *The Romance of the Rose* (3rd ed., trans. Dahlberg).

Lovejoy, Arthur O. (1955a): "The Chinese Origin of a Romanticism", repr. in *Essays in the History of Ideas.*

-- (1955b): "The First Gothic Revival", repr. in *ibid.*

Lowic, Lawrence (1983): "The Meaning and Significance of the Human Analogy in Francesco di Giorgio's Trattato", *J. Society of Architectural Historians,* v.42.

Luecke, D. (1994): in eds. Rykwert and Engel: *Leon Battista Alberti.*

MacDonald, William L. (1982): *The Architecture of the Roman Empire An Introductory Study.*(rev.ed)

Machover, Karen (1949): *Personality Projection in the Drawing of the Human Figure.*

Mack, Charles (1974): "The Rucellai Palace: Some New Proposals", *Art Bulletin,* v.56.

-- (1987): *Pienza: the Creation of a Renaissance City.*

Magnus, Olaus (1996): *Historia de Gentibus Septentrionalibus,* (trans. Fisher and Higgins).

Mainzer, Klaus (1996): *Symmetries of Nature.*

Malins, Edward (1966): *English Landscaping and Literature 1660-1840.*

Mancini, G. (1882):*Vita di Leon Battista Alberti.*

Manetti, Antonio (1970): *The Life of Brunelleschi,* (ed. Saalman).

Martin, Constance (1988): "William Scoresby (1789-1857) and the open polar sea", *Arctic* v.41.

Marvell, Andrew (1927): *The Poems and Letters of Andrew Marvell* (ed. Margoliouth).

Mason, B. J. (1992): "Snow crystals, natural and man- made", *Contemporary Physics,* v. 33.

Masson, Georgina (1961): *Italian Gardens.*

Mateer, David (2000): *Courts, Patrons and Poets.*

Mattusch, Carol C. (1988): *Greek Bronze Statuary.*

McBeath, Michael, Diane Schiano and Barbara Tversky (1997): "Three-dimensional Bilateral symmetry bias in judgments of figural identity and orientation", *Psychological Science* v.8.

McCann, A. M. (1978): *Roman Sarcophagi in the Metropolitan Museum of Art.*

McCarthy, Michael (1987): *Origins of the Gothic Revival.*

McManus, I.C. (2004): "Right-Left and the Scrotum in Greek Sculpture", *Laterality,* v.2.

-- (2005): "Symmetry and Asymmetry in Aesthetics and the Arts", *European Review,* v. 13.

Meiss, Millard (1951): *Painting in Florence and Siena after the Black Death.*

Michelis, P.A. (1955): "Refinements in Architecture", *J. of Aesthetics and Art Criticism,*v.14.

Millon, H. (1958): "The Architectural Theory of Francesco di Giorgio", *Art Bulletin*.

-- (1972): "Rudolf Wittkower's 'Architectural Principles', its influence on the development and interpretation of modern architecture", *J. Society of Architectural Historians*, v.31.

-- (1994): "Models in Renaissance Architecture" in Millon and Lampugnani, eds., *The Renaissance. From Brunelleschi to Michelangelo. The Representation of Architecture*.

Milton, John (1958): *The Poems of John Milton*, (ed. Darbishire).

Mitten, David Gordon and Suzannah F. Doeringer (1967): *Master Bronzes From The Classical World*.

Mogono, Choji and Chung Woo Lee (1966): "Meteorological Classification of Natural Snow Crystals", *J. of the Faculty of Science, Hokkaido University*, Ser.VII, II:4.

Mokhopadhyay, Swapna (2009): "The decorative impulse: ethnomathematics and Tlingit basketry", *ZDM Mathematics Education*, v. 41.

Molini, Giuseppe (1820): *La Metropolitana fiorentina illustrata*.

Montesquieu (1777): *The Complete Works of M. de Montesquieu*.

Montesquieu (1825): *Oeuvres* (ed. De Plancy).

Morgan, Luke (2006): *Nature as Model: Salomon de Caus and early 17th century landscape design*.

Morolli, Luchinat and Marchetti, eds. (1992): *L'Architettura di Lorenzo il Magnifico*.

Morris, William (2004): *News from Nowhere* (Dover reprint).

Morrison, Alan S, J. Kirshner and A. Molho (1985): "Epidemics in Renaissance Florence", *Am. J. Publish Health*, v.75.

Muet, Pierre Le (1623): *Manière de bâtir pour toutes sortes de personnes*.

-- (1670): *The Art of Fair Building*, (trans. Pricke).

Mullett, Charles F. (1936): "The English Plague Scare of 1720-1723", *Osiris*, v.2.

Murray, Ciaran (1998): "Sharawadgi Resolved", *Garden History*, v.26.

Nakaya, Ukichiro, (1954): *Snow Crystals, natural and artificial*.

Naredi-Rainer, Paul (1977): "Exkurs zum Problem der Proportionen bei Alberti", *Zeitschrift fuer Kunstgeschichte*, v.40.

Negra, Ricardo Della (2004): *La Cupola di Santa Maria del Fiore. Il rilievo fotogrammatico*.

Nocentinni, Carlo (1992): in eds., Morolli, Luchinat and Marchetti, *L'Architettura di Lorenzo il Magnifico*.

Norman, Diana, (1995): *Siena, Florence and Padua. Art, Society and Religion 1280-1400*.

Oechslin, Werner (1985): "Symmetrie – Eurythmie: oder, 'Ist Symmetrie schön?", *Daidalos*, v.15.

Ogden, H. V. S. (1949): "The principles of variety and contrast in seventeenth century aesthetics, and Milton's poetry", *J. of the History of Ideas*, v.10.

Onians, John, (1992): "Architecture, Metaphor and Mind", *Architectural History*, v.35.

Ostwald, Michael J (2000): "Under Siege: the Golden Mean in Architecture", *Nexus Network Journal*, v.2.

Palladio, Andrea (1570): *I Quattro Libril dell' Architettura.*

-- (1997): *The Four Books on Architecture* (trans. Tavernor and Schofield).

Panofsky, Erwin (1955): *Meaning in the Visual Arts.*

-- (1957): *Gothic Architecture and Scholasticism.*

-- (1972): *Renaissance and Renascences in Western Art.*

Paret, Peter (1997): *Imagined Battles. Reflections of War in European Art.*

Pasteur, Louis (1874): *Works*, v.I. (from *Comptes Rendus de l'Académie des Sciences*, June 1, 1874).

Payne, Alina (1994): "Rudolf Wittkower and architectural principles in the age of modernism", *J. Society of Architectural Historians*, v.53.

-- (1999): *The Architectural Treatise in the Renaissance.*

Pelt, Robert and Carroll Westfall (1993): *Architectural Principles in the Age of Historicism.*

Pennick, Nigel (2012): *The Sacred Architecture of London.*

Penrose, Frances Cranmer (1888): *An Investigation of the Principles of Athenian Architecture or the results of a survey conducted chiefly with reference to the optical refinements exhibited in the construction of ancient buildings in Athens.* (New and enlarged ed.)

Perrault, Claude (1993): *Ordonnance for the five kinds of columns after the methods of the ancients* (trans. McEwen).

Perry, Ellen E. (2000): "Notes on *Diligentia* as a term of Roman Art Criticism", *Classical Philology*, v.95.

Petkau, Karen (n.d.): "Baskets: Carrying a Culture. The Distinctive Regional Styles Of Basketmaking Nations in the Pacific Northwest", langleymuseum.org/baskets/pd fs/carrying-a-culture11.pdf downloaded Feb.4, 2010.

Pevsner, N. (1964): *The Englishness of English Art.*

-- (1974): *The Picturesque Garden and its influence outside the British Isles.*

-- and M. Aitchison (2010): *Visual Planning and the Picturesque.*

Pfaff, Christopher A. (2003): *The Argive Heraion, v.1: The Architecture of the Classical Temple of Hera.*

Philipp, Hanna (1999): "Curvature: Remarks of a Classical Archaeologist" in Haselberger, *supra*.

Picard, Gilbert Charles (1970): *Roman Painting.*

Pius II (1962): eds. Gragg and Gable, *Memoirs of a Renaissance Pope.*

-- (2003): ed. Meserve, *Pius II Commentaries*, v.1.

Plato (1966): trans. Fowler, *Plato in Twelve Volumes*, v. 1.

Pliny (1952): *Letters* (Loeb ed.)

Plommer, Hugh (1960): "The Archaic Acropolis: Some Problems", *J. Hellenic Studies*, v.80.

Poeschke, J., and C. Syndikus, eds., (2008): *Leon Battista Alberti Humanist Architekt Kunsttheoretiker.*

Pope, Alexander (1831): *The Poetical Works of Alexander Pope* (Aldine ed.)

Pope-Hennessy, John (1980): *The Study and Criticism of Italian Sculpture.*

-- (1991): *Paradiso. The illustrations to Dante's Divine Comedy by Giovanni di Paolo.*

Portoghesi, Palo (1972): *Rome of the Renaissance* (trans. Sanders).

Powell, Melissa S. and C. Jill Grady, eds., (2010): *Huichol Art and Culture: balancing the world.*

Prak, N.L. (1966): "Measurements of Amiens Cathedral", *J. Society of Architectural Historians*, v.25.

Prochaska, Frank (2013): *The Memoirs of Walter Bagehot.*

Prest, John (1981): *The Garden of Eden, the Botanic Garden and the Re-Creation of Paradise.*

Puffer, E. D. (1905): *The Psychology of Beauty.*

Ragghianti, Licia Collobi (1979): *National Archaeological Museum Athens.*

Ramberg, Walter Dodd (1960): "Some Aspects of Japanese Architecture", *Perspecta*, v.6.

Redford, Bruce (2002): "The Measure of Ruins: Dilettanti in the Levant 1750-1770", *Harvard Library Bulletin* v.13.

Reichard, Gladys A. (1922): "The Complexity of Rhythm in Decorative Art", *American Anthropologist* n.s., v.24.

-- (1933): *Melanesian Design. A study of style in wood and tortoiseshell carving.*

Reynolds, Joshua (1997): *Discourses on Art*, ed. Robert R. Wark.

Richards, Charles M. (n.d.): "Ralph Cudworth", *Internet Encyclopedia of Philosophy*, accessed Aug. 27, 2013.

Richter, Gisela A. M. (1946): *Attic Red-Figured Vases. A Survey.*

Robertson, D. S. (1954) *Handbook of Greek and Roman Architecture.*

Robison, Elwin C: (1998-1999): "Structural Implications in Palladio's Use of Harmonic Proportions", *Annali di architettura1*, vv.10-11.

Rochberg, George (1997): "Polarity in Music: Symmetry and Asymmetry and their Consequences", *Proceedings of the American Philosophical Society*, v.141.

Romanes, G. R. (1882): *Animal Intelligence* (2nd ed.)

Rosen, Joe (1975): *Symmetry Discovered. Concepts and applications in nature and science.*

Rossini, Orietta (2007): *Ara Pacis.*

Ruskin, John (1903-1912): *Complete Works* (eds. Cook and Wedderburn).

Rykwert, Joseph (1972): *On Adam's House in Paradise. The Idea of the Primitive Hut in Architectural History.*

-- Engel, Anne, eds., (1994): *Leon Battista Alberti*.

Saalman, Howard (1959): "Early Renaissance Architectural Theory and Practice in Antonio Filarete's *Trattato di Archittetura*", *Art Bulletin*, v.41.

Sackville-West, Vita (1929): *Andrew Marvell*.

Samonà, Giuseppe et al (1977): *Piazza San Marco l'architettura la storia e funzioni* (2nd. ed.)

Schneider, Lambert A. (1973): *Asymmetrie griecheischer Koepfe vom 5.Jh. bis zum Hellenismus*.

Scholfield, P. H: (1958): *The Theory of Proportion in Architecture*.

Scoresby, William (1820): *An account of the arctic regions*.

Scranton, Robert L. (1967): "The Architecture of the Sanctuary of Apollo Hylates at Kourion", *Trans. American Philosophical Society* N.S. v.57.

-- (1974): "Vitruvius' Art of Architecture", *Hesperia*, v.43.

Seligman, G. (1980): *Snow Structure and Ski Field* [1936] (repr. ed.)

Serle, J. (1745): *A Plan of Mr. Pope's Garden, as it was left at his death: with a plan and perspective view of the grotto. All taken by J. Serle, his Gardener* (Augustan Reprint Society ed).

Serlio, Sebastiano (1982): *The Five Books of Architecture*, Peake trans. (Dover ed.)

-- (1996, 2001): *Serlio on Architecture*, (ed. and trans., Hart and Hicks.)

Shaftesbury, Earl of (1749): *Characteristicks of Men, Manners, Opinions, Times*.

Shaw, Joseph (1978): "Evidence from the Minoan Tripartite Shrine", *American J. of Archaeology*, v.82.

Shelby, L. R. (1972): "The Geometrical Knowledge of Medieval Master Masons", *Speculum* v.47.

Shepard, Anna O (1948): *The Symmetry of Abstract Design with special reference to ceramic decoration*. (Contributions to American Anthropology and History no.47. Carnegie Institute of Washington Publication no.574.)

Sherbo, Arthur (1972): "Paradise Lost IV. 239", *Modern Language Review*, v.67.

Shrewsbury, J.F.D. (1970): *A History of the Bubonic Plague in the British Isles*.

Shute, John (1563): *The First and Chief Groundes of Architecture…*

Sieveking, A.F., ed. (1908): *Sir William Temple upon the Gardens of Epicurus, with other XVIIth Century Garden Essays*.

Simson, Otto von (1962): *The Gothic Cathedral. Origins of Gothic Architecture and the medieval concept of order*. (2nd ed.)

Six, J. (1885): "Some Archaic Gorgons in the British Museum". *J. Hellenic Studies* v.6.

Smith, C. (1992): *Architecture in the Culture of Early Humanism: ethics, aesthetics, and eloquence, 1400-1470*.

Smith, Graham (2000): "Gaetano Baccani's 'Systematization' of the Piazza del Duomo in Florence", *J. Society of Architectural Historians*, v.59.

Soles, Jeffrey T. (1991): "The Gournia Palace", *American J. of Archaeology*, v.95.

Spectator (1891): *The Spectator* ed. Morley.

Spence, Joseph (1964): *Anecdotes, Observations and Characters of Books and Men* (repr. ed.)

Spenser, Edmund (1993): *Edmund Spenser's Poetry* (eds. Maclean and Prescott, 3rd. ed.)

Stendhal (1962): *Memoirs of a Tourist* (trans. Seager).

Stern, Judith (2000): "The Eichmann Trial and its Influence on Psychology and Psychiatry", *Theoretical Inquiries in Law*, v.1.

Stevens, Gorham (1943): "The Curve of the North Stylobate of the Parthenon", *Hesperia*, v.12.

Stewart, Ian, (2001): *What Shape Is A Snowflake?*

Stewering, Roswitha (2000): "Architectural Representation in the 'Hypnerotomachia Poliphili'", *J. Society of Architectural Historians*, v.59.

Stockstad, M., and J. Stannard (1983): *Gardens of the Middle Ages.*

Streatfield, David C., and Alistair Duckworth, eds. (1981): *Landscape in the Gardens and Literature of eighteenth-century England.*

Striker, Cecil L. (1981): *The Myrelaion (Bodrum Camii) in Istanbul.*

Strong, Roy (1998): *The Renaissance Garden in England.*

Stuart, James, and Nicholas Revett (2008): *Antiquities of Athens. (repr. ed.)*

Sturgis, Russell (1905): *A Dictionary of Architecture and Building.*

Summers, David (1981): *Michelangelo and the language of art.*

Sutton, Peter (1988): *Dreamings: The Art of Aboriginal Asia.*

Sydow, Eckart von (1932): *Die Kunst der Naturvölker und der Vorzeit.*

Tavernor, Robert (1998): *On Alberti and the Art of Building.*

Taylor, Rabun (2003): *Roman Builders A Study in Architectural Process.*

Tellez, Trinidad Ruiz and Anders Pape Moller (2006): "Fluctuating Asymmetry of Leaves in *Digitalis thapsi* under Field and Common Garden Conditions", *International Journal of Plant Sciences*, v. 167.

Temko, Allan (1959): *Notre-Dame of Paris* (Viking Compass ed.)

Temple, William (1731): *Works*, (2nd ed.)

Thacker, Christopher (1979): *History of Gardens.*

Thiersch, August (1902): "Die Proportionen in der Architektur" in ed. Durm, *Handbuch der Architektur*, v.4.

Thompson, D'Arcy (2005): *On Growth and Form* (repr. of abridged edition, 1961).

Thornton, Peter (1998): *Form and Decoration. Innovation in the decorative arts 1470-1870.*

Tietze-Conrat, E. (1955): *Mantegna. Paintings, Drawings, Engravings.*

Tobin, Richard (1981): "The Doric Groundplan", *American J. of Archaeology*, v.85.

Torbrügge, Walter (1968): *Prehistoric European Art.*

Trachtenberg, Marvin (1997): *Dominion of the Eye. Urbanism, Art, and Power in Early Modern Florence.*

Tuchman, Barbara (1978): *A Distant Mirror. The Calamitous 14th Century.*

Tunnard, Christopher (1978): *A World with a View.*

Turner, A. Richard (1966): *The Vision of Landscape in Renaissance Italy.*

Vasari, Giorgio (1908): *Le vite dei più celebri pittori, scultori e architetti* (ed.Salani).

-- (1996): *Lives of the Painters, Sculptors and Architects* (trans. de Vere).

Venturi, Robert (1977): *Complexity and Contradiction in Architecture* (2nd ed.)

Vermeule, Cornelius Clarkson (1977): *Greek Sculpture and Roman Taste.*

Vershbow (2013): *The Collection of Arthur and Charlotte Vershbow* Part One (Christie's NY catalog).

Vickers, Michael (1987):"Eighteenth-Century Taste and the Study of Greek Vases", *Past and Present*, v.116.

Villard de Honnecourt (1959): *The Sketchbook of Villard de Honnecourt* (ed. Bowie).

Vinci, Leonardo da (1958): *The Notebooks of Leonardo da Vinci* (ed. MacCurdy).

Viollet-le-Duc, E-E. (1987): *Lectures on Architecture.*

Vitruvius (1931): ed. and trans. Frank Granger, *Vitruvius on Architecture.*

Voloshinov, Alexander (1996): "Symmetry as Superprinciple of Science and Art", *Leonardo*, v.29.

Walpole, Horace (1891): *Letters of Horace Walpole* (ed. Cunningham).

-- (1995): *The History of the Modern Taste in Gardening* (repr. ed.)

Ward-Perkins, John, and Amanda Claridge (1978): *Pompeii AD 79.*

Washburn, Dorothy and Donald W. Crowe (1988): *Symmetries of Culture.*

Washburn, Dorothy K. (1995):"Symmetry Clues to the Puebloan Lifeway", in *Symmetry: Culture and Growth*, v. 6.

-- (1999) "Perceptual Anthropology: the cultural salience of symmetry", *American Anthropologist*, v. 101.

Watkins, R. N. (1972): "Petrarch and the Black Death", *Studies in the Renaissance*, v.19

Webster, T. B. L.(1939): "Tondo composition in Archaic and Classical Greek Art" *J. of Hellenic Studies*, v.59.

Weil-Garris, and John F. D'Amico (1980): "The Renaissance Cardinal's Ideal Palace" in ed. Henry A. Millon, *Studies in Italian Art and Architecture 15th through 18th centuries*. Memoirs of the American Academy in Rome, v.35.

Weinberger, Martin (1941): "The First Façade of the Cathedral of Florence", *J. of the Cortauld and Warburg Institutes*, v.4.

Weyl, Hermann (1952): *Symmetry.*

White, John (1973): "Giotto's Use of Architecture in 'The Expulsion of Joachim' and 'The Entry into Jerusalem' at Padua", *Burlington Magazine*, v.115.

Wiencke, Martha Heath (2000): *The architecture, stratification, and pottery of Lerna*, v.III.

Williman, Daniel (ed.) 1982: *The Black Death The Impact of the Fourteenth-Century Plague.* Medieval and Renaissance Texts and Studies, v.13.

Wilson Jones, Mark (2001): "Doric Measure and Architectural Design 2", *A. J. Archeology*, v.4.

-- (2003): *Principles of Roman Architecture*.

Wilson, Michael I. (1977): *The English Country House and its furnishings*.

Winckelmann, Johann Joachim (1968): *History of Ancient Art* (trans. Alexander Gode).

Wittkower, Rudolf (1949): *Architectural Principles in the Age of Humanism*, First ed.

-- (1952): *Architectural Principles in the Age of Humanism*, Second ed.

-- (1962): *Architectural Principles in the Age of Humanism*, Third ed.

-- (1971): *Architectural Principles in the Age of Humanism*, Fourth ed.

-- (1974a)*: Gothic vs. Classic. Architectural projects in seventeenth-century Italy*.

-- (1974b): *Palladio and English Palladianism*.

-- (1978): "Changing Concept of Proportion", *Idea and Image*.

-- (1940-1941): "Alberti's Approach to Antiquity in Architecture", *J. of the Warburg and Courtauld Institutes*, v. 4.

Wölfflin, Heinrich (1889): "Zur Lehre von den Proportionen" in *Kleine Schriften* (ed. Gantner).

-- (1946): "Prolegomena zu einer Psychologie der Architektur", *Kleine Schriften* (ed. Gantner).

Woodbridge, Homer (1940): *Sir William Temple. The man and his work*.

Woodford, Susan (1988): *Introduction to Greek Art*.

Wotton, Henry (1968): *Elements of Architecture* (repr. ed.)

Wu, Nancy, editor (2002): *Ad Quadratum: The practical application of geometry in medieval architecture*.

Wyman, Jeffries (1866): *Notes on the Cells of Bees*.

Yeroulanou, Marina (1998): "Metopes and Architecture: The Hephaiston and the Parthenon", *Annual of the British School of Athens*, v.93.

Zarnecki, George (1975): *Art of the Medieval World*.

Zocchi, Giuseppe (1757): *Vedute delle ville, e d'altri luoghi della Toscana* (3rd.ed.)

Printed in Great Britain
by Amazon.co.uk, Ltd.,
Marston Gate.